Mastering Machine AWS

Advanced machine learning in Python using SageMaker, Apache Spark, and TensorFlow

Dr. Saket S.R. Mengle
Maximo Gurmendez

BIRMINGHAM - MUMBAI

Mastering Machine Learning on AWS

Commissioning Editor: Sunith Shetty
Acquisition Editor: Devika Battike
Content Development Editor: Nathanya Dias
Technical Editor: Utkarsha S. Kadam
Copy Editor: Safis Editing
Project Coordinator: Kirti Pisat
Proofreader: Safis Editing
Indexer: Priyanka Dhadke
Graphics: Jisha Chirayil
Production Coordinator: Shraddha Falebhai

First published: May 2019

Production reference: 1150519

Published by Packt Publishing Ltd.
Livery Place
35 Livery Street
Birmingham
B3 2PB, UK.

ISBN 978-1-78934-979-5

www.packtpub.com

I would like to dedicate this book in memory of my dad. Thanks for being there for me and supporting my dreams.

*– **Dr. Saket S.R. Mengle***

This book is dedicated to Mateo and Paulina, who are my constant source of inspiration, joy and purpose.

*– **Maximo Gurmendez***

`mapt.io`

Mapt is an online digital library that gives you full access to over 5,000 books and videos, as well as industry leading tools to help you plan your personal development and advance your career. For more information, please visit our website.

Why subscribe?

- Spend less time learning and more time coding with practical eBooks and Videos from over 4,000 industry professionals

- Improve your learning with Skill Plans built especially for you

- Get a free eBook or video every month

- Mapt is fully searchable

- Copy and paste, print, and bookmark content

Packt.com

Did you know that Packt offers eBook versions of every book published, with PDF and ePub files available? You can upgrade to the eBook version at `www.packt.com` and as a print book customer, you are entitled to a discount on the eBook copy. Get in touch with us at `customercare@packtpub.com` for more details.

At `www.packt.com`, you can also read a collection of free technical articles, sign up for a range of free newsletters, and receive exclusive discounts and offers on Packt books and eBooks.

Contributors

About the authors

Dr. Saket S.R. Mengle holds a PhD in text mining from Illinois Institute of Technology, Chicago. He has worked in a variety of fields, including text classification, information retrieval, large-scale machine learning, and linear optimization. He currently works as senior principal data scientist at dataxu, where he is responsible for developing and maintaining the algorithms that drive dataxu's real-time advertising platform.

> *I would like to thank my wife, Sharvari, who gives me strength and inspires me to be the best version of myself every day. This book would have not been possible without her love and support. I would also like to thank my parents, Subhash and Rashmi Mengle, who taught me the value of hard work. I would like to express my appreciation to my advisor, Dr. Nazli Goharian, and Dr. Ophir Frieder, who introduced me to the world of Machine Learning.*

Maximo Gurmendez holds a master's degree in computer science/AI from Northeastern University, where he attended as a Fulbright Scholar. Since 2009, he has been working with dataxu as data science engineering lead. He's also the founder of Montevideo Labs (a data science and engineering consultancy). Additionally, Maximo is a computer science professor at the University of Montevideo and is director of its data science for business program.

> *I'd like to deeply thank my wife Maggie for her sustained support, encouragement and patience, especially throughout the long work days and busy weekends that writing this book implied. Additionally, I'd like to thank my mother, Margarita, who taught me the importance of learning, caring and hard-work through her own example. Finally, I'd like to express my gratitude to the dataxu team from whom I learned so much in the past ten years.*

About the reviewer

Chirag Nayyar helps organizations initiate their digital transformation using the public cloud. He has been actively working on cloud platforms since 2013, providing consultancy to many organizations, ranging from small and mid-size businesses to enterprises. He holds a wide range of certifications from all major public cloud platforms. He also runs a meet-up group and is a regular speaker at various cloud events. He has also reviewed *Hands-On Machine Learning on Google Cloud Platform* and *Google Cloud Platform Cookbook*, by Packt Publishing.

Packt is searching for authors like you

If you're interested in becoming an author for Packt, please visit `authors.packtpub.com` and apply today. We have worked with thousands of developers and tech professionals, just like you, to help them share their insight with the global tech community. You can make a general application, apply for a specific hot topic that we are recruiting an author for, or submit your own idea.

Table of Contents

Preface

AWS is constantly driving new innovations that empower data scientists to explore a variety of machine learning cloud services. This book is your comprehensive reference for learning about and implementing advanced machine learning algorithms in AWS.

As you go through this book, you'll gain insights into how these algorithms can be trained, tuned, and deployed in AWS using Apache Spark on Elastic MapReduce, SageMaker, and TensorFlow. While you focus on algorithms such as XGBoost, linear models, Factorization Machines, and deep networks, the book will also provide you with an overview of AWS, as well as detailed practical applications that will help you solve real-world problems. Every practical application includes a series of companion notebooks with all the necessary code to run on AWS. In the next few chapters, you will learn how to use SageMaker and EMR notebooks to perform a range of tasks, from smart analytics and predictive modeling through to sentiment analysis.

By the end of this book, you will be equipped with the skills you need to effectively handle machine learning projects and implement and evaluate algorithms on AWS.

Who this book is for

This book is for data scientists, machine learning developers, deep learning enthusiasts and AWS users who want to build advanced models and smart applications on the cloud using AWS and its integration services. Some understanding of machine learning concepts, Python programming and AWS will be beneficial.

What this book covers

Chapter 1, *Getting Started with Machine Learning for AWS*, introduces machine learning to the readers. It explains why it is necessary for data scientists to learn about machine learning and how AWS can help them to solve various real-world problems. We also discuss the AWS services and tools that we will be covered in the book.

Chapter 2, *Classifying Twitter Feeds with Naive Bayes*, introduces the basics of the Naive Bayes algorithm and presents a text classification problem that will be addressed by the use of this algorithm and language models. We'll provide examples explaining how to apply Naive Bayes using scikit-learn and Apache Spark on SageMaker's BlazingText. Additionally, we'll explore how to use the ideas behind Bayesian reasoning in more complex scenarios. We will use the Twitter API to stream tweets from two different political candidates and predict who wrote them. We will use scikit-learn, Apache Spark, SageMaker, and BlazingText.

Chapter 3, *Predicting House Value with Regression Algorithms*, introduces the basics of regression algorithms and applies them to predict the price of houses given a number of features. We'll also introduce how to use logistic regression for classification problems. Examples in SageMaker for scikit-learn and Apache Spark will be provided. We'll be using the Boston Housing Price dataset https://www.kaggle.com/c/boston-housing/, along with scikit-learn, Apache Spark, and SageMaker.

Chapter 4, *Predicting User Behavior with Tree-Based Methods*, introduces decision trees, random forests, and gradient boosted trees. We will explore how to use these algorithms to predict when users will click on ads. Additionally, we will explain how to use AWS EMR and Apache Spark to engineer models at a large scale. We will use the Adform click prediction dataset (https://doi.org/10.7910/DVN/TADBY7, Harvard Dataverse, V2). We will use the xgboost, Apache Spark, SageMaker, and EMR libraries.

Chapter 5, *Customer Segmentation Using Clustering Algorithms*, introduces the main clustering algorithms by exploring how to apply them for customer segmentation based on consumer patterns. Through AWS SageMaker, we will show how to run these algorithms in skicit-learn and Apache Spark. We will use the e-commerce data from Fabien Daniel (https://www.kaggle.com/fabiendaniel/customer-segmentation/data) and scikit-learn, Apache Spark, and SageMaker.

Chapter 6, *Analyzing Visitor Patterns to Make Recommendations*, presents the problem of finding similar users based on their navigation patterns in order to recommend custom marketing strategies. Collaborative filtering and distance-based methods will be introduced with examples in scikit-learn and Apache Spark on AWS SageMaker. We will use Kwan Hui Lim's Theme Park Attraction Visits Dataset (https://sites.google.com/site/limkwanhui/datacode), Apache Spark, and SageMaker.

Chapter 7, *Implementing Deep Learning Algorithms*, introduces the reader to the main concepts behind deep learning and explains why it has become so relevant in today's AI-powered products. The aim of this chapter is to not discuss the theoretical details of deep learning, but to explain the algorithms with examples and provide a high-level conceptual understanding of deep learning algorithms. This will give the readers a platform to understand what they are implementing in the next chapters.

Chapter 8, *Implementing Deep Learning with TensorFlow on AWS*, goes through a series of practical image-recognition problems and explains how to address them with TensorFlow on AWS. TensorFlow is a very popular deep learning framework that can be used to train deep neural networks. This chapter will explain how TensorFlow can be installed by readers and used to train deep learning models using toy datasets. In this chapter, we'll use the MNIST handwritten digits dataset (http://yann.lecun.com/exdb/mnist/), along with TensorFlow and SageMaker.

Chapter 9, *Image Classification and Detection with SageMaker*, revisits the image classification problem we dealt with in the previous chapters, but using SageMaker's image classification algorithm and object detection algorithm. We'll use the following datasets:

- Caltech256 (http://www.vision.caltech.edu/Image_Datasets/Caltech256/)

We'll also use AWS Sagemaker.

Chapter 10, *Working with AWS Comprehend*, explains the functionality of an AWS tool called Comprehend, which is an NLP tool that performs various useful tasks.

Chapter 11, *Using AWS Rekognition*, explains how to use Rekognition, which is an image recognition tool that uses deep learning. The readers will learn an easy way of applying image recognition in their applications.

Chapter 12, *Building Conversational Interfaces Using AWS Lex*, explains that AWS Lex is a tool that allows programmers to build conversational interfaces. This chapter introduces the readers to topics such as natural language understanding using deep learning.

Chapter 13, *Creating Clusters on AWS*, discusses that one of the key problems in deep learning is understanding how to scale and parallelize learning on multiple machines. In this chapter, we'll examine different ways to create clusters of learners. In particular, we'll focus on how to parallelize deep learning pipelines through distributed TensorFlow and Apache Spark.

Chapter 14, *Optimizing Models in Spark and SageMaker*, explains that the models that are trained on AWS can be further optimized to run smoothly in production environments. In this section, we will discuss various tricks that our readers can use to improve the performance of their algorithms.

Chapter 15, *Tuning Clusters for Machine Learning*, explains that many data scientists and machine learning practitioners face the problem of scale when attempting to run machine learning data pipelines at scale. In this chapter, we focus primarily on EMR, which is a very powerful tool for running very large machine learning jobs. There are many ways to configure EMR, and not every setup works for every scenario. We will go through the main configurations of EMR and explain how each configuration works for different objectives. Additionally, we'll present other ways to run big data pipelines through AWS.

Chapter 16, *Deploying Models Built on AWS*, discusses deployment. At this point, readers will have their models built on AWS and would like to ship them to production. We understand that there are a variety of different contexts in which models should be deployed. In some cases, it's as easy as generating a CSV of actions that would be fed to some system. Often, we just need to deploy a web service that's capable of making predictions. However, there are many times in which we need to deploy these models to complex, low-latency, or edge systems. We will go through the different ways you can deploy machine learning models to production.

To get the most out of this book

This book covers a number of different frameworks, such as Spark and Tensorflow. However it is not meant to be a comprehensive guide for each. Instead we focus on the way AWS empowers practical machine learning through the use of the different frameworks. We encourage the readers to refer to other books with framework-specific content when necessary.

Download the example code files

You can download the example code files for this book from your account at `www.packt.com`. If you purchased this book elsewhere, you can visit `www.packt.com/support` and register to have the files emailed directly to you.

You can download the code files by following these steps:

1. Log in or register at `www.packt.com`.
2. Select the **SUPPORT** tab.
3. Click on **Code Downloads & Errata**.
4. Enter the name of the book in the **Search** box and follow the onscreen instructions.

Once the file is downloaded, please make sure that you unzip or extract the folder using the latest version of:

- WinRAR/7-Zip for Windows
- Zipeg/iZip/UnRarX for Mac
- 7-Zip/PeaZip for Linux

The code bundle for the book is also hosted on GitHub at `https://github.com/PacktPublishing/Mastering-Machine-Learning-on-AWS`. In case there's an update to the code, it will be updated on the existing GitHub repository.

We also have other code bundles from our rich catalog of books and videos available at `https://github.com/PacktPublishing/`. Check them out!

Download the color images

We also provide a PDF file that has color images of the screenshots/diagrams used in this book. You can download it here: `http://www.packtpub.com/sites/default/files/downloads/9781789349795_ColorImages.pdf`.

Conventions used

There are a number of text conventions used throughout this book.

`CodeInText`: Indicates code words in text, database table names, folder names, filenames, file extensions, pathnames, dummy URLs, user input, and Twitter handles. Here is an example: "The following screenshot shows the first few lines of our `df` dataframe."

A block of code is set as follows:

```
vectorizer = CountVectorizer(input=dem_text + gop_text,
                             stop_words=stop_words,
                             max_features=1200)
```

Any command-line input or output is written as follows:

```
wget -O /tmp/adform.click.2017.01.json.gz
https://dataverse.harvard.edu/api/access/datafile/:persistentId/?persistent
Id=doi:10.7910/DVN/TADBY7/JCI3VG
```

Bold: Indicates a new term, an important word, or words that you see onscreen. For example, words in menus or dialog boxes appear in the text like this. Here is an example: "You can also train a custom NER algorithm in AWS Comprehend using the **Customization | Custom entity recognition** option in the left menu."

Warnings or important notes appear like this.

Tips and tricks appear like this.

Get in touch

Feedback from our readers is always welcome.

General feedback: If you have questions about any aspect of this book, mention the book title in the subject of your message and email us at customercare@packtpub.com.

Errata: Although we have taken every care to ensure the accuracy of our content, mistakes do happen. If you have found a mistake in this book, we would be grateful if you would report this to us. Please visit www.packt.com/submit-errata, selecting your book, clicking on the Errata Submission Form link, and entering the details.

Piracy: If you come across any illegal copies of our works in any form on the Internet, we would be grateful if you would provide us with the location address or website name. Please contact us at copyright@packt.com with a link to the material.

If you are interested in becoming an author: If there is a topic that you have expertise in and you are interested in either writing or contributing to a book, please visit `authors.packtpub.com`.

Reviews

Please leave a review. Once you have read and used this book, why not leave a review on the site that you purchased it from? Potential readers can then see and use your unbiased opinion to make purchase decisions, we at Packt can understand what you think about our products, and our authors can see your feedback on their book. Thank you!

For more information about Packt, please visit `packt.com`.

Section 1: Machine Learning on AWS

1

The objective of this section is to introduce readers to machine learning in the context of AWS cloud computing and services. We expect our audience to have some basic knowledge of machine learning. However, we'll describe the nature of a typical successful machine learning project and the challenges often faced. We will provide an overview of the different AWS services and provide examples of typical machine learning pipelines, along with the key aspects to consider in order to create smart AI-powered products.

This section contains the following chapter:

- Chapter 1, *Getting Started with Machine Learning for AWS*

Getting Started with Machine Learning for AWS

1

In this book, we focus on all three aspects of data science by explaining **machine learning** (ML) algorithms in business applications, demonstrating how they can be implemented in a scalable environment and how to evaluate models and present evaluation metrics as business **Key Performance Indicators** (KPI). This book shows how **Amazon Web Services** (AWS) Machine Learning tools can be effectively used on large datasets. We present various scenarios where mastering machine learning algorithms in AWS helps data scientists to perform their jobs more effectively.

Let's take a look at the topics we will cover in this chapter:

- How AWS empowers data scientists
- Identifying candidate problems that can be solved using machine learning
- Machine Learning project life cycle
- Deploying models

How AWS empowers data scientists

The number of digital data records that are stored on the internet has a lot in the last decade. Due to the drop in storage costs, and new sources of digital data, it is predicted that the amount of digital data available in 2025 will be 163 zettabytes (1,630,000,000,000 terabytes). Moreover, the amount of data that is generated every day is increasing at an alarming pace, with almost 90% of current data only being generated during the last two years. With more than 3.5 billion people with access to the internet, this data is not only generated by professionals and large companies, but by each of the 3.5 billion internet users.

Moreover, since companies understand the importance of data, they store all of their transactional data in the hope of analyzing it and uncovering interesting trends that could help their business make important decisions. Financial investors also crave storing and understanding every bit of information they can get about companies and train their quantitative analysts or **quants** to make investment decisions.

It is up to the data scientists of the world to analyze this data and find gems of information from it. In the last decade, the data science team has become one of the most important teams in every organization. When data science teams were first created, most of the data would fit in Microsoft Excel sheets and the task was to find statistical trends in the data and provide actionable insights to business teams. However, as the amount of data has increased and machine learning algorithms have become more sophisticated and potent, the scope of data science teams has expanded.

In the following diagram, we can see the three basic skills that a data scientist needs:

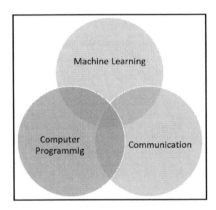

The job description for a data scientists from company to company. However, in general, a data scientist needs the following three crucial skills:

- **Machine learning**: Machine learning algorithms provide tools to analyze and learn from a large amount of data and provide predictions or recommendations from that data. It is an important tool for analyzing structured (databases) and unstructured (text documents) data and inferring actionable insights from them. A data scientist should be an expert in a plethora of machine learning algorithms and should understand what algorithm should be applied in a given situation. As data scientists have access to a large library of algorithms that can solve a given problem, they should know which algorithms should be used in each situation.

- **Computer programming**: A data scientist should be an adept programmer who can write code to access various machine learning and statistical libraries. There are a lot of programming languages such as Scala, Python, and R that provide a number of libraries that let us apply machine learning algorithms on a dataset. Hence, knowledge of such tools helps a data scientist to perform complex tasks in a feasible time. This is crucial in a business environment.

- **Communication**: Along with discovering trends in the data and building complex machine learning models, a data scientist is also tasked with explaining these findings to business teams. Hence, a data scientist must not only possess good communication skills but also good analytics and visualization skills. This will help them present complex data models in a way that is easily understood by people not familiar with machine learning. This also helps data scientists to convey their findings to business teams and provide them with guidance on expected outcomes.

Using AWS tools for machine learning

Machine learning research spans decades and has deep roots in mathematics and statistics. ML algorithms can be used to solve problems in many business applications. In application areas such as advertising, predictive algorithms are used to predict where to discover the further customers based on trends from previous purchasers. Regression algorithms are used to predict stock prices based on prior trends. Services such as Netflix use recommendation algorithms to study the history of a user and enhance the discoverability of new shows that they may be interested in. **Artificial Intelligence** (**AI**) applications such as self-driving cars rely heavily on image recognition algorithms that utilize deep learning to effectively discover and label objects on the road. It is important for a data scientist to understand the nuances of different machine learning algorithms and understand where they should be applied. Using pre-existing libraries helps a data scientist to explore various algorithms for a given application area and evaluate them. AWS offers a large number of libraries that can be used to perform machine learning tasks, as explained in the Machine Learning algorithms and deep learning algorithms parts of this book.

Identifying candidate problems that can be solved using machine learning

It is also important for data scientists to be able to understand the scale of data that they are working with. There might be tasks related to medical research that span thousands of patients with hundreds of features that can be processed on a single node device. However, tasks such as advertising, where companies collect several petabytes of data on customers based on every online advertisement that is served to the user, may require several thousand machines to compute and train machine learning algorithms. Deep learning algorithms are GPU-intensive and require a different type of machine than other machine learning algorithms. In this book, for each algorithm, we supply a description of how it is implemented simply using Python libraries and then how it can be scaled on large AWS clusters using technologies such as Spark and AWS SageMaker. We also discuss how TensorFlow is used for deep learning applications.

It is crucial to understand the customer of their machine learning-related tasks. Although it is challenging for data scientists to find which algorithm works for a specific application area, it is also important to gather evidence on how that algorithm enhances the application area and present it to the product-owners. Hence, we also discuss how to evaluate each algorithm and visualize the results where necessary. AWS offers a large array of tools for evaluating machine learning algorithms and presenting the results.

Finally, a data scientist also needs to be able to make decisions on what types of machines are best fitted for their needs on AWS. Once the algorithm is implemented, there are important considerations on how it can be deployed on large clusters in the most economical way. AWS offers more than 25 hardware alternatives, called **instance types**, which can be selected. We will discuss case studies on how an application is deployed on production clusters and various issues a data scientist can face during this process.

Machine learning project life cycle

A typical machine learning project life cycle starts by understanding the problem at hand. Typically, someone in the organization (possibly a data scientist or business stakeholder) feels that some part of their business can be improved by the use of machine learning. For example, a music streaming company could conjecture that providing recommendations of songs similar to those played by a user would improve user engagement with the platform. Once we understand the business context and possible business actions to take, a data science team will need to consider several aspects during the project life cycle.

The following diagram describes various steps in a machine learning project life cycle:

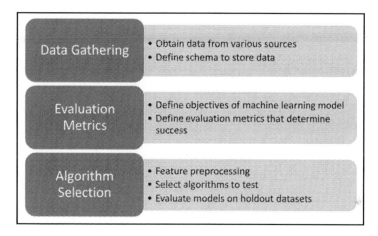

Data gathering

We need to obtain data and organize it appropriately for the current problem (in our example, this could mean building a dataset linking users to songs they've listened to in the past). Depending on the size of the data, we might pick different technologies for storing the data. For example, it might be fine to train on a local machine using scikit-learn if we're working through a few million records. However, if the data doesn't fit on a single computer, then we must consider AWS solutions such as S3 for storage and Apache Spark, or SageMaker's built-in algorithms for model building.

Evaluation metrics

Before applying a machine learning algorithm, we need to consider how to assess the effectiveness of our strategy. In some cases, we can use part of our data to simulate the performance of the algorithm. However, on other occasions, the only viable way to evaluate the application of an algorithm is by doing some controlled testing (A/B testing) and determining whether the use cases in which the algorithm was applied resulted in a better outcome. In our music streaming example, this could mean selecting a panel of users and recommending songs to them using the new algorithm. We can run statistical tests to determine whether these users effectively stayed longer on the platform. Evaluation metrics should be determined based on the business KPI and should show significant improvement over existing processes.

Algorithm selection

We need to iterate on the complex problem of the creating the algorithm. This entails exploring the data to gain a deep understanding of the underlying variables. Once we have an idea of the kind of algorithm we want to apply, we'll need to further prepare the data, possibly combining it with other data sources (for example, census data). In our example, this could mean creating a song similarity matrix. Once we have the data, we can train a model (capable or making predictions) and test that model against holdout data to see how it performs. There are many considerations in this process that make it complex:

- How the data is encoded (for example, how the song matrix is constructed)
- What algorithm is used (example, collaborative filtering or content-based filtering)
- What parameter values your model takes (for example, values for smoothing constants or prior distributions)

Our goal in this book is to make this step easier for you by presenting iterations a data scientist would undergo in the task of creating a successful model using real-world applications as examples.

Deploying models

Once we generate a model that abides by our initial KPI requirements, we need to deploy it in the production environment. This could be something as simple as creating a list of neighborhoods and political issues to address on each neighborhood or something as complex as shipping the model to thousands of machines to make real-time decisions about which advertisements to buy for a particular marketing campaign. Once deployed to production, it is important to keep on monitoring those KPIs to make sure we're still solving the problem we aimed for initially. Sometimes, the model could have negative effects due to the change in trends and another model needs to be trained. For instance, listeners over time may lose interest in continually hearing the same music style and the process must start all over again.

Summary

In this chapter, we first learned how AWS empowers machine learning practitioners and data scientists. We then looked at the various AWS tools that are available for machine learning, after which we learned about the machine learning life cycle. And finally, we learned how to deploy models.

In the next chapter, we will discuss various popular machine learning algorithms and see how to implement them at scale on AWS. Before continuing to the next chapter we advice readers who are new to AWS to go through the appendix, getting started with AWS, which covers the process of creating a new AWS account.

Exercise

1. Define three applications you can identify on your mobile phone that implement machine learning. For each of the application, define what the project life cycle is based on the steps presented in this chapter.
2. Search for three data scientist job positions and carefully review the job requirements. For each of the requirements, classify whether the skill falls under communication, machine learning, or computer programming.
3. As a data scientist, it is important to be aware of the applications around you that are generating data that can be used for machine learning. Based on the electronic devices you use, make a list of data that you generate every day. Define three machine learning applications that can use the data that you generate.

2
Section 2: Implementing Machine Learning Algorithms at Scale on AWS

In this section, we will discuss various popular machine learning algorithms and how they work. We will provide examples of situations in which they work well and when they should be avoided. The reader will learn about different machine learning algorithms and will be able to work with simple examples in scikit-learn and scale them into Apache Spark in the context of AWS. After reading the section, we expect readers to have a working knowledge of machine learning algorithms and how to implement them at scale in AWS.

This section contains the following chapters:

2
Classifying Twitter Feeds with Naive Bayes

Machine learning (ML) plays a major part in analyzing large datasets and extracting actionable insights from the data. ML algorithms perform tasks such as predicting outcomes, clustering data to extract trends, and building recommendation engines. Knowledge of ML algorithms helps data scientists to understand the nature of data they are dealing with and plan what algorithms should be applied to achieve desired outcomes from the data. Although multiple algorithms are available to perform any tasks, it is important for data scientists to know the pros and drawbacks of different ML algorithms. The decision to apply ML algorithms can be based on various factors, such as the size of the dataset, the budget for the clusters used for training and deployment of ML models, and the cost of error rates. Although AWS offers a large number of options in terms of selecting and deploying ML models, a data scientist has to knowledgeable in terms of what algorithms should be used in different situations.

In this part of the book, we present various popular ML algorithms and examples of applications where they can be applied effectively. We will explain the advantages and disadvantages of each algorithm and situations when these algorithms should be selected in AWS. As this book is written with data science students and professionals in mind, we will present a simple example of how the algorithms can be implemented using simple Python libraries, and then deployed on AWS clusters using Spark and AWS SageMaker for larger datasets. These chapters should help data scientists to get familiar with the popular ML algorithms and help them understand the nuances of implementing these algorithms in big data environments on AWS clusters.

Chapter 2, *Classifying Twitter Feeds with Naive Bayes,* Chapter 3, *Predicting House Value with Regression Algorithms,* Chapter 4, *Predicting User Behavior with Tree-Based Methods,* and Chapter 5, *Customer Segmentation Using Clustering Algorithms* present four classification algorithms that can be used to predict an outcome based on a feature set. Chapter 6, *Analyzing Visitor Patterns to Make Recommendations,* explains clustering algorithms and demonstrates how they can be used for applications such as customer segmentation.

Chapter 7, *Implementing Deep Learning Algorithms*, presents a recommendation algorithm that can be used to recommend new items to users based on their purchase history.

This chapter will introduce the basics of the Naive Bayes algorithm and present a text classification problem that will be addressed by the use of this algorithm and language models. We'll provide examples on how to apply it on `scikit-learn`, Apache Spark, and on SageMaker's BlazingText. Additionally, we'll explore how to further use the ideas behind Bayesian reasoning in more complex scenarios.

In this chapter, we will cover the following topics:

- Classification algorithms
- Naive Bayes classifier
- Classifying text with language models
- Naive Bayes — pros and cons

Classification algorithms

One of the popular subsets of ML algorithms are the classification algorithms. They are also referred to as supervised learning algorithms. For this approach, we assume that we have a rich dataset of features and events associated with those features. The task of the algorithm is to predict an event given a set of features. The event is referred to as a class variable. For example, consider the following dataset of features related to weather and if it snowed on that day:

Table 1: Sample dataset

Temperature (in °F)	Sky condition	Wind Speed (in MPH)	Snowfall
Less than 20	Sunny	30	False
20-32	Sunny	6	False
32-70	Cloudy	20	False
70 and above	Cloudy	0	False
20-32	Cloudy	10	True
32-70	Sunny	15	False
Less than 20	Cloudy	8	True
32-70	Sunny	7	False
20-32	Cloudy	11	False
Less than 20	Sunny	13	True

In the dataset, a weather station has information about the temperature, the sky condition, and the wind speed for the day. They also have records of when they received snowfall. The classification problem they are working on is to predict snowfall based on features such as temperature, sky condition, and wind speed.

Let's discuss some terminology that is used in ML datasets. For the example table, if the classification problem is to predict snowfall, then the snowfall feature is referred to as a **class** or **target** variable. Non-class values are referred to as attribute or feature variables. Each row in this dataset is referred to as an observation.

Feature types

There are three types of features that are available in a classification dataset. The reason why data scientists need to be able to differentiate between different features is that not every ML algorithm supports each type of feature. So, if the type of feature set does not match the desired algorithm, then the features need to be preprocessed to transform the feature that the classification algorithm can process.

Nominal features

Nominal or **categorical** features are features that can have a finite set of categorical values, and these values cannot be ordered in any specific order. In the example dataset, the **sky condition** feature is a nominal feature. In the table, the value of the nominal feature is either **Sunny** or **Cloudy**. Other examples of nominal features are gender and color. Nominal features can be converted into continuous variables by using techniques such as one-hot encoding.

Ordinal features

Ordinal features, similar to nominal features, also have a finite set of categorical values. However, unlike nominal features, these categorical values can be put into a specific order. In the previous example, the **Temperature** feature is an ordinal feature. The labels in this category can be ordered from coldest to warmest. Ordinal features can be converted into continuous variables by interpolating the range values to a defined scale.

Continuous features

Continuous features can have infinite possible values. Unlike nominal and ordinal features, which can only have a discrete set of values, continuous variables are numerical variables, and are not compatible with some ML algorithms. However, continuous features can be converted into ordinal features using a technique called **discretization**.

Although we will not discuss techniques to transform features from one form to another here, we will demonstrate how it can be done in our example sections. We have selected example datasets in this book where feature transformation is required. You should not only learn about these various transformation techniques from this book, but also observe how a data scientist analyzes a dataset and uses specific feature transformation techniques based on the application. We have also provided examples to apply these techniques at scale in Python and AWS SageMaker.

Naive Bayes classifier

Naïve Bayes classifier is a ML algorithm based on Bayes' theorem. The algorithm is comparable to how a belief system evolves. Bayes' theorem was initially introduced by an English mathematician, Thomas Bayes, in 1776. This algorithm has various applications, and has been used for many historic tasks for more than two centuries. One of the most famous applications of this algorithm was by Alan Turing during the Second World War, where he used Bayes' theorem to decrypt the German Enigma code. Bayes' theorem has also found an important place in ML for algorithms such as Bayesian Net and Naive Bayes algorithm. Naïve Bayes algorithm is very popular for ML due to its low complexity and transparency in why it makes the prediction.

Bayes' theorem

In this section, we will first introduce Bayes' theorem and demonstrate how it is applied in ML.

Bayes' theorem calculates the probability of an event given a condition, such that we have prior knowledge about the event, the condition, and the probability of the condition when the event occurs. In our snow prediction example, the event is when snow occurs. A condition would be when the temperature is between 20°F and 32°F. And, based on the data, we can calculate the likelihood of temperature being 20°F and 32°F when it snows. Using this data, we can predict the probability of snow given the temperature being between 20°F and 32°F.

Assume that we have a class variable C and a condition variable x. Bayes' theorem is presented in formula 1. We also present a given simple way to remember different components of the algorithm in formula 2.

Formula 1

$$P(C|x) = \frac{P(C) \cdot P(x|C)}{P(x)}$$

Formula 2

$$Posterior = \frac{Prior \cdot Likelihood}{Evidence}$$

There are four terms that you need to remember from this formula.

Posterior $P(C|x)$

The **posterior** probability is the chance of an event occurring given the existence of feature variable x.

Likelihood $P(x|C)$

Likelihood is the probability of a condition occurring for a given event. In our example, likelihood means what the probability is of the temperature being between 20°F to 32°F when it snows. Based on the data in the dataset, there is a 66.66% probability that the temperature is 20°F-30°F when it snows. Training data can be used to calculate the probability of each discrete value in the feature set.

Prior probability $P(C)$

The **prior** probability is the overall probability of the event in the dataset. In our example, this would be the overall probability that it snows in the dataset. Prior probability is important in cases where the datasets are unbalanced, that is, the number of instances of one class variable in the dataset is significantly higher than the other. This leads to bias in the likelihood variable. Prior probabilities are used to renormalize these probabilities by taking the bias in the dataset into account. For example, in our dataset, the prior probability of a snow event is 30% and the prior probability of it not snowing is 70%. The probability of cloudy conditions when it snows is 66%, while the likelihood of cloudy conditions when it does not snow is 42.8%.

However, by taking the prior probabilities into account, although cloudy conditions are more likely when it snows than when it does not, after multiplying the priors, the posterior probability of snow when it is cloudy is 19% and the probability of not snowing when it is cloudy is 30%. By multiplying the prior probabilities to the likelihood events, we inform our posterior probability that there is a higher probability of it not snowing than snowing.

Evidence $P(x)$

The **evidence** variable is the probability of a condition in the dataset. In our example, the probability of temperature being 70°F or above is only 10%. Rare events have low evidence probability. Evidence probabilities boost posterior probabilities of rare events. For the purpose of the Naïve Bayes classifier, we do not need to consider the evidence variable, since it is not dependent on the class variable.

So, Bayes' theorem is used to calculate the probability of an event given a single condition. However, when we train ML algorithms, we use one or more features to predict the probability of an event. In the next section, we will explain Naïve Bayes algorithm and how it utilizes posterior probabilities of multiple features variables.

How the Naive Bayes algorithm works

The Naive Bayes algorithm uses Bayes' theorem to calculate the posterior probability of every condition in the dataset and uses these probabilities to calculate the conditional probability of an event given a set of conditions. The Naive Bayes algorithm assumes that each conditional feature is independent of each other. This is an important assumption that helps simplify how the conditional probability is calculated. The independence assumption is the reason why the algorithm gets the name, Naive Bayes.

In this section, instead of considering one x feature variable, we consider a vector of features, $X = (x_1, x_2, \ldots, x_n)$, where n is the number of feature variables used to calculate the class probability. We represent the conditional probability of a class variable for the x vector in formula 3:

Formula 3

$$P(C \mid x_1, x_2, \ldots, x_n)$$

As we have assumed that each feature variable is independent of each other, the conditional probability of a class variable can be calculated as follows:

Formula 4

$$P(C \,|\, x_1, x_2 .. x_n) = \prod_{i=1}^{n} P(C \,|\, x_i)$$

Based on posterior probability calculations shown in the previous sections, this formula can be rewritten as follows:

Formula 5

$$P(C \,|\, x_1, x_2 .. x_n) = P(C) \prod_{i=1}^{n} P(x_i \,|\, C)$$

Formula 5 explains how a probability of event C is calculated based on the $X = (x_1, x_2, \ldots, x_n)$ feature variables. An interesting thing to note in this formula is how easy it is to calculate each element from the dataset. Also, since the evidence probability from Bayes' theorem is not dependent on the class variable, it is not used in the Naive Bayes formula.

The Naive Bayes algorithm only requires one pass over the dataset during the training phase to calculate the probability of the value of a feature for each event. During the prediction phase, we calculate the probability of each event given the instance of the features and predict the event with the highest probability. Formula 6 shows how the prediction of a Naïve Bayes classifier is calculated when *k* events are possible. **Argmax** in the formula means that the event with maximum probability is selected as the prediction:

Formula 6

$$Prediction = argmax_{k \in 1..K} \, P(C_k) \prod_{i=1}^{n} P(x_i \,|\, C)$$

Naïve Bayes classifier is a multiclass classifier that can be used to train on a dataset where two or more class variables need to be predicted. In the next chapters, we will present some examples of binary classifiers that only work with two class variables needs to be predicted. However, we will show you the methodologies of applying binary classifiers to multiclass problems.

Classifying text with language models

Text classification is an application of classification algorithms. However, the text is a combination of words in a specific order. Hence, you can observe that a text document with a class variable is not similar to the dataset that we presented in table 1, in the *Classification algorithms* section.

A text dataset can be represented as shown in table 2.

Table 2: Example of a Twitter dataset

Tweet	Account
The simplest way to protect Americans from gun violence is to actually talk about common-sense gun laws.	Democrats
This cannot be who we are as a country. We need to find out what happened and ensure it never happens again (`https://t.co/RiY7sjMfJK`))	Democrats
Over the weekend, President Trump visited Arlington National Cemetery to honor fallen soldiers.	Republicans
This President has made it clear that he will secure this country—`@SecNielsen`.	Republicans

For this chapter, we have built a dataset based on tweets from two different accounts. We also have provided code in the following sections so that you can create your own datasets to try this example. Our purpose is to build a smart application that is capable of predicting the source of a tweet just by reading the tweet text. We will collect several tweets by the United States Republican Party (`@GOP`) and the Democratic Party (`@TheDemocrats`) to build a model that can predict which party wrote a given tweet. In order to do this, we will randomly select some tweets from each party and submit them through the model to check whether the prediction actually matched reality.

Collecting the tweets

We will start by using the `Twython` library to access the Twitter API and collect a series of tweets, labeling them with the originating political party.

The details of the implementation can be found in our GitHub repository in the following Jupyter Notebook:

```
chapter2/collect_tweets.ipynb
```

We need to invoke the following method in the `Twython` library to save tweets from `@GOP` and `@TheDemocrats` onto some text files, `gop.txt` and `dems.txt` respectively:

```
twitter.get_user_timeline(screen_name='GOP', tweet_mode='extended',
count=500)
```

Each file contains 200 tweets. The following are some excerpts from the `dems.txt` file:

- `This cannot be who we are as a country. We need to find out what happened and ensure it never happens again.`
- `RT @AFLCIO: Scott Walker. Forever a national disgrace.`

Preparing the data

Now that we have the source data in text files, we need to convert it to a format that can be used as an input for a ML library. Most general-purpose ML packages, such as `scikit-learn` and Apache Spark, only accept a matrix of numbers as input. Hence, feature transformation is required for a text dataset. A common approach is to use language models such as **bag of words (BoW)**. In this example, we build a BoW for each tweet and construct a matrix in which each row represents a tweet and each column signals the presence of a particular word. We also have a column for the label that can distinguish tweets from `Republicans` (1) or `Democrats` (0), as we can see in the following table:

Table 3: Converting text dataset to structured dataset

	Immigration	Medicaid	Terrorism	Class
Tweet 1	0	1	0	0
Tweet 2	1	0	1	1
Tweet 3	0	0	1	0

Table 2 represents the matrix that can be derived from tweets. However, there are many points to remember when generating such a matrix. Due to the number of terms in the language lexicon, the number of columns in the matrix can be very high. This poses a problem in ML known as the **curse of dimensionality** (see section X). There are several ways to tackle this problem; however, as our example is fairly small in terms of data, we will only briefly discuss methods to reduce the number of columns.

- **Stopwords**: Certain common words might add no value to our task (for example, the words **the**, **for**, or **as**). We call these words stopwords, and we shall remove these words from `dems.txt` and `gop.txt`.

- **Stemming**: There may be many variants of a word that are used in the text. For example, argue, argued, argues, and arguing all stem from the word **argue**. Techniques such as stemming and lemmatization can be used to find the stem of the word and replace variants of that word with the stem.
- **Tokenization**: Tokenization can be used to combine various words into phrases so that the number of features can be reduced. For example, **tea party** has a totally different meaning, politically, than the two words alone. We won't consider this for our simple example, but tokenization techniques help in finding such phrases.

Another issue to consider is that words appearing more than once in a tweet have equal importance on a training row. There are ways to utilize this information by using multinomial or term frequency-inverse document frequency (TFIDF) models. Since tweets are relatively short text, we will not consider this aspect in our implementation.

The table 2 matrix describes the words you would find for each class (that is each political party). However, when we want to predict the source of the tweet, the inverse problem is posed. Given a specific bag of words, we're interested in assessing how likely it is that the terms are used by one party or another. In other words, we know the probability of a bag of words given a particular party, and we are interested in the reverse: the probability of a tweet being written by a party given a bag of words. This is where the Naive Bayes algorithm is applied.

Building a Naive Bayes model through SageMaker notebooks

Let's get started with SageMaker notebooks. This tool will help us run the code that will train our model. SageMaker, among other things, allows us to create notebook instances that host Jupyter Notebooks. Jupyter is a web UI that allows a data scientist or programmer to code interactively by creating paragraphs of code that are executed on demand. It works as an IDE, but with the additional ability to render the output of the code in visually relevant forms (for example, charts, tables, and markdown), and also supports writing paragraphs in different languages within the same notebook. We will use notebooks extensively throughout this book, and we recommend its use as a way to share and present data science findings. It allows users to achieve reproducible research, as the code necessary for a particular research objective can be validated and reproduced by re-running the code paragraphs in the notebook.

You can learn more on SageMaker's AWS console page at `https://console.aws.amazon.com/sagemaker/home?region=us-east-1#/dashboard`.

Let's look at what Sagemaker's AWS console page looks in the following screenshot:

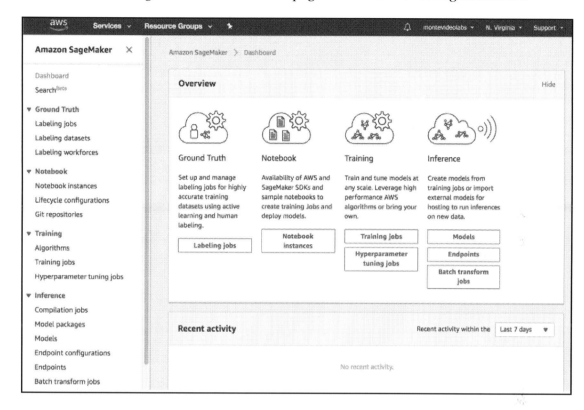

Click on **Add repository**, choose your authentication mechanism and add the repository found at `https://github.com/mg-um/mastering-ml-on-aws`:

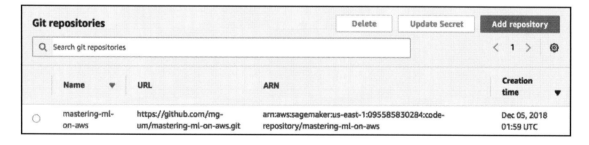

Before creating the notebook instance, it is possible that you would want to attach a Git repository so that the notebooks available with this book are attached to the notebook, and so are made available immediately as you will see later:

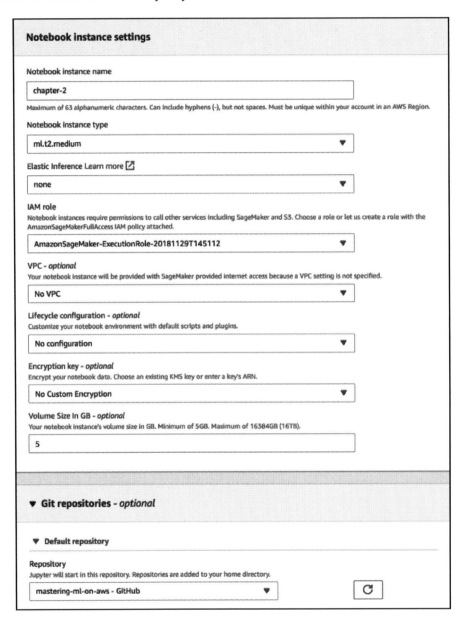

We can now proceed to launch a notebook instance. There are several options to configure the hardware, networking, and security of the server that will host the notebook. However, we will not go into much detail for now, and will accept the defaults. The AWS documentation is an excellent resource if you want to limit the access or power-up your machine.

Since we attached the Git repository, once you open Jupyter, you should see the notebooks we created for this book, and you can re-run them, modify them, or improve them:

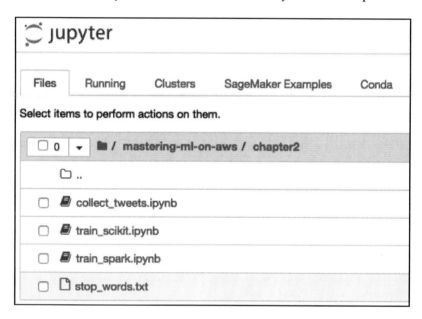

In this section, we focus on the train_scikit Python notebook and go over code snippets to explain how we can build and test a model for out tweet classification problem. We encourage you to run all the paragraphs of this notebook to get an idea of the purpose of this notebook.

The first thing we will do is load the stopwords and the two sets of tweets into variables:

```
import pandas as pd
import numpy as np
from sklearn.feature_extraction.text import CountVectorizer
from scipy import sparse

SRC_PATH = '/home/ec2-user/SageMaker/mastering-ml-on-aws/chapter2/'
stop_words = [word.strip() for word in open(SRC_PATH +
'stop_words.txt').readlines()]
with open(SRC_PATH + 'dem.txt', 'r') as file:
```

```
        dem_text = [line.strip('\n') for line in file]
with open(SRC_PATH + 'gop.txt', 'r') as file:
        gop_text = [line.strip('\n') for line in file]
```

We will then proceed to use the utilities in scikit-learn to construct our matrix. In order to do that, we will use a CountVectorizer class, which is a class that knows how to allocate the different words into columns while at the same time filtering the stopwords. We will consider both sets of tweets; for our example, we'll just use the first 1200 words:

```
vectorizer = CountVectorizer(input=dem_text + gop_text,
                             stop_words=stop_words,
                             max_features=1200)
```

Through vectorizer we can now construct two matrices, one for republican party tweets and one for democratic party tweets:

```
dem_bow = vectorizer.fit_transform(dem_text)
gop_bow = vectorizer.fit_transform(gop_text)
```

These two bag-of-words matrices (dem_bow and gop_bow) are represented in a sparse data structure to minimize memory usage, but can be examined by converting them to arrays:

```
>>> gop_bow.toarray()

array([[0, 0, 1, ..., 0, 1, 0],
       [0, 0, 0, ..., 0, 0, 1],
       [0, 1, 0, ..., 0, 0, 0],
       ...,
       [0, 0, 0, ..., 0, 0, 0],
       [0, 1, 0, ..., 0, 0, 0],
       [0, 0, 0, ..., 0, 1, 0]], dtype=int64)
```

In order to train our model, we need to provide two arrays. The BoWs matrix (for both parties), which we will call x, and the labels (class variables) for each of the tweets. To construct this, we will vertically stack both matrices (for each party):

```
x = sparse.vstack((dem_bow, gop_bow))
```

To construct the labels vector, we will just assemble a vector with ones for Democrat positions and zeros for Republican positions:

```
ones = np.ones(200)
zeros = np.zeros(200)
y = np.hstack((ones, zeros))
```

Before we train our models, we will split the tweets (rows on our x matrix) randomly, so that some are used to build a model and others are used to check whether the model predicts the correct political party (label):

```
from sklearn.model_selection import train_test_split
x_train, x_test, y_train, y_test = train_test_split(x, y, test_size=0.25,
random_state=42)
```

Now that we have our training and testing datasets, we proceed to train our model using Naive Bayes (a Bernoulli Naive Bayes, since our matrices are ones or zeros):

```
from sklearn.naive_bayes import BernoulliNB
naive_bayes = BernoulliNB()
model = naive_bayes.fit(x_train, y_train)
```

As you can see in the preceding code, it is very simple to fit a Naive Bayes model. We need to provide the training matrices and the labels. A model is now capable of predicting the label (political party) of arbitrary tweets (as long as we have them as a BoWs matrix representation). Fortunately, we had separated some of the tweets for testing, so we can run these through the model and see how often the model predicts the right label (note that we know the actual party that wrote the tweet for every tweet in the testing dataset).

To get the predictions it's as simple as invoking the predict method of the model:

```
y_predictions = model.predict(x_test)
```

Now, we can see how many of the predictions match the ground truth:

```
from sklearn.metrics import accuracy_score
accuracy_score(y_test, y_predictions)
```

The output score of the code block is 0.95.

In this example, we are using accuracy as an evaluation metric. Accuracy can be calculated using formula 7:

Formula 7

$$Accuracy = \frac{Total\,Number\,of\,Correct\,Predictions}{Total\,Number\,of\,predictions}$$

There are various evaluation metrics that a data scientist can use to evaluate ML algorithm. We will present evaluation measures such as precision, recall, F1 measure, **root mean squared error** (**RMSE**), and **area under curve** (**AUC**) in our next chapters for different examples. Evaluation metrics should be selected based on the business need of implementing an algorithm, and should indicate whether or not the ML algorithm is performing at the standards required to achieve a task.

Since this is the first example we are working on, we will use the simplest evaluation measure, which is accuracy. As specified in formula 7, accuracy is the ratio of correct predictions to the total number of predictions made by the classifier. It turns out that our Naive Bayes model is very accurate, with an accuracy of 95%. It is possible that some words, such as the names of members of each party, can quickly make the model give a correct prediction. We will explore this using decision trees in Chapter 4, *Predicting User Behavior with Tree-Based Methods*.

 Note that, during this process, we had to prepare and transform the data in order to fit a model. This process is very common, and both scikit-learn and Spark support the concept of pipelines, which allow the data scientist to declare the necessary transformations needed to build a model without having to manually obtain intermediary results.

In the following code snippet, we can see an alternative way to produce the same model by creating a pipeline with the following two stages:

- Count vectorizer
- Naive Bayes trainer

```
from sklearn.pipeline import Pipeline
x_train, x_test, y_train, y_test = train_test_split(dem_text + gop_text, y,
test_size=0.25, random_state=5)
pipeline = Pipeline([('vect', vectorizer), ('nb', naive_bayes)])
pipeline_model = pipeline.fit(x_train, y_train)
y_predictions = pipeline_model.predict(x_test)
accuracy_score(y_test, y_predictions)
```

This allows our modeling to be a bit more concise and declarative. By calling the pipeline.fit() method, the library applies any necessary transformations or estimations necessary. Note that, in this case, we split the raw texts (rather than the matrices) as the fit() method now receives the raw input. As we shall see in the next section, pipelines can contain two kinds of stages, Transformers and Estimators, depending on whether the stage needs to compute a model out of the data, or simply transform the data declaratively.

Naïve Bayes model on SageMaker notebooks using Apache Spark

In the previous section *Classifying text with language models,* we saw how you can train a model with `scikit-learn` on a SageMaker notebook instance. This is feasible for examples as small as the ones we collected from Twitter. What if, instead, we had hundreds of terabytes worth of tweet data? For starters, we would not be able to store the data in a single machine. Even if we could, it would probably take too long to train on such large dataset. Apache Spark solves this problem for us by implementing ML algorithms that can read data from distributed datasets (such as AWS S3) and can distribute the computing across many machines. AWS provides a product called **Elastic MapReduce** (**EMR**) that is capable of launching and managing clusters on which we can perform ML at scale.

Many of the ML algorithms require several passes over the data (although this is not the case for Naive Bayes). Apache Spark provides a way to cache the datasets in memory, so that one can efficiently run algorithms that require several passes over the data (such as **logistic regression** or **decision trees**, which we will see in the following chapters). We will show how to launch EMR clusters in `Chapter 4`, *Predicting User Behavior with Tree-Based Methods,* however, in this section, we will present how similar it is to work with Apache Spark compared to `scikit-learn`. In fact, many of the interfaces in Apache Spark (such as pipelines, Transformers, and Estimators) were inspired by `scikit-learn`.

Apache Spark supports four main languages: R, Python, Scala, and Java. In this book we will use the Python flavor, also called PySpark. Even though our spark code will run on a single machine (that is, will run on our SageMaker notebook instance), it could run on multiple machines without any code changes if our data was larger and we had a Spark Cluster (in `Chapter 4`, *Predicting User Behavior with Tree-Based Methods,* we will dive into creating Spark Clusters with EMR).

In Spark, the first thing we need to do is to create a Spark session. We do this by first creating a Spark context, and then creating a session for SQL-like manipulation of data:

```
from pyspark.context import SparkContext
from pyspark.sql import SQLContext

sc = SparkContext('local', 'test')
sql = SQLContext(sc)
```

Since we will run Spark locally (on a single machine) we specify `local`. However, if we were to run this on a cluster, we would need to specify the master address of the cluster instead. Spark works with abstractions called DataFrames that allow us to manipulate huge tables of data using SQL-like operations.

Our first task will be to define DataFrames for our raw data:

```
from pyspark.sql.functions import lit

dems_df = sql.read.text("file://" + SRC_PATH + 'dem.txt')
gop_df = sql.read.text("file://" + SRC_PATH + 'gop.txt')
corpus_df = dems_df.select("value",
lit(1).alias("label")).union(gop_df.select("value", lit(0).alias("label")))
```

In the first two lines, we create DataFrames out of our raw tweets. We also create `corpus_df`, which contains both sources of tweets, and add the label by creating a column with a literal of 1 for Democrats and 0 for `Republicans`:

```
>>> corpus_df.select("*").limit(2).show()

+--------------------+-----+
|               value|label|
+--------------------+-----+
|This ruling is th...|  1 . |
|No president shou...|  1 . |
+--------------------+-----+
```

Spark works in a lazy fashion, so, even though we defined and unioned the DataFrame, no actual processing will happen until we perform the first operation on the data. In our case, this will be the splitting of the DataFrame into testing and training:

```
train_df, test_df = corpus_df.randomSplit([0.75, 0.25])
```

Now, we are ready to train our model. Spark supports the same concept of pipelines. We will build a pipeline with the necessary transformations for our model. It's very similar to our previous example, except that Spark has two separate stages for tokenization and stop words remover:

```
from pyspark.ml import Pipeline
from pyspark.ml.feature import CountVectorizer, Tokenizer, StopWordsRemover
tokenizer = Tokenizer(inputCol="value", outputCol="words")
stop_words_remover = StopWordsRemover(inputCol="words",
outputCol="words_cleaned")
vectorizer = CountVectorizer(inputCol="words_cleaned",
outputCol="features")
cleaning_pipeline = Pipeline(stages = [tokenizer, stop_words_remover,
vectorizer])
cleaning_pipeline_model = cleaning_pipeline.fit(corpus_df)
cleaned_training_df = cleaning_pipeline_model.transform(train_df)
cleaned_testing_df = cleaning_pipeline_model.transform(test_df)
```

A Spark ML pipeline consists of a series of stages. Each stage can be a Transformer or an Estimator. Transformers apply a well-defined transformation on a dataset, while Estimators have the added capability of producing models by traversing the dataset. `NaiveBayes` and `CountVectorizer` are examples of Estimators, while tokenizer and `StopWordsRemover` are examples of Transformers. Models, in turn, are Transformers, because they can provide predictions for all elements in a dataset as a transformation.

As you can see in the preceding code, we defined a pipeline with all the necessary stages to clean the data. Each stage will transform the original DataFrame (which only has two columns value, which are the raw tweet text and label) and add more columns.

In the following code, the relevant columns used at training time are the features (a sparse vector representing the BoWs exactly like our `scikit-learn` example) and the label:

```
>>> cleaned_training_df.show(n=3)

+-----------+-----+-------------+-------------+--------------------+
| value     |label| . words .   |words_cleaned| features           |
+-----------+-----+-------------+-------------+--------------------+
|#Tuesday...| 1 . |[#tuesday...]|[#tuesday... |(3025,[63,1398,18...|
|#WorldAI...| 1 . |[#worlda....]|[#worldai... |(3025,[37,75,155,...|
|@Tony4W....| 1 . |[.@tony4w...]|[.@tony4w... |(3025,[41,131,160...|
+-----------+-----+-------------+-------------+--------------------+
```

By specifying these columns to the `NaiveBayes` classifier we can train a model:

```
from pyspark.ml.classification import NaiveBayes
naive_bayes = NaiveBayes(featuresCol="features", labelCol="label")
```

The model is a transformer that can provide predictions for each row in our training DataFrame:

```
naive_bayes_model = naive_bayes.fit(cleaned_training_df)
predictions_df = naive_bayes_model.transform(cleaned_testing_df)

>>> predictions_df.select("features", "label",
"prediction").limit(3).show()
+--------------------+-----+----------+
| features           |label|prediction|
+--------------------+-----+----------+
|(3025,[1303,1858,...| 1 . | 1.0      |
|(3025,[1,20,91,13...| 1 . | 1.0      |
|(3025,[16,145,157...| 1 . | 1.0      |
+--------------------+-----+----------+
```

Similar to our previous example, we can evaluate the accuracy of our models. By using the `MulticlassClassificationEvaluator` class and specifying the actual and predicted labels, we can obtain `accuracy`:

```
from pyspark.ml.evaluation import MulticlassClassificationEvaluator
evaluator = MulticlassClassificationEvaluator(
    labelCol="label", predictionCol="prediction", metricName="accuracy")
evaluator.evaluate(predictions_df)
```

The output is 0.93, which is similar to the results we had on `scikit-learn`.

Using SageMaker's BlazingText built-in ML service

We saw how to perform ML tasks using `scikit-learn` and Apache Spark libraries. However, sometimes it's more appropriate to use a ML service. SageMaker provides ways for us to create, tune, and deploy models supporting a variety of built-in ML algorithms by just invoking a service. In a nutshell, you need to place the data in S3 (an Amazon service to store large amounts of data) and call the SageMaker service providing all the necessary details (actual ML algorithm, the location of the data, which kind and how many machines should be used for training). In this section, we go through the process of training our model for predicting tweets through SageMaker's BlazingText ML service. BlazingText is an algorithm that supports text classification using word2vec, which is a way to transform words into vectors in a way that captures precise syntactic and semantic word relationships. We won't dive into the details of SageMaker's architecture yet, but we will present the reader how we would use this AWS service as an alternative to `scikit-learn` or Spark.

We will start by importing the SakeMaker libraries, creating a session, and obtaining a role (which is the role that the notebook instance is using (see `https://aws.amazon.com/blogs/aws/iam-roles-for-ec2-instances-simplified-secure-access-to-aws-service-apies-from-ec2`).

Additionally, we specify the S3 bucket we will be using to store all our data and models:

```
import sagemaker
from sagemaker import get_execution_role
import json
import boto3

sess = sagemaker.Session()
role = get_execution_role()
bucket = "mastering-ml-aws"
prefix = "chapter2/blazingtext"
```

The next step is to put some data in S3 for training. The expected format for BlazingText is to have each line in the __label__X TEXT format. In our case, this means prefixing each tweet by a label representing the originating party:

```
__label__1 We are forever g..
__label__0 RT @AFLCIO: Scott Walker.
__label__0 Democrats will hold this
__label__1 Congratulations to hundreds of thousands ...
```

To do that, we perform some preprocessing of our tweets and prefix the right label:

```
with open(SRC_PATH + 'dem.txt', 'r') as file:
    dem_text = ["__label__0 " + line.strip('\n') for line in file]

with open(SRC_PATH + 'gop.txt', 'r') as file:
    gop_text = ["__label__1 " + line.strip('\n') for line in file]
corpus = dem_text + gop_text
```

We then proceed to create the sets for training and testing as text files:

```
from sklearn.model_selection import train_test_split
corpus_train, corpus_test = train_test_split(corpus, test_size=0.25,
random_state=42)

corpus_train_txt = "\n".join(corpus_train)
corpus_test_txt = "\n".join(corpus_test)

with open('tweets.train', 'w') as file:
    file.write(corpus_train_txt)
with open('tweets.test', 'w') as file:
    file.write(corpus_test_txt)
```

Once we have our training and validation text files, we upload them into S3:

```
train_path = prefix + '/train'
validation_path = prefix + '/validation'

sess.upload_data(path='tweets.train', bucket=bucket, key_prefix=train_path)
sess.upload_data(path='tweets.test', bucket=bucket,
key_prefix=validation_path)

s3_train_data = 's3://{}/{}'.format(bucket, train_path)
s3_validation_data = 's3://{}/{}'.format(bucket, validation_path)
```

We then proceed to instantiate `Estimator`, by specifying all the necessary details: the type and amount of machines to be used for training, as well as the location of the path in S3 where the models will be stored:

```
container = sagemaker.amazon.amazon_estimator.get_image_uri('us-east-1',
"blazingtext", "latest")

s3_output_location = 's3://{}/{}/output'.format(bucket, prefix)
bt_model = sagemaker.estimator.Estimator(container,
                                    role,
                                    train_instance_count=1,
train_instance_type='ml.c4.4xlarge',
                                    train_volume_size = 30,
                                    train_max_run = 360000,
                                    input_mode= 'File',
                                    output_path=s3_output_location,
                                    sagemaker_session=sess)
```

As we discussed in the previous section *Naive Bayes model on SageMaker notebooks using Apache Spark* section, an estimator is capable of creating models by processing training data. The next step will be to fit the model providing the training data:

```
bt_model.set_hyperparameters(mode="supervised", epochs=10, min_count=3,
learning_rate=0.05, vector_dim=10, early_stopping=False, patience=5,
min_epochs=5, word_ngrams=2) train_data =
sagemaker.session.s3_input(s3_train_data, distribution='FullyReplicated',
content_type='text/plain', s3_data_type='S3Prefix') validation_data =
sagemaker.session.s3_input(s3_validation_data,
distribution='FullyReplicated', content_type='text/plain',
s3_data_type='S3Prefix') data_channels = {'train': train_data,
'validation': validation_data}
bt_model.fit(inputs=data_channels, logs=True)
```

Before we train the model we need to specify the hyperparameters. We won't go into much detail about this algorithm in this section, but the reader can find the details in `https://docs.aws.amazon.com/sagemaker/latest/dg/blazingtext.html`.

This particular algorithm also takes the validation data, as it runs over the data several times (epochs) to improve the error. Once we fit the model, we can deploy the model as a web service so that applications can use it:

```
predictor = bt_model.deploy(initial_instance_count = 1,instance_type =
'ml.m4.xlarge')
```

In our case, we will just hit the endpoint to get the predictions and evaluate the accuracy:

```
corpus_test_no_labels = [x[11:] for x in corpus_test]
payload = {"instances" : corpus_test_no_labels}
response = predictor.predict(json.dumps(payload))
predictions = json.loads(response)
print(json.dumps(predictions, indent=2))
```

After running the preceding code we get the following output:

[{ "prob": [0.5003], "label": ["__label__0"] }, { "prob": [0.5009], "label": ["__label__1"] }...

As you can see in the preceding code, each prediction comes along with a probability (which we will ignore for now). Next, we compute how many of these labels matched the original one:

```
predicted_labels = [prediction['label'][0] for prediction in predictions]
predicted_labels[:4]
```

After running the preceding code we get the following output:

['__label__0', '__label__1', '__label__0', '__label__0']

Then run the next line of code:

```
actual_labels = [x[:10] for x in corpus_test]
actual_labels[:4]
```

As you can see in the following output from the previous code block, some of the labels matched the actual while some don't:

['__label__1', '__label__1', '__label__0', '__label__1']

Next, we run the following code to build a boolean vector containing true or false depending on whether the actual matches the predicted result:

```
matches = [(actual_label == predicted_label) for (actual_label,
predicted_label) in zip(actual_labels, predicted_labels)]
matches[:4]
```

After running the preceding code we get the following output:

[False, True, True, False]

After we run the preceding output, we will run the following code to calculate the ratio of cases that match out of the total instances:

```
matches.count(True) / len(matches)
```

The following output from the previous block shows the accuracy score:

```
0.61
```

We can see that the accuracy is lower than in our previous examples. This is for many reasons. For starters, we did not invest too much in data preparation in this case (for example, no stopwords are used in this case). However, the main reason for the lower accuracy is due to the fact we're using such little data. These models work best on larger datasets.

Naive Bayes – pros and cons

In this section, we present the advantages and disadvantages in selecting the Naive Bayes algorithm for classification problems:

Pros

- **Training time**: Naive Bayes algorithm only requires one pass on the entire dataset to calculate the posterior probabilities for each value of the feature in the dataset. So, when we are dealing with large datasets or low-budget hardware, Naive Bayes algorithm is a feasible choice for most data scientists.

- **Prediction time**: Since all the probabilities are pre-computed in the Naive Bayes algorithm, the prediction time of this algorithm is very efficient.

- **Transparency**: Since the predictions of Naive Bayes algorithms are based on the posterior probability of each conditional feature, it is easy to understand which features are influencing the predictions. This helps users to understand the predictions.

Cons

- **Prediction accuracy**: The prediction accuracy of the Naive Bayes algorithm is lower than other algorithms we will discuss in the book. Algorithm prediction accuracy is dataset dependent, a lot of research works have proved that algorithms such as random forest, **support vector machines (SVMs)**, and **deep neural networks (DNNs)** outperform Naive Bayes algorithm in terms of classification accuracy.

- **Assumption of independence**: Since we assume that each feature is independent of each other, this algorithm may lose information for features that are dependent on each other. Other advanced algorithms do use this dependence information when calculating predictions.

Summary

In this chapter, we introduced you to why ML is a crucial tool in a data scientist's repository. We discussed what a structured ML dataset looks like and how to identify the types of features in the dataset.

We took a deep dive into Naive Bayes classification algorithm, and studied how Bayes' theorem is used in Naive Bayes algorithm. Using Bayes' theorem, we can predict the probability of an event occurring based on the values of each feature, and select the event that has the highest probability.

We also presented an example of a Twitter dataset. We hope that you learned how to think about a text classification problem, and how to build a Naive Bayes classification model to predict the source of a tweet. We also presented how the algorithm can be implemented in SageMaker, and how it can also be implemented using Apache Spark. This code base should help you tackle any text classification problems in the future. As the implementation is presented using SageMaker services and Spark, it can scale to datasets that can be gigabytes or terabytes in size.

We will look at how to deploy the ML models on actual production clusters in later chapters.

Exercises

1. Bayes' Theorem is not only useful for the Naive Bayes algorithm, but is also used for other purposes. Find two more algorithms where Bayes' theorem is applied, and explain how they are different than the Naive Bayes algorithm.

2. In this chapter, we presented an example of a binary classifier. Based on our code to download tweets, create a new dataset where you download tweets from five different sources and build a Naive Bayes model that can predict the source of each tweet.

3. Identify scenarios for when you would use `scikit-learn`, Apache Spark, or SageMaker services for a particular problem.

3
Predicting House Value with Regression Algorithms

This chapter will introduce the basics of regression algorithms and apply them to predict the price of houses given a number of features. We'll also introduce how to use logistic regression for classification problems. Examples in SageMaker Notebooks for scikit-learn, Apache Spark, and SageMaker's linear learner will be provided.

In this chapter, we will cover the following topics:

- Predicting the price of houses
- Understanding linear regression
- Evaluating regression models
- Implementing linear regression through scikit-learn
- Implementing linear regression through Apache Spark
- Implementing linear regression through SageMaker's linear learner
- Understanding logistic regression
- Pros and cons of linear models

Predicting the price of houses

In this chapter, we will consider the problem of trying to predict the value of houses in Boston's suburbs based on a number of variables, such as the number of rooms and house age. The details of the dataset can be found here: https://www.kaggle.com/c/boston-housing/. This problem is different to the one we considered in the last chapter, as the variable we're trying to predict (price in dollars) is continuous. Models that are able to predict continuous quantities are called **regressors**, or **regression algorithms**. There are many such algorithms, but in this chapter, we will focus on the simplest (but very popular) kind, linear regressors.

Understanding linear regression

Regression algorithms are an important algorithm in a data scientist's toolkit as they can be used for various non-binary prediction tasks. The linear regression algorithm models the relationship between a dependent variable that we are trying to predict with a vector of independent variables. The vector of variables is also called the regressor in the context of regression algorithms. Linear regression assumes that there is a linear relationship between the vector of independent variables and the dependent variable that we are trying to predict. Hence, linear regression models learn the unknown variables and constants of a linear function using the training data, such that the linear function best fits the training data.

Linear regression can be applied in cases where the goal is to predict or forecast the dependent variable based on the regressor variables. We will use an example to explain how linear regression trains based on data.

The following table shows a sample dataset where the goal is to predict the price of a house based on three variables:

Floor Size	Number of Bedrooms	Number of Bathrooms	House Price
2500	4	2	6,00,000
2800	4	2	6,50,000
2700	4	3	6,50,000
4500	6	4	8,00,000
3500	4	2	7,50,000
3000	5	4	7,60,000
2000	3	2	5,00,000
4100	4	3	8,10,000

In this dataset, the variables `Floor Size`, `Number of Bedrooms`, and `Number of Bathrooms` are assumed as independent in linear regression. Our goal is to predict the `House Price` value based on the variables.

Let's simplify this problem. Let's only consider the `Floor Size` variable to predict the house price. Creating linear regression from only one variable or regressor is referred to as **a simple linear regression**. If we create a scatterplot from the two columns, we can observe that there is a relationship between these two variables:

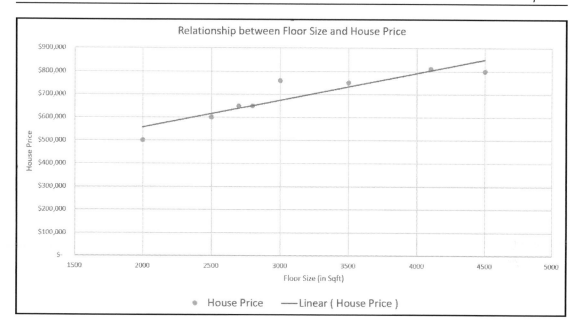

Although there is not an exact linear relationship between the two variables, we can create an approximate line that represents the trend. The aim of the modeling algorithm is to minimize the error in creating this approximate line.

As we know, a straight line can be represented by the following equation:

$$y = \beta_0 + \beta_1 x$$

Hence, the approximately linear relationship in the preceding diagram can also be represented using the same formula, and the task of the linear regression model is to learn the value of β_0 and β_1. Moreover, since we know that the relationship between the predicted variable and the regressors is not strictly linear, we can add a random error variable to the equation that models the noise in the dataset. The following formula represents how the simple linear regression model is represented:

$$y = \beta_i x + \beta_0 + \varepsilon$$

Now, let's consider the dataset with multiple regressors. Instead of just representing the linear relationship between one variable x and y, we will represent a set of regressors as $X = (x_1, x_2 \ldots x_n)$. We will assume that a linear relationship between the dependent variable y and the regressors X is linear. Thus, a linear regression model with multiple regressors is represented by the following formula:

$$y = \sum_{i=1}^{n} \beta_{1i} x_i + \beta_{0i} + \varepsilon_i$$

Linear regression, as we've already discussed, assumes that there is a linear relationship between the regressors and the dependent variable that we are trying to predict. This is an important assumption that may not hold true in all datasets. Hence, for a data scientist, using linear regression may look attractive due to its fast training time. However, if the dataset variables do not have a linear relationship with the dependent variable, it may lead to significant errors. In such cases, data scientists may also try algorithms such as Bernoulli regression, Poisson regression, or multinomial regression to improve prediction precision. We will also discuss logistic regression later in this chapter, which is used when the dependent variable is binary.

During the training phase, linear regression can use various techniques for parameter estimation to learn the values of β_0, β_1, and ε. We will not go into the details of these techniques in this book. However, we recommend that you try using these parameter estimation techniques in the examples that follow and observe their effect on the training time of the algorithm and the accuracy of prediction.

To fit a linear model to the data, we first need to be able to determine how well a linear model fits the data. There are various models being developed for parameter estimation in linear regression. Parameter estimation is the process of estimating the values of β_0, β_1, and ε. In the following sections, will briefly explain these two estimation techniques.

Linear least squares estimation

Linear least squares (LLS) is an estimation approach that's used to estimate parameters based on the given data. The optimization problem of the LLS estimation can be explained as follows:

$$min_{\beta 0, \beta 1} : \sum_{x=1}^{n} [y_i - (\beta_0 + \beta_1 x_i)]^2$$

LLS is a set of formulations that are used to get solutions to the statistical problem of linear regression by estimating the values of β_0 and β_1. LLS is an optimization methodology for getting solutions for linear regression. It uses the observed values of x and y to estimate the values of β_0 and β_1. We encourage you to explore LLS solutions to understand how it estimates the linear regression parameters. However, as the focus of this book is to introduce you to these concepts and help you apply them in AWS, we won't go into detail about this methodology.

Maximum likelihood estimation

Maximum likelihood estimation (**MLE**) is a popular model that's used for estimating the parameters of linear regression. MLE is a probabilistic model that can predict what values of the parameters have the maximum likelihood to recreate the observed dataset. This is represented by the following formula:

$$l(parameters|data) = \sum_{i=1}^{n} f(data_i|parameters)$$

For linear regression, our assumption is that the dependent variable has a linear relationship with the model. MLE assumes that the dependent variable values have a normal distribution. The idea is to predict the parameters for each observed value of X so that it models the value of y. We also estimate the error for each observed value that models how different the linear predicted value of y is from the actual value.

Gradient descent

The **gradient descent algorithm** is also popular for estimating parameters for linear regression. The gradient descent algorithm is used to minimize a function. Based on what we are predicting, we start with a set of initial values for the parameters and iteratively move toward the parameters to minimize the error in the function. The function to iteratively make steps in minimizing error is called **gradient**. The idea is to descend the gradient toward the lowest point in the gradient plane. Different types of gradient descent algorithms include **batch gradient descent**, which looks at all observed examples in each example, and **stochastic gradient descent**, where we iterate with only one observation at a time. For this reason, batch gradient descent is more accurate than stochastic gradient descent, but is much slower and hence not suitable for larger datasets.

There is a vast amount of research being done on regression algorithms as it is very well suited for predicting continuous variables. We encourage you to learn more about linear regression libraries and try different variants that are provided in the library to calculate the efficiency and effectiveness of the test datasets.

Evaluating regression models

Unlike the Naive Bayes classification model, the regression model provides a numerical output as a prediction. This output can be used for binary classification by predicting the value for both the events and using the maximum value. However, in examples such as predicting a house value based on regressors, we cannot use evaluation metrics that rely on just predicting whether we got the answer correct or incorrect. When we are predicting a numerical value, the evaluation metrics should also quantify the value of error in prediction. For example, if the house value is 600,000 and model A predicts it as 700,000 and model B predicts it as 1,000,000, metrics such as precision and recall will count both these predictions as false positives. However, for regression models, we need evaluation metrics that can tell us that model A was closer to the actual value than model B. Therefore, in this section, we will present three metrics that are used for such numerical predictions.

Mean absolute error

Mean absolute error (MAE) is the mean of the absolute values of the error. It can be represented with the following formula:

$$MAE = \frac{1}{n} \sum_{i=1}^{n} |y_i - \hat{y}_i|$$

MAE provides an average error between two vectors. In our case, MAE is the difference between the actual value of y and the predicted value $\hat{y}$. MAE is used by a lot of researchers since it gives a clear interpretation of the errors in the model's prediction.

Mean squared error

Mean squared error (MSE) is the mean of squares of the error values and is represented by the following formula:

$$MSE = \frac{1}{n}\sum_{i=1}^{n}(y_i - \hat{y}_i)^2$$

MSE is useful in cases where the errors are very small. MSE incorporates both how far the predicted values are from the truth and also the variance in the predicted values.

Root mean squared error

Root mean squared error (RMSE) is the square root of the mean squared errors and is represented by the following formula:

$$RMSE = \sqrt{\frac{1}{n}\sum_{i=1}^{n}(y_i - \hat{y}_i)^2}$$

RMSE, similar to MSE, captures the variance in predictions. However, in RMSE, since we take the square root of the squared error values, the error can be comparable to MSE, and also keep the advantages of MSE.

R-squared

Another popular metric that's used in regression problems is the R-squared score, or coefficient of determination. This score measures the proportion of the variance in the dependent variable that is predictable from the independent variables:

$$R^2(y, \hat{y}) = 1 - \frac{\sum_{i=0}^{n-1}(y_i - \hat{y}_i)}{\sum_{i=0}^{n-1}(y_i - \bar{y}_i)}$$

Here, y represents the vector of actual values, while y_i and $\hat{y}_i$ represents the vector of predicted values. The mean actual value is $\bar{y}$. The denominator of the quotient measures how actual values typically differ from the mean, while the numerator measures how actual values differ from predicted values. Note that differences are squared, similar to MSE, and so large differences are penalized heavily.

In a perfect regressor, the numerator is 0, so the best possible value for R^2 is 1.0. However, we can see arbitrarily large negative values when the prediction errors are significant.

All four types of evaluation metrics are implemented in machine learning packages and are demonstrated in the following code examples.

Implementing linear regression through scikit-learn

Like we did in the previous chapter, we will show you how you can quickly use `scikit-learn` to train a linear model straight from a SageMaker notebook instance. First, you must create the notebook instance (choosing `conda_python3` as the kernel).

1. We will start by loading the training data into a `pandas` dataframe:

```
housing_df = pd.read_csv(SRC_PATH + 'train.csv')
housing_df.head()
```

The preceding code displays the following output:

	ID	crim	zn	indus	chas	nox	rm	age	dis	rad	tax	ptratio	black	lstat	medv
0	1	0.00632	18.0	2.31	0	0.538	6.575	65.2	4.0900	1	296	15.3	396.90	4.98	24.0
1	2	0.02731	0.0	7.07	0	0.469	6.421	78.9	4.9671	2	242	17.8	396.90	9.14	21.6
2	4	0.03237	0.0	2.18	0	0.458	6.998	45.8	6.0622	3	222	18.7	394.63	2.94	33.4
3	5	0.06905	0.0	2.18	0	0.458	7.147	54.2	6.0622	3	222	18.7	396.90	5.33	36.2

2. The last column (`medv`) stands for median value and represents the variable that we're trying to predict (dependent variable) based on the values from the remaining columns (independent variables).

As usual, we will split the dataset for training and testing:

```
from sklearn.model_selection import train_test_split

housing_df_reordered = housing_df[[label] + training_features]

training_df, test_df = train_test_split(housing_df_reordered,
                                        test_size=0.2)
```

3. Once we have these datasets, we will proceed to construct a linear regressor:

```
from sklearn.linear_model import LinearRegression

regression = LinearRegression()

training_features = ['crim', 'zn', 'indus', 'chas', 'nox',
                     'rm', 'age', 'dis', 'tax', 'ptratio', 'lstat']

model = regression.fit(training_df[training_features],
                       training_df['medv'])
```

We start by constructing an estimator (in this case, linear regression) and fit the model by providing the matrix of training values, (`training_df[training_features]`), and the labels, (`raining_df['medv']`).

4. After fitting the model, we can use it to get predictions for every row in our testing dataset. We do this by appending a new column to our existing testing dataframe:

```
test_df['predicted_medv'] =
model.predict(test_df[training_features])
test_df.head()
```

The preceding code displays the following output:

	ID	crim	zn	indus	chas	nox	rm	age	dis	rad	tax	ptratio	black	lstat	medv	predicted_medv
74	110	0.26363	0.0	8.56	0	0.520	6.229	91.2	2.5451	5	384	20.9	391.23	15.55	19.4	20.058458
310	473	3.56868	0.0	18.10	0	0.580	6.437	75.0	2.8965	24	666	20.2	393.37	14.36	23.2	20.850997
264	404	24.80170	0.0	18.10	0	0.693	5.349	96.0	1.7028	24	666	20.2	396.90	19.77	8.3	13.150412
207	311	2.63548	0.0	9.90	0	0.544	4.973	37.8	2.5194	4	304	18.4	350.45	12.64	16.1	18.640210
283	440	9.39063	0.0	18.10	0	0.740	5.627	93.9	1.8172	24	666	20.2	396.90	22.88	12.8	11.553577

5. It's always useful to check our predictions graphically. One way to do this is by plotting the predicted versus actual values as a scatterplot:

```
test_df[['medv', 'predicted_medv']].plot(kind='scatter',
                                         x='medv',
                                         y='predicted_medv')
```

The preceding code displays the following output:

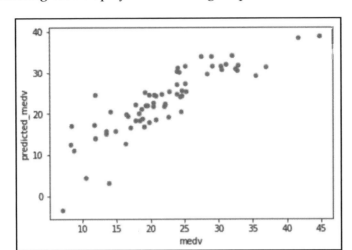

Note how the values are located mostly on the diagonal. This is a good sign, as a perfect regressor would yield all data points exactly on the diagonal (every predicted value would be exactly the same as the actual value).

6. In addition to this graphical verification, we obtain an evaluation metric that tells us how good our model is at predicting the values. In this example, we use R-squared evaluation metrics, as explained in the previous section, which is available in scikit-learn.

Let's look at the following code block:

```
from sklearn.metrics import r2_score

r2_score(test_df['medv'], test_df['predicted_medv'])

0.695
```

A value near 0.7 is a decent value. If you want to get a sense of what a good R2 correlation is, we recommend you play this game: http://guessthecorrelation.com/.

Our linear model will create a predicted price by multiplying the value of each feature by a coefficient and adding up all these values, plus an independent term, or intercept.

We can find the values of these coefficients and intercept by accessing the data members in the model instance variable:

```
model.coef_

array([-7.15121101e-02, 3.78566895e-02, -4.47104045e-02, 5.06817970e+00,
       -1.44690998e+01, 3.98249374e+00, -5.88738235e-03, -1.73656446e+00,
       1.01325463e-03, -6.18943939e-01, -6.55278930e-01])

model.intercept_
32.20
```

It is usually very convenient to examine the coefficients of the different variables as they can be indicative of the relative importance of the features in terms of their independent predictive ability.

By default, most linear regression algorithms such as `scikit-learn` or Spark will automatically do some degree of preprocessing (for example, it will scale the variables to prevent features with large values to introduce bias). Additionally, these algorithms support regularization parameters and provide you with options to choose the optimizer that's used to efficiently search for the coefficients that maximize the R2 score (or minimize some loss function).

Implementing linear regression through Apache Spark

You are likely interested in training regression models that can take huge datasets as input, beyond what you can do in `scikit-learn`. Apache Spark is a good candidate for this scenario. As we mentioned in the previous chapter, Apache Spark can easily run training algorithms on a cluster of machines using **Elastic MapReduce (EMR)** on AWS. We will explain how to set up EMR clusters in the next chapter. In this section, we'll explain how you can use the Spark ML library to train linear regression algorithms.

1. The first step is to create a dataframe from our training data:

```
housing_df = sql.read.csv(SRC_PATH + 'train.csv', header=True,
inferSchema=True)
```

The following image shows the first few rows of the dataset:

```
+---+-------+----+-----+----+-----+-----+----+------+---+---+-------+------+-----+----+
| ID|   crim|  zn|indus|chas|  nox|   rm| age|   dis|rad|tax|ptratio| black|lstat|medv|
+---+-------+----+-----+----+-----+-----+----+------+---+---+-------+------+-----+----+
|  1|0.00632|18.0| 2.31|   0|0.538|6.575|65.2|  4.09|  1|296|   15.3| 396.9| 4.98|24.0|
|  2|0.02731| 0.0| 7.07|   0|0.469|6.421|78.9|4.9671|  2|242|   17.8| 396.9| 9.14|21.6|
|  4|0.03237| 0.0| 2.18|   0|0.458|6.998|45.8|6.0622|  3|222|   18.7|394.63| 2.94|33.4|
|  5|0.06905| 0.0| 2.18|   0|0.458|7.147|54.2|6.0622|  3|222|   18.7| 396.9| 5.33|36.2|
+---+-------+----+-----+----+-----+-----+----+------+---+---+-------+------+-----+----+
```

2. Typically, Apache Spark requires the input dataset to have a single column with a vector of numbers representing all the training features. In Chapter 2, *Classifying Twitter Feeds with Naive Bayes,*we used the CountVectorizer to create such a column. In this chapter, since the vector values are already available in our dataset, we just need to construct such a column using a VectorAssembler transformer:

```
from pyspark.ml.feature import VectorAssembler

training_features = ['crim', 'zn', 'indus', 'chas', 'nox',
                     'rm', 'age', 'dis', 'tax', 'ptratio', 'lstat']

vector_assembler = VectorAssembler(inputCols=training_features,
                                   outputCol="features")

df_with_features_vector = vector_assembler.transform(housing_df)
```

The following screenshot shows the first few rows of the df_with_features_vector dataset:

```
+---+-------+----+-----+----+-----+-----+----+------+---+---+-------+------+-----+----+--------------------+
| ID|   crim|  zn|indus|chas|  nox|   rm| age|   dis|rad|tax|ptratio| black|lstat|medv|            features|
+---+-------+----+-----+----+-----+-----+----+------+---+---+-------+------+-----+----+--------------------+
|  1|0.00632|18.0| 2.31|   0|0.538|6.575|65.2|  4.09|  1|296|   15.3| 396.9| 4.98|24.0|[0.00632,18.0,2.3...|
|  2|0.02731| 0.0| 7.07|   0|0.469|6.421|78.9|4.9671|  2|242|   17.8| 396.9| 9.14|21.6|[0.02731,0.0,7.07...|
|  4|0.03237| 0.0| 2.18|   0|0.458|6.998|45.8|6.0622|  3|222|   18.7|394.63| 2.94|33.4|[0.03237,0.0,2.18...|
+---+-------+----+-----+----+-----+-----+----+------+---+---+-------+------+-----+----+--------------------+
```

Note how the vector assembler created a new column called features, which assembles all the features that are used for training as vectors.

3. As usual, we will split our dataframe into testing and training:

```
train_df, test_df = df_with_features_vector.randomSplit([0.8, 0.2],
                                                         seed=17)
```

4. We can now instantiate our regressor and fit a model:

```
from pyspark.ml.regression import LinearRegression

linear = LinearRegression(featuresCol="features", labelCol="medv")
linear_model = linear.fit(train_df)
```

5. By using this model, we find predictions for each value in the test dataset:

```
predictions_df = linear_model.transform(test_df)
predictions_df.show(3)
```

The output of the above `show()` command is:

```
+---+-------+----+-----+----+-----+-----+-----+------+---+---+-------+------+-----+----+--------------------+------------------+
| ID|   crim|  zn|indus|chas|  nox|   rm|  age|   dis|rad|tax|ptratio| black|lstat|medv|            features|        prediction|
+---+-------+----+-----+----+-----+-----+-----+------+---+---+-------+------+-----+----+--------------------+------------------+
|  7|0.08829|12.5| 7.87|   0|0.524|6.012| 66.6|5.5605|  5|311|   15.2| 395.6|12.43|22.9|[0.08829,12.5,7.8...|21.273530243958177|
| 24|0.98843| 0.0| 8.14|   0|0.538|5.813|100.0|4.0952|  4|307|   21.0|394.54|19.88|14.5|[0.98843,0.0,8.14...|13.894245541490553|
| 44|0.15936| 0.0| 6.91|   0|0.448|6.211|  6.5|5.7209|  3|233|   17.9|394.46| 7.44|24.7|[0.15936,0.0,6.91...|25.209683694484067|
+---+-------+----+-----+----+-----+-----+-----+------+---+---+-------+------+-----+----+--------------------+------------------+
```

6. We can easily find the `R2` value by using a `RegressionEvaluator`:

```
from pyspark.ml.evaluation import RegressionEvaluator

evaluator = RegressionEvaluator(labelCol="medv",
                                predictionCol="prediction",
                                metricName="r2")
evaluator.evaluate(predictions_df)
```

In this case, we get an `R2` of `0.688`, which is a similar result to that of `scikit-learn`.

Implementing linear regression through SageMaker's linear Learner

Another alternative within AWS for training regression models is to use SageMaker's API to build linear models. In the previous chapter, we explained the basics of this service when we considered how to use BlazingText for our text classification problem. Similarly, we will use Linear Learners in this section and go through the same process, which basically entails three steps:

1. Stage the training and testing data in S3
2. Invoke the API to train the model

3. Use the model to obtain predictions

Unlike what we did in `Chapter 2`, *Classifying Twitter Feeds with Naive Bayes*, instead of deploying an endpoint (that is, a web service) to obtain predictions, we will use a batch transformer, which is a service that's capable of obtaining bulk predictions given a model and some data in S3. Let's take a look at the following steps:

1. Assuming that we have prepared the training and testing datasets in a similar way to the previous sections, we will create a SageMaker session and upload our training and testing data to S3:

```python
import sagemaker
from sagemaker import get_execution_role
import json
import boto3

sess = sagemaker.Session()
role = get_execution_role()

bucket = "mastering-ml-aws"
prefix = "chapter3/linearmodels"

train_path = prefix + '/train'
validation_path = prefix + '/validation'


sess.upload_data(path='training-housing.csv',
                bucket=bucket,
                key_prefix=train_path)
sess.upload_data(path='testing-housing.csv',
                bucket=bucket,
                key_prefix=validation_path)

s3_train_data = 's3://{}/{}'.format(bucket, train_path)
s3_validation_data = 's3://{}/{}'.format(bucket, validation_path)
```

2. Once the data is in S3, we can proceed to instantiate the estimator:

```python
from sagemaker.amazon.amazon_estimator import get_image_uri
from sagemaker.session import s3_input

container = get_image_uri(boto3.Session().region_name, 'linear-learner')
s3_output_location = 's3://{}/{}/output'.format(bucket, prefix)

linear = sagemaker.estimator.Estimator(container,
                                       role,
```

```
                                                  train_instance_count=1,
        train_instance_type='ml.c4.xlarge',
        output_path=s3_output_location,

                                              sagemaker_session=sess)
```

3. Next, we need to set the hyperparameters. Linear Learner in SageMaker takes a large set of options, which can be found here `https://docs.aws.amazon.com/` `sagemaker/latest/dg/ll_hyperparameters.html`. In `Chapter 14`, *Optimizing SageMaker and Spark Machine Learning Models*, we will dive into how to find suitable values for these parameters:

```
linear.set_hyperparameters(feature_dim=len(training_features),
predictor_type='regressor',
mini_batch_size=1)

linear.fit({'train': s3_input(s3_train_data,
content_type='text/csv'),
'test': s3_input(s3_validation_data,
content_type='text/csv')})
```

4. Once we fit the model, we can instantiate a transformer, which is capable of computing predictions for our test dataset in `S3`:

```
transformer = linear.transformer(instance_count=1,
instance_type='ml.m4.xlarge', output_path=s3_output_location)

transformer.transform(s3_validation_data, content_type='text/csv')
transformer.wait()
```

This will create a file in s3 called `testing-housing.csv.out` with the following format:

```
{"score":18.911674499511719}
{"score":41.916255950927734}
{"score":20.833599090576172}
{"score":38.696208953857422}
```

5. We can download this file and build a pandas dataframe with the predictions:

```
predictions = pd.read_json('testing-housing.csv.out',lines=True)
```

The following screenshot shows the first few predictions:

	score
0	18.911674
1	41.916256
2	20.833599
3	38.696209
4	30.833647

6. Given that these scores follow the exact order found in the testing dataset, we can then proceed to put together the actual and predicted columns by merging the data series:

```
evaluation_df = pd.DataFrame({'actual':list(test_df[label]),
'predicted':list(predictions['score'])})
```

The preceding code displays the following output:

	actual	predicted
0	14.3	18.911674
1	50.0	41.916256
2	23.2	20.833599
3	46.0	38.696209
4	30.8	30.833647

7. With this data frame, we can calculate the R2 score:

```
from sklearn.metrics import r2_score

r2_score(evaluation_df['actual'], evaluation_df['predicted'])
```

The result was 0.796, which is in line with the previous estimates, with a slight improvement.

Understanding logistic regression

Logistic regression is a widely used statistical model that can be used to model a binary dependent variable. In linear regression, we assumed that the dependent variable is a numerical value that we were trying to predict. Consider a case where the binary variable has values of true and false. In logistic regression, instead of calculating the value of numerical output using the formula we used in the *Linear regression* section, we estimate the log odds of a binary event labeled True using the same formulation. The function that converts log odds to the probability of the event labeled 1 occurring is called the **logistic function**.

The unit of measurement for log-odds scale is called **logit**. Log-odds are calculated using the following formula:

$$log(\frac{p(y = True)}{1 - p(y = True)}) = \sum_{i=0}^{n} \alpha_i \cdot x_i + \beta_i$$

Thus, using the same methodology as linear regression, logistic regression is used for binary dependent variables by calculating the odds of the True event occurring. The main difference between linear regression and logistic regression is that linear regression is used to predict the values of the dependent variable, while logistic regression is used to predict the probability of the value of the dependent variable. Hence, as we emphasize in most of this book, data scientists should look at what they want to predict and choose the algorithms accordingly.

The logistic regression algorithm is implemented in most popular machine learning packages, and we will provide an example of how to use it in Spark in the following section.

Logistic regression in Spark

The `chapter3/train_logistic` notebook shows how we can instantiate a `LogisticRegression` Spark Trainer instead of `NaiveBayes` for the Twitter dataset we dealt with in `Chapter 2`, *Classifying Twitter Feeds with Naive Bayes* and obtain a model just as good as the one we constructed:

```
from pyspark.ml.classification import LogisticRegression
logistic_regression = LogisticRegression(featuresCol="features",
                                         labelCol="label")
logistic_model = logistic_regression.fit(cleaned_training_df)
```

Pros and cons of linear models

Regression models are very popular in machine learning and are widely applied in many areas. Linear regression's main advantage is its simplicity to represent the dataset as a simple linear model. Hence, the training time for linear regression is fast. Similarly, the model can be inspected by data scientists to understand which variable is contributing to the decisions of the overall model. Linear regression is recommended in cases where the problem statement is simple and fewer variables are used for predictions. As the complexity of the dataset increases, linear regression may generate significant errors if the data has a lot of noise in it.

Linear regression makes a bold assumption that the dependent variable has a linear relationship with the regressors. If this does not hold true, then the linear regression algorithm may not be able to fit the data well. There are variants such as quadratic regressions that can solve this issue. However, this leads to complexity in the model and hence significantly increases training time.

Summary

In this chapter, we started with the basics of regression algorithms and applied them to predict the price of houses. We then learned how to evaluate regression models, were introduced to linear regression through various libraries such as `scikit-learn`, Apache Spark and SageMaker's linear learner, and, finally, we saw how to use logistic regression for classification problems, and the pros and cons of linear models.

In the next chapter, we will predict user behavior with tree-based methods.

4
Predicting User Behavior with Tree-Based Methods

This chapter will introduce decision trees, random forests, and gradient-boosted trees. Decision trees methodology is a popular technique used in data science that provides a visual representation of how the information in the training set can be represented as a hierarchy. Traversing the hierarchy based on an observation helps you to predict the probability of that event. We will explore how to use these algorithms can be used to predict when a user may click on online advertisement based on existing advertising click records. Additionally, we will show how to use AWS **Elastic MapReduce** (**EMR**) with Apache Spark and the SageMaker XGBoost service to engineer models in the context of big data.

In this chapter, we will cover the following topics:

- Understanding decision trees
- Understanding random forests algorithms
- Understanding gradient boosting algorithms
- Predicting clicks on log streams

Understanding decision trees

Decision trees graphically show the decisions to be made, the observed events that may occur, and the probabilities of the outcomes given a specific set of observable events occurring together. Decision trees are used as a popular machine learning algorithm, where, based on a dataset of observable events and the known outcomes, we can construct a decision tree that can represent the probability of an event occurring.

The following table shows a very simple example of how decision trees can be generated:

Car Make	Year	Price
BMW	2015	>$40K
BMW	2018	>$40K
Honda	2015	<$40K
Honda	2018	>$40K
Nissan	2015	<$40K
Nissan	2018	>$40K

This is a very simple dataset that is represented by the following decision tree:

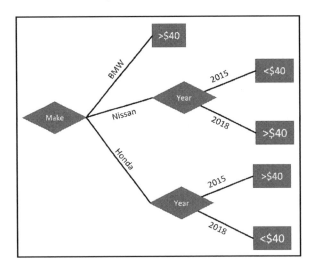

The aim of the machine learning algorithm is to generate decision trees that best represent the observations in the dataset. For a new observation, if we traverse the decision tree, the leaf nodes represent the class variable or event that is most likely to occur. In the preceding example, we have a dataset that has information regarding the make and the year of a used car. The class variable (also called the **feature label**) is the price of the car. We can observe in the dataset that, irrespective of the year variable value, the price of a BMW car is greater than $40,000. However, if the make of the car is not BMW, the cost of the car is determined by the year the car was produced. The example is based on a very small amount of data. However, the decision tree represents the information in the dataset, and if we have to determine the cost of a new car where the make is BMW and year is 2015, then we can predict that the cost is greater than $40,000. For more complex decision trees, the leaf nodes also have a probability associated with them that represents the probability of the class value occurring. In this chapter, we will study algorithms that can be used to generate such decision trees.

Recursive splitting

Decision trees can be built by recursively splitting the dataset into subsets. During each split, we evaluate splits based on all the input attributes and use a cost function to determine which split has the lowest cost. The cost functions generally evaluate the loss of information when we split the dataset into two branches. This partitioning of the dataset into smaller subsets is also referred to as recursive partitioning. The cost of splitting the datasets into subsets is generally determined by how records with similar class variables are grouped together in each dataset. Hence, the most optimal split would be when observations in each subset will have the same class variable values.

Such recursive splitting of decision trees is a top-down approach in generating decision trees. This is also a greedy algorithm since we made the decision at each point on how to divide the dataset, without considering how it may affect the later splits.

In the preceding example, we made the first split based on the make of the car. This is because one of our subsets, where the make is BMW, has a 100% probability of the price of the car being greater than $40,000. Similarly, if we had made a split based on the year, we would also get a subset of the year equal to 2018 that also has a 100% probability of the cost of the car is greater than $40,000. Hence, for the same dataset, we can generate multiple decision trees that represent the dataset. There are various cost functions that we will look at that generate different decision trees based on the same dataset.

Types of decision trees

There are following two main types of decision trees that most data scientists have to work with based on the class variables in the dataset:

- **Classification trees:** Classification trees are decision trees that are used to predict discrete values. This means that the class variable of the dataset used to generate classification trees is a discrete value. The preceding example regarding car prices at the start of this section is a classification tree as it only has two values of the class variable.
- **Regression trees:** Regression trees are decision trees that are used to predict real numbers, such as the example in *Chapter 3, Predicting House Value with Regression Algorithms*, where we were predicting the price of the house.

The term **Classification and Regression Trees (CART)** is used to describe the algorithm for generating decision trees. CART is a popular algorithm for decision trees. Other popular decision tree algorithms include ID3 and C4.5. These algorithms are different from each other in terms of the cost functions they use for splitting the dataset and the criteria used to determine when to stop splitting.

Cost functions

As discussed in the section on *Recursive splitting*, we need cost functions to determine whether splitting on a given input variable is better than other variables. The effectiveness of these cost functions is crucial for the quality of the decision trees being built. In this section, we'll discuss two popular cost functions for generating a decision tree.

Gini Impurity

Gini Impurity is defined as the measurement of the likelihood of incorrect classification of a random observation, given the random observation is classified based on the distribution of the class variables in the dataset. Consider a dataset with J class variables, and p_i is the fraction of observations in the dataset labeled as i. *Gini Impurity* can be calculated using the following formula:

$$GiniImpurity = \sum_{i=1}^{J} p_i \cdot (1 - p_i) = 1 - \sum_{i=1}^{J} p_i^2 \qquad .. 4.1$$

Gini Impurity tells us the amount of noise present in the dataset, based on the distributions of various class variables.

For example, in the car price dataset presented at the start of *Understanding Decision Trees* section, we have two class variables: greater than 40,000 and less than 40,000. If we had to calculate the Gini Impurity of the dataset, it could be calculated as shown in the following formula:

$$GiniImpurity = 1 - (p_{>40K}^2 + p_{<40K}^2) = 1 - (0.5^2 + 0.5^2) = 0.5$$

Hence, there is a lot of noise in the base dataset since each class variable has 50% of the observations.

However, when we create a branch where the make of the car, the Gini Impurity of that subset of the dataset is calculated as follows:

$$GiniImpurity(BMW) = 1 - (p_{>40K}{}^2 + p_{<40K}{}^2) = 1 - (1^2 + 0^2) = 0$$

$$GiniImpurity(Nissan) = 1 - (p_{>40K}{}^2 + p_{<40K}{}^2) = 1 - (0.5^2 + 0.5^2) = 0.5$$

$$GiniImpurity(Honda) = 1 - (p_{>40K}{}^2 + p_{<40K}{}^2) = 1 - (0.5^2 + 0.5^2) = 0.5$$

Since the branch of for BMW only contains class values of >40K, there is no noise in the branch and the value of Gini Impurity is 0. Note that when the subset of the data only has one class value, the Gini Impurity value is always 0.

Gini Impurity is used to calculate the Gini Index for each attribute. The Gini Index is a weighted sum of all the values of an attribute on which we create branches. For an attribute, a, that has K unique values, Gini Gain is calculated using formula below. p_i is the fraction of observations in the dataset where the value of the attribute, a, is i:

$$Gini\_Index(a) = \sum_{i=1}^{K} p_i . Gini\_Impurity_i$$

Hence, in our preceding example, the Gini Index for the *Make* attribute that has three distinct values is calculated as follows:

$$Gini\_Index(Make) = \sum_{i=1}^{K} p_i . Gini\_Impurity_i = 0.33.Gini\_impurity(BMW) + 0.33.Gini\_impurity(Honda) + 0.33.Gini\_impurity(Nissan) = 0.33$$

Similarly, we calculate the Gini Index for other attributes. In our example, the Gini Index for the *Year* attribute is 0.4422. We encourage you to calculate this value on your own. Our aim is to pick the attribute that generates the lowest Gini Index score. For a perfect classification, where all the class values in each branch are the same, the Gini Index score will be 0.

Information gain

Information gain is based on the concept of entropy, which is commonly used in physics to represent the unpredictability in a random variable. For example, if we have an unbiased coin, the entropy of the coin is represented as *1*, as it has the highest unpredictability. However, if a coin is biased, and has a 100% chance of heads, the entropy of the coin is 0.

This concept of entropy can also be used to determine the unpredictability of the class variable in a given branch. The entropy, denoted as *H*, of a branch is calculated using the formula below. $H(T)$ represents the entropy of the attribute. J is the number of class variables in the dataset. p_i is the fraction of observations in the dataset that belong to the class, i:

$$H(T) = -\sum_{i=1}^{J} p_i log_2 p_i$$

Step 1: In our example, for the entire dataset, we can calculate the entropy of the dataset as follows.

$$H(T) = -\sum_{i=1}^{J} p_i log_2 p_i = p_{<40K} . log_2 p_{<40K} + p_{>40K} . log_2 p_{>40K} = 0.5.log_2 0.5 + 0.5.log_2 0.5 = 1$$

Step 2: In our decision tree, we split the tree based on the make of the car. Hence, we also calculate the entropy of each branch of the tree, as follows:

$$H(BMW) = -p_{<40K} . log_2 p_{<40K} - p_{>40K} . log_2 p_{>40K} = -0.log_2 0 - 1.log_2 1 = 0$$

$$H(Honda) = -\sum_{i=1}^{J} p_i log_2 p_i = p_{<40K} . log_2 p_{<40K} + p_{>40K} . log_2 p_{>40K} = 0.5.log_2 0.5 + 0.5.log_2 0.5 = 1$$

$$H(Nissan) = -\sum_{i=1}^{J} p_i log_2 p_i = p_{<40K} . log_2 p_{<40K} + p_{>40K} . log_2 p_{>40K} = 0.5.log_2 0.5 + 0.5.log_2 0.5 = 1$$

Step 3: Based on the entropy of the parent and the branches, we can evaluate the branch using a measure called **information gain**. For a parent branch, T, and attribute, a, information gain is represented as follows:

$$IG(T, a) = H(T) - H(T|a)$$

$H(T|a)$ is the weighted sum of the entropy of the children. In our example, $H(T|a)$ of the *Make* attribute is calculated as follows:

$$H(T|Make) = 0.33.H(BMW) + 0.33.H(Honda) + 0.33.H(Nissan) = 0.66$$

Hence, the information gain for the *Make* attribute is calculated as follows:

$$IG(T, a) = H(T) - H(T|a) = 1 - 0.66 = 0.34$$

Similarly, we can calculate the information gain score for other attributes. The attribute with the highest information gain should be used to split the dataset for the highest quality of a decision tree. Information gain is used in the ID3 and C4.5 algorithms.

Criteria to stop splitting trees

As decision tree generation algorithms are recursive, we need a criterion that indicates when to stop splitting the trees. There are various criteria we can set to stop splitting the trees. Let us now look at the list of commonly used criteria:

- **Number of observations in the node**: We can set criteria to stop the recursion in a branch if the number of observations is less than a pre-specified amount. A good rule of thumb is to stop the recursion when there is fewer than 5% of the total training data in a branch. If we over split the data, such that each node only has one data point, it leads to overfitting the decision tree to the training data. Any new observation that has not been previously seen will not be accurately classified in such trees.
- **Purity of the node**: In the *Gini Impurity* section, we learned to calculate the likelihood of error in classifying a random observation. We can also use the same methodology to calculate the purity of the dataset. If the purity of the subset in a branch is greater than a pre-specified threshold, we can stop splitting based on that branch.
- **The depth of the tree**: We can also pre-specify the limit on the depth of the tree. If the depth of any branch exceeds the limit, we can stop splitting the branch further.

- **Pruning trees**: Another strategy is to let the trees grow fully. This avoids the branch splitting being terminated prematurely, without looking ahead. However, after the full tree is built, it is likely that the tree is large and there may be overfitting in some branches. Hence, pruning strategies are applied to evaluate each branch of the tree; any branch that introduces less than the pre-specified amount of impurity in the parent branch is eliminated. There are various techniques to prune decision trees. We encourage our readers to explore this topic further in the libraries that they implement their decision trees in.

Understanding random forest algorithms

There are two main disadvantages to using decision trees. First, the decision trees use algorithms that make a choice to split on an attribute based on a cost function. The decision tree algorithm is a greedy algorithm that optimizes toward a local optimum when making every decision regarding splitting the dataset into two subsets. However, it does not explore whether making a suboptimal decision while splitting over an attribute, would lead to a more optimal decision tree in the future. Hence, we do not get a globally optimum tree when running this algorithm. Second, decision trees tend to overfit to the training data. For example, a small sample of observations available in the dataset may lead to a branch that provides a very high probability of a certain class event occurring. This leads to the decision trees being really good at generating correct predictions for the dataset that was used for training. However, for observations that they have never seen before, decision trees may not be accurate due to overfitting to the training data.

To tackle these issues, the random forest algorithm can be used to improve the accuracy of the existing decision tree algorithms. In this approach, we divide the training data into random subsets and create a collection of decision trees, each based on a subset. This tackles the issue of overfitting, as we no longer rely on one tree to make the decision that has overfit to the entire training set. Secondly, this also helps with the issue of splitting on only one attribute based on a cost function. Different decision trees in random forests may make decisions on splitting based on different attributes, based on the random sample they are training on.

During the prediction phase, the random forest algorithm gets a probability of an event from each branch and uses a voting methodology to generate a prediction. This helps us suppress predictions from trees that may have overfitted or made sub-optimal decisions when generating the trees. Such an approach to divide the training set into random subsets and train multiple machine learning models is known as **Bagging**. The Bagging approach can also be applied to other machine learning algorithms.

Understanding gradient boosting algorithms

Gradient boosting algorithms are also used to address the disadvantages of the decision tree algorithm. However, unlike the random forests algorithm, which trains multiple trees based on random subsets of training data, gradient-boosting algorithms train multiple trees sequentially by reducing the errors in the decision trees. Gradient boosting decision trees are based on a popular machine learning technique called **Adaptive Boosting**, where we learn why a machine learning model is making errors, and then train a new machine learning model that reduces the errors from the previous models.

Gradient boosting algorithms discover patterns in the data that are difficult to represent in the decision trees, and add a greater weight to the training examples, which can lead to correct predictions. Thus, similar to random forests, we generate multiple decision trees from subsets of the training data. However, during each step, the subset of training data is not selected randomly. Instead, we create a subset of training data, where the examples that would lead to fewer errors in decision trees are prioritized. We stop this process when we cannot observe patterns in errors that may lead to more optimizations.

Examples of how random forest algorithms and gradient-boosting algorithms are implemented are provided in the next section.

Predicting clicks on log streams

In this section, we will show you how to use tree-based methods to predict who will click on a mobile advertisement given a set of conditions, such as region, where the ad is shown, time of day, location of the banner, and the application delivering the advertisement.

The dataset we will use throughout the rest of the chapter is obtained from *Shioji, Enno, 2017, Adform click prediction dataset,* https://doi.org/10.7910/DVN/TADBY7, *Harvard Dataverse, V2.*

The main task is to build a classifier capable of predicting whether a user will click on an advertisement given the conditions. Having such a model is very useful for ad-tech platforms that select which ads to show to users and when. These platforms can use these models to only show ads to users who are likely to click on the ad being delivered.

The dataset is large enough (5 GB) to justify the use of technologies that span multiple machines to perform the training. We will first look at how to use AWS EMR to carry out this task with Apache Spark. We will also show how to do this with SageMaker services.

Introduction to Elastic MapReduce (EMR)

EMR is an AWS service that allows us to run and scale Apache Spark, Hadoop, HBase, Presto, Hive, and other big data frameworks. We will cover more EMR details in `Chapter 15`, *Tuning Clusters for Machine Learning*. However, for now, let's think of EMR as a service that allows us to launch several interconnected machines with running software, such as Apache Spark, that coordinates distributed processing. EMR clusters have a master and several slaves. The master typically orchestrates the jobs, whereas the slaves process and combine the data to provide the master with a result. This result can range from a simple number (for example, a count of rows) to a machine learning model capable of making predictions. The Apache Spark Driver is the machine that coordinates the jobs necessary to complete the operation. The driver typically runs on the master node but it can also be configured to run on a slave node. The Spark executors (the demons that Spark uses to crunch the data) typically run on the EMR slaves.

EMR can also host notebook servers that connect to the cluster. This way, we can run our notebook paragraphs and this will trigger any distributed processing through Apache Spark. There are two ways to host notebooks on Apache Spark: EMR notebooks and JupyterHub EMR Application. We will use the first method in this chapter, and will cover JupyterHub in `Chapter 15`, *Tuning Clusters for Machine Learning*.

Through EMR notebooks, you can launch the cluster and the notebook at the same time through the **EMR notebooks** link on the console (`https://console.aws.amazon.com/elasticmapreduce/home`).

You can create the cluster and notebook simultaneously by clicking on the **Create Notebook** button, as seen in the following screenshot:

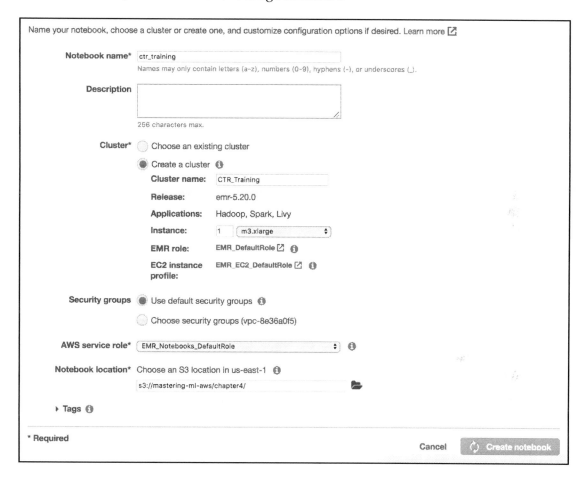

Once you create the notebook, it will click on the **Open** button, as shown in the following screenshot:

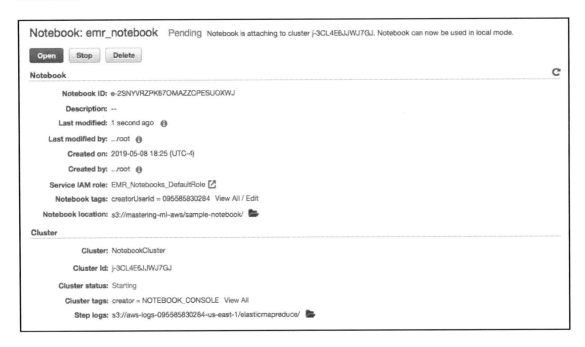

Clicking on the **Open** button opens the notebook for us to start coding. The notebook is a standard Jupyter Notebook as it can be seen in the following screenshot:

Alternatively, you can create the cluster separately and attach the notebook to the cluster. The advantage of doing so is that you have access to additional advanced options.

We recommend at least 10 machines (for instance, 10 m5.xlarge nodes) to run the code from this chapter in a timely fashion. Additionally, we suggest you increase the Livy session timeout if your jobs take longer than an hour to complete. For such jobs, the notebook may get disconnected from the cluster. Livy is the software responsible for the communication between the notebook and the cluster. The following screenshot shows the create cluster options including a way to extend the Livy session timeout:

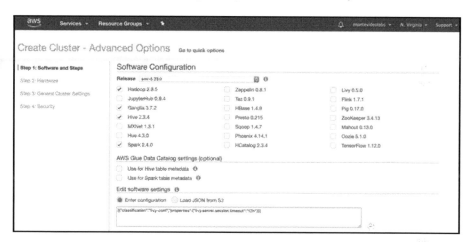

On `Chapter 15`, *Tuning Clusters for Machine Learning,* we will cover more details regarding cluster configuration.

Training with Apache Spark on EMR

Let's now explore the training with Apache Spark on EMR.

Getting the data

The first step is to upload the data to EMR. You can do this straight from the notebook or download the dataset locally and then uploaded it to S3 using the command-line tools from AWS (awscli). In order to use the command-line tools from AWS, you need to create AWS access keys on the IAM console. Details on how to do that can be found here: `https://docs.aws.amazon.com/IAM/latest/UserGuide/id_credentials_access-keys.html`.

Once you have your AWS access and secret keys, you can configure them by executing `aws configure` on the command line.

First, we will get a portion of the dataset through the following `wget` command:

```
wget -O /tmp/adform.click.2017.01.json.gz
https://dataverse.harvard.edu/api/access/datafile/:persistentId/?persistent
Id=doi:10.7910/DVN/TADBY7/JCI3VG
```

Next, we will unzip and upload the CSV dataset onto a `s3` bucket called `mastering-ml-aws` as shown by the following command:

```
gunzip /tmp/adform.click.2017.01.json.gz

aws s3 cp /tmp/adform.click.2017.01.json s3://mastering-ml-aws/chapter4/training-data/adform.click.2017.01.json
```

Once the data is in S3, we can come back to our notebook and start coding to train the classifier.

Preparing the data

The EMR notebooks, as opposed to the examples we ran locally in previous chapters (`Chapter 2`, *Classifying Twitter Feeds with Naive Bayes and* `Chapter 3`, *Predicting House Value with Regression Algorithms)* have implicit variables to access the Spark context. In particular, the Spark session is named `spark`. The first paragraph run will always initialize the context and trigger the Spark driver.

In the following screenshot, we can see the spark application starting and a link to the Spark UI:

```
In [1]:  s3_train_path = 's3://mastering-ml-aws/chapter4/training-data'

         VBox()

         Starting Spark application
```

ID	YARN Application ID	Kind	State	Spark UI	Driver log	Current session?
1	application_1556298146643_0008	pyspark	idle	Link	Link	✔

```
         SparkSession available as 'spark'.
```

The next step is to load our dataset and explore the different the first few rows by running the following snippet:

```
ctr_df = spark.read.json(s3_train_path)
ctr_df.show(5)
```

The output of the above show command is:

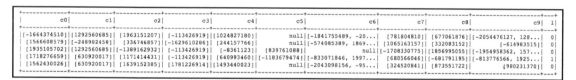

The `spark.read.json` method, the first command from the preceding code block, reads the JSON data into a dataset similar to what we've done before with CSV using `spark.read.csv`. We can observe our dataset has 10 features and an `l` column indicating the label which we're trying to predict, that is, if the user clicked (1) or didn't click (0) in the advertisement. You might realize that some features are multivalued (more than one value in a cell) and some are null. To simplify the code examples in this chapter we will just pick the first five features by constructing a new dataset and name these features `f0` through `f4` while also replacing null features with the value `0` and only taking the first value in the case of multivalued features:

```
df = ctr_df.selectExpr("coalesce(c0[0],0) as f0",
                       "coalesce(c1[0],0) as f1",
                       "coalesce(c2[0],0) as f2",
                       "coalesce(c3[0],0) as f3",
                       "coalesce(c4[0],0) as f4",
                       "l as click")
```

The `selectExpr` command above allows us to use SQL-like operations. In this particular case we will use coalesce operation which transforms any null expressions into the value 0. Also note that we're always just taking the first value for multivalued features.

Generally, it's a bad idea to discard features as they might carry important predictive value. Likewise, replacing nulls for a fixed value can also be sub-optimal. We should consider common imputation techniques for missing values such as replacing with a point estimate (medians, modes, and means are commonly used). Alternatively, a model can be trained to fill in the missing value from the remaining features. In order to keep our focus on using trees in this chapter, we won't go deeper on the issue of missing values.

Our `df` dataset now looks as follows:

```
+-----------+----------+-----------+-----------+----------+-----+
|         f0|        f1|         f2|         f3|        f4|click|
+-----------+----------+-----------+-----------+----------+-----+
|-1664374510|1292560685| 1963151207| -113426919|1024827180|    0|
| 1566608579|-248982458|  336746857|-1629610286| 244157766|    0|
| 1935105702|1292560685|-1389162932| -113426919|  -8361123|    0|
| 1718276659| 630920017| 1171414431| -113426919| 640993460|    1|
| 1562430026| 630920017| 1639152385| 1781226914|1493440023|    0|
+-----------+----------+-----------+-----------+----------+-----+
```

Now we do something quite Spark specific, which is to reshuffle the different portions of the CSV into different machines and cache them in memory. The command to do such thing is as follows:

```
df = df.repartition(100).cache()
```

Since we will repeatedly iterate on processing the same dataset, by loading it in memory, it will significantly speed up any future operation made for `df`. The repartitioning helps to make sure the data is better distributed throughout the cluster, hence increasing the parallelization.

The `describe()` method builds a dataframe with some basic stats (`min`, `max`, `mean`, `count`) of the different fields in our dataset, as seen in the following screenshot:

```
+-------+-------------------+-------------------+-------------------+------------------+-------------------+-------------------+
|summary|                 f0|                 f1|                 f2|                f3|                 f4|              click|
+-------+-------------------+-------------------+-------------------+------------------+-------------------+-------------------+
|  count|           12000000|           12000000|           12000000|          12000000|           12000000|           12000000|
|   mean|-6.610412663970825E7|2.5049429668800482E8|-2.915904354482062E8|5.459869260236725E7|-6.716129061083934E7|        0.18310175|
| stddev|1.2294656059145813E9|1.287445524252859E9|1.2580392622053525E9|8.234483651283175E8|1.2429134469135067E9|0.3867499342101606|
|    min|         -2145952914|         -2125813709|         -2145112401|        -2134594413|         -2147400218|                  0|
|    max|          2146734164|          2136145316|          2145529900|         2102865870|          2147086554|                  1|
+-------+-------------------+-------------------+-------------------+------------------+-------------------+-------------------+
```

We can observe that most features range from low negative values to very large integers, suggesting these are anonymized feature values for which a hash function was applied. The field we're trying to predict is `click`, which is `1` when the user clicked on the advertisement and 0 when the user didn't click. The mean value for the click column informs us that there is certain degree of label imbalance (as about 18% of the instances are clicks). Additionally, the `count` row tell us that there is a total of 12,000,000 rows on our dataset.

Another useful inspection is to understand the cardinality of the categorical values. The following screenshot from our notebooks shows the different number of unique values each feature gets:

```
df.select("f0").distinct().count()

2497

df.select("f1").distinct().count()

178

df.select("f3").distinct().count()

68

df.select("f4").distinct().count()

17572
```

As you can see, the f4 feature is an example of a category that has many distinct values. These kinds of features often require special attention, as we will see later in this section.

Decision trees and most of Spark ML libraries require our features to be numerical only. It happens by chance that our features are already in numerical form, but these really represent categories which were hashed into numbers. In Chapter 2, *Classifying Twitter Feeds with Naive Bayes*, we learned that in order to train a classifier, we need to provide a vector of numbers. For this reason, we need to transform our categories into numbers in our dataset to include them in our vectors. This transformation is often called **feature encoding**. There are two popular ways to do this: through one-hot encoding or categorical encoding (also called **string indexing**).

In the following generic examples, we assume that the `site_id` feature could only take up to three distinct values: `siteA`, `siteB`, and `siteC`. These examples will also illustrate the case in which we have string features to encode into numbers (not integer hashes as in our dataset).

Categorical encoding

Categorical encoding (or string indexing) is the simplest kind of encoding, in which we assign a number to each site value. Let's look at an example in the following table:

site_id	site_id_indexed
siteA	1
siteB	2
siteC	3

One-hot encoding

In this kind of encoding, we create new binary columns for each possible site value and set the value as 1 when the value is present, as shown in the following table:

site_id	siteA	siteB	siteC
siteA	1	0	0
siteB	0	1	0
siteC	0	0	1

Categorical encoding is simple; however, it may create an artificial ordering of the features, and some ML algorithms are sensitive to that. One-hot encoding has the additional benefit of supporting multi-valued features (for example, if a row has two sites, we can set a 1 in both columns). However, one-hot encoding adds more features to our dataset, which increases the dimensionality. Adding more dimensions to our dataset makes the training more complex and may reduce its predictive ability. This is known as the **curse of dimensionality**.

Let's see how we would use categorical encoding on a sample of our dataset to transform the C1 feature (a categorical feature) into numerical values:

```
from pyspark.ml.feature import StringIndexer

string_indexer = StringIndexer(inputCol="f0", outputCol="f0_index")
string_indexer_model = string_indexer.fit(df)
ctr_df_indexed = string_indexer_model.transform(df).select('f0','f0_index')
ctr_df_indexed.show(5)
```

The preceding code first instantiates a `StringIndexer` that will encode column `f0` into a new column `f0_index` upon fitting, goes through the dataset and finds distinct feature values that assign an index based on the popularity of such values. Then we can use the `transform()` method to get indices for each value. The output of the preceding final `show()` command is shown in the following screenshot:

```
+-----------+--------+
|        f0 |f0_index|
+-----------+--------+
| -130745722|   178.0|
|-1322326169|     0.0|
| -130745722|   178.0|
|-1248885727|     8.0|
|  571589560|   877.0|
+-----------+--------+
only showing top 5 rows
```

In the above screenshot we can see the numerical value that each raw (hashed) categorical value was assigned to.

To perform one-hot encoding on the values, we use the `OneHotEncoder` transformer:

```
from pyspark.ml.feature import OneHotEncoder

encoder = OneHotEncoder(inputCol="f0_index", outputCol="f0_encoded")
encoder.transform(ctr_df_indexed).distinct().show(5)
```

The preceding commands generates the following output:

```
+-----------+--------+-------------------+
|        f0 |f0_index|         f0_encoded|
+-----------+--------+-------------------+
|-1910840705|   118.0|  (2496,[118],[1.0])|
|-1713169383|   242.0|  (2496,[242],[1.0])|
| 1590237751|  1216.0|(2496,[1216],[1.0])|
|-1156005499|   337.0|  (2496,[337],[1.0])|
| 1707433888|   388.0|  (2496,[388],[1.0])|
+-----------+--------+-------------------+
only showing top 5 rows
```

Note how the different `f0` values get mapped to the corresponding boolean vector. We did the encoding for just one feature; however, for training, we need to go through the same process for several features. For this reason, we built a function that builds all the indexing and encoding stages necessary for our pipeline:

```
def categorical_one_hot_encoding_stages(columns):
    indexers = [StringIndexer(inputCol=column,
                              outputCol=column + "_index",
```

```
                                 handleInvalid='keep')
                 for column in columns]
    encoders = [OneHotEncoder(inputCol=column + "_index",
                              outputCol=column + "_encoded")
                 for column in columns]
    return indexers + encoders
```

The following code builds a training pipeline, including the `DecisionTree` estimator:

```
from pyspark.ml.feature import OneHotEncoder
from pyspark.ml.feature import StringIndexer
from pyspark.ml.feature import ChiSqSelector
from pyspark.ml import Pipeline
from pyspark.ml.feature import VectorAssembler
from pyspark.ml.classification import DecisionTreeClassifier

categorical_columns = ['f0','f1','f2','f3','f4']
encoded_columns = [column + '_encoded' for column in categorical_columns]

categorical_stages =
categorical_one_hot_encoding_stages(categorical_columns) vector_assembler =
VectorAssembler(inputCols=encoded_columns,
                                 outputCol="features")
selector = ChiSqSelector(numTopFeatures=100, featuresCol="features",
                         outputCol="selected_features", labelCol="click")
decision_tree = DecisionTreeClassifier(labelCol="click",
                                       featuresCol="selected_features")

pipeline = Pipeline(stages=categorical_stages + [vector_assembler,
selector,
                                        decision_tree])
```

In the preceding code,`VectorAssembler` constructs a vector with all features that require encoding as well as the numerical features (`VectorAssembler` can take as input columns that can be vectors or scalars so you can use numerical features directly if existent in your dataset). Given the high number of one-hot-encoded values, the feature vector can be huge and make the trainer very slow or require massive amounts of memory. One way to mitigate that is to use a **chi-squared** feature selector. In our pipeline, we have selected the best 100 features. By best, we mean the features that have more predictive power—note how the chi-squared estimator takes both the features and the label to decide on the best features. Finally, we include the decision engine estimator stage, which is the one that will actually create the classifier.

If we attempt to string index features with very large cardinality, the driver will collect all possible values (in order to keep a value-to-index dictionary for transformation). In such an attempt, the driver will most likely run out of memory as we're looking at millions of distinct values to keep. For these cases, you need other strategies, such as keeping only the features with the most predictive ability or considering only the most popular values. Check out our article, which includes a solution to this problem at `https://medium.com/dataxutech/how-to-write-a-custom-spark-classifier-categorical-naive-bayes-60f27843b4ad`.

Training a model

Our pipeline is now constructed, so we can proceed to split our dataset for testing and training and then we fit the model:

```
train_df, test_df = df.randomSplit([0.8, 0.2], seed=17)
pipeline_model = pipeline.fit(train_df)
```

Once this is executed, the Spark Driver will figure out the best plan for distributing the processing necessary to train the model across many machines.

By following the Spark UI link shown at the beginning of this section, we can see the status of the different jobs running on EMR:

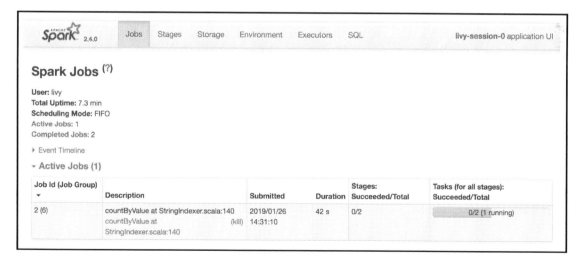

Once the model is trained, we can explore the decision tree behind it. We can do this by inspecting the last stage of the pipeline (that is, the decision tree model).

The following code snippet shows the result of outputting the decision tree in text format:

```
print(pipeline_model.stages[-1].toDebugString)

DecisionTreeClassificationModel (uid=DecisionTreeClassifier_3cc3252e8007)
of depth 5 with 11 nodes
  If (feature 3 in {1.0})
   Predict: 1.0
  Else (feature 3 not in {1.0})
   If (feature 21 in {1.0})
    Predict: 1.0
   Else (feature 21 not in {1.0})
    If (feature 91 in {1.0})
     Predict: 1.0
    Else (feature 91 not in {1.0})
     If (feature 27 in {1.0})
      Predict: 1.0
     Else (feature 27 not in {1.0})
      If (feature 29 in {1.0})
       Predict: 1.0
      Else (feature 29 not in {1.0})
       Predict: 0.0
```

Note how each decision is based on a feature that takes a value of 0 or 1. This is because we have used one-hot encoding on our pipeline. If we had used the categorical encoding (string indexing), we would have seen a condition that involves several indexed values, such as the following example:

```
If (feature 1 in {3.0,4.0,5.0,6.0,7.0,8.0,9.0,10.0,17.0,27.0})
      Predict: 0.0
Else (feature 1 not in {3.0,4.0,5.0,6.0,7.0,8.0,9.0,10.0,17.0,27.0})
      Predict: 1.0
```

Evaluating our model

Contrary to our Twitter classification problem in Chapter 2, *Classifying Twitter Feeds with Naive Bayes*, the label in this dataset is very skewed. This is because there are only a few occasions where users decide to click on ads. The accuracy measurement we used in Chapter 2, *Classifying Twitter Feeds with Naive Bayes*, would not be suitable, as a model that never predicts a click would still have very high accuracy (all non-clicks would result in correct predictions). Two possible alternatives for this case could be to use metrics derived from the ROC or **precision-recall curves**, which can be seen in the following section.

Area Under ROC Curve

The **Receiver Operating Characteristic (ROC)** is a representation of a trade-off between true-positive rates and false-positive rates. True-positive rates describe how good a model is at predicting a positive class when the actual class is positive. True-positive rates are calculated as the ratio of true positives predicted by a model, to the sum of true positives and false negatives. False-positive rates describe how often the model predicts the positive class, when the actual class is negative. False-positive rates are calculated as the ratio of false positives, to the sum of false positives and true negatives. ROC is a plot where the x axis is represented by the false-positive rate with a range of 0-1, while the y axis is represented as the true-positive rate. **Area Under Curve (AUC)** is the measure of the area under the ROC curve. AUC is a measure of predictiveness of a classification model.

Three examples of receiver operator curves are seen in the following screenshot:

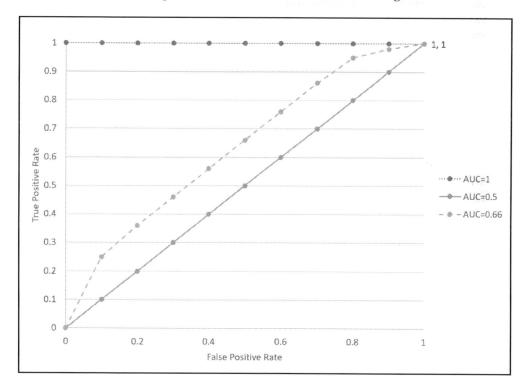

In the preceding plot, the dotted line represents an example of when AUC is 1. Such AUCs occur when all the positive outcomes are classified correctly. The solid line represents the AUC that is 0.5. For a binary classifier, the AUC is 0.5 when the predictions coming from the machine learning model are similar to randomly generating an outcome. This indicates that the machine learning model is no better than a random-number generator in predicting outcomes. The dashed line represents the AUC that is 0.66. This happens when a machine learning model predicts some examples correctly, but not all. However, if the AUC is higher than 0.5 for the binary classifier, the model is better than just randomly guessing the outcome. However, if it is below 0.5, this means that the machine learning model is worse than a random-outcome generator. Thus, AUC is a good measure of comparing machine learning models and evaluating their effectiveness.

Area under the precision-recall curve

The precision-recall curve represents a tradeoff between precision and recall in a prediction model. **Precision** is defined as the ratio of true positives to the total number of positive predictions made by the model. **Recall** is defined as the ratio of positive predictions to the total number of actual positive predictions.

 Note that the precision-recall curve does not model true negative values. This is useful in cases of the unbalanced dataset. ROC curves may provide a very optimistic view of a model if the model is good at classifying true negatives and generates a smaller number of false positives.

The following plot shows an example of a precision-recall curve:

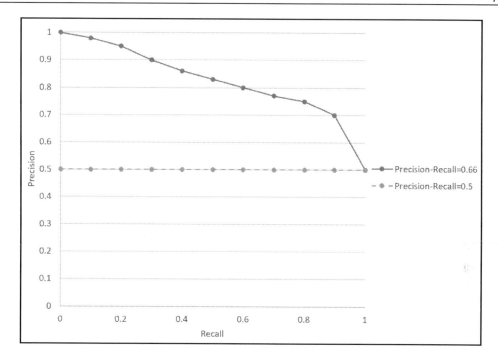

In the preceding screenshot, the dashed line shows when the area under precision-recall curve is `0.5`. This indicates that the precision is always 0.5, which is similar to a random-number generator. The solid line represents the precision-recall curve that is better than random. The precision recall curve also can be used to evaluate a machine learning model, similar to the ROC area. However, the precision-recall curve should be used when the dataset is unbalanced, and the ROC should be used when the dataset is balanced.

So, going back to our example, we can use Spark's `BinaryClassificationEvaluator` to calculate the scores by providing the actual and predicted labels on our test dataset. First we will apply the model on our test dataset to get the predictions and scores:

```
test_transformed = pipeline_model.transform(test_df)
```

By applying the previous transformation `test_transformed` will have all columns included in `test_df` plus an additional one called `rawPrediction` which will have a score which can be used for evaluation:

```
from pyspark.ml.evaluation import BinaryClassificationEvaluator

evaluator = BinaryClassificationEvaluator(rawPredictionCol="rawPrediction",
                                          labelCol="click")
evaluator.evaluate(test_transformed,
                   {evaluator.metricName: "areaUnderROC"})
```

The output of the preceding command is 0.43. The fact that we got an ROC metric lower than 0.5 means that our classifier is even worse than random classifier and hence it is not a good model for predicting clicks! In the next section, we will show how to use ensemble models to improve our predictive ability.

Training tree ensembles on EMR

Decision trees can be useful for understanding the decisions made by our classifier, especially when decision trees are small and readable. However, decision trees tend to overfit the data (by learning the details of the training dataset and not being able to generalize on new data). For this reason, ML practitioners tend to use tree ensembles, such as random forests and gradient-boosted trees, which are explained in the previous sections in this chapter under *Understanding gradient boosting algorithms* and *Understanding random forest algorithms*.

In our code examples, to use random forests or gradient boosted trees, we just need to replace the last stage of our pipeline with the corresponding constructor:

```
from pyspark.ml.classification import RandomForestClassifier

random_forest = RandomForestClassifier(labelCol="click",
                                        featuresCol="features")

pipeline_rf = Pipeline(stages=categorical_stages + \
                          [vector_assembler, random_forest])
```

Note how we get a better ROC value with random forests on our sampled dataset:

```
rf_pipeline_model = pipeline_rf.fit(train_df)

evaluator.evaluate(rf_pipeline_model.transform(test_df),
                  {evaluator.metricName: "areaUnderROC"})

>> 0.62
```

We can see that now we get a ROC greater than 0.5 which means that our model has improved an is now better than random guessing. Similarly, you can train a gradient boosted tree with the `pyspark.mllib.tree.GradientBoostedTrees` class.

Training gradient-boosted trees with the SageMaker services

In the *Training a model* and *Evaluating our model* sections, we learned how to build and evaluate a random forest classifier using Spark on EMR. In this section, we will see how to train a gradient boosted tree using the SageMaker services through the SageMaker notebooks. The XGBoost SageMaker service allows us to train gradient-boosted trees in a distributed fashion. Given that our clickthrough data is relatively large, it will be convenient to use such a service.

Preparing the data

In order to use the SageMaker services, we will need to place our training and testing data in S3. The documentation at `https://docs.aws.amazon.com/sagemaker/latest/dg/xgboost.html` requires us to drop the data as CSV files where the first column indicates the training label (target feature) and the rest of the columns represent the training features (other formats are supported but we will use CSV in our example). For splitting and preparing the data in this way, EMR is still the best option as we want our data preparation to be distributed as well. Given our testing and training Spark datasets from the last *Preparing the data* section, we can apply the pipeline model, not for getting predictions in this case, but instead, for obtaining the selected encoded features for each row.

In the following snippet, for both `test_df` and `train_df` we apply the model transformation:

```
test_transformed = model.transform(test_df)
train_transformed = model.transform(train_df)
```

The following screenshot shows the last three columns of the `test_transformed` dataframe:

selected_features	probability	rawPrediction
(0.0, 0.0, 0.0, 0.0, 0.0, 0.0, 0.0, 0.0, 1.0, ...	[0.8323081791819823, 0.16769182081801767]	[2677329.0, 539423.0]
(0.0, 0.0, 0.0, 0.0, 0.0, 0.0, 0.0, 0.0, 0.0, ...	[0.8323081791819823, 0.16769182081801767]	[2677329.0, 539423.0]
(0.0, 0.0, 0.0, 0.0, 0.0, 0.0, 0.0, 0.0, 0.0, ...	[0.8323081791819823, 0.16769182081801767]	[2677329.0, 539423.0]
(0.0, 0.0, 0.0, 0.0, 0.0, 0.0, 0.0, 0.0, 0.0, ...	[0.8323081791819823, 0.16769182081801767]	[2677329.0, 539423.0]

The transformed datasets includes the feature vector column (named `selected_features` with a size of 100). We need to transform these two columns into a CSV with 101 columns (the `click` and the `selected_features` vectors flattened out). A simple transformation in Spark allows us to do this. We define a `deconstruct_vector` function, which we will use to obtain a Spark dataframe with the label and each vector component as a distinct column. We then save that to S3 both for training and testing as a CSV without headers, as SageMaker requires.

In the following code snippet, we provide the `deconstruct_vector` function as well as the series of transformations needed to save the dataframe:

```
def deconstruct_vector(row):
    arr = row['selected_features'].toArray()
    return tuple([row['click']] + arr.tolist())

df_for_csv = train_transformed.select("click", "selected_features") \
                .rdd.map(deconstruct_vector).toDF()

df_for_csv.write.csv('s3://mastering-ml-aws/chapter4/train-trans-vec-csv-1/',
                header=False)
```

In a similar fashion, we will save an additional CSV file that will not include the label (just the features) under the `s3://mastering-ml-aws/chapter4/test-trans-vec-csv-no-label` path. We will use this dataset to score the testing dataset through the SageMaker batch transform job in the next section, *Training with SageMaker XGBoost*.

Training with SageMaker XGBoost

Now that our datasets for training and testing are in S3 in the right format, we can launch our SageMaker notebook instance and start coding our trainer. Let's perform the following steps:

1. Instantiate the SageMaker session, container, and variables with the location of our datasets:

```
import sagemaker
from sagemaker import get_execution_role
import boto3

sess = sagemaker.Session()
role = get_execution_role()
container = sagemaker.amazon.amazon_estimator.get_image_uri('us-east-1',
'xgboost',
```

```
'latest')

s3_validation_data = \
    's3://mastering-ml-aws/chapter4/test-trans-vec-csv-1/'
s3_train_data = \
    's3://mastering-ml-aws/chapter4/train-trans-vec-csv-1/'
s3_test_data = \
    's3://mastering-ml-aws/chapter4/test-trans-vec-csv-no-label/'
s3_output_location = \
    's3://mastering-ml-aws/chapter4/sagemaker/output/xgboost/'
```

2. Create a classifier by instantiating a SageMaker estimator and providing the basic parameters, such as the number and type of machines to use (details can be found in the AWS documentation at `https://sagemaker.readthedocs.io/en/stable/estimators.html`):

```
sagemaker_model = sagemaker.estimator.Estimator(container,
    role,
    train_instance_count=1,
    train_instance_type='ml.c4.4xlarge',
    train_volume_size=30,
    train_max_run=360000,
    input_mode='File',
    output_path=s3_output_location,
    sagemaker_session=sess)
```

3. Set the hyperparameters of our trainer. The details can be found in the documentation (and we will cover it in more detail in Chapter 14, *Optimizing SageMaker and Spark Machine Learning Models*). The main parameter to look at here is the objective, which we have set for binary classification (using a logistic regression score, which is the standard way XGBoost performs classification). XGBoost can also be used for other problems, such as regressions or multi-class classification:

```
sagemaker_model.set_hyperparameters(objective='binary:logistic',
    max_depth=5,
    eta=0.2,
    gamma=4,
    min_child_weight=6,
    subsample=0.7,
    silent=0,
    num_round=50)
```

4. Before fitting the model, we need to specify the location and format of the input (there are a couple of formats accepted; we have chosen CSV for our example):

```
train_data = sagemaker.session.s3_input(s3_train_data,
    distribution='FullyReplicated',
    content_type='text/csv',
    s3_data_type='S3Prefix')

validation_data = sagemaker.session.s3_input(s3_validation_data,
    distribution='FullyReplicated',
    content_type='text/csv',
    s3_data_type='S3Prefix')

data_channels = {'train': train_data,
                 'validation': validation_data}

sagemaker_model.fit(inputs=data_channels,
                    logs=True)
```

5. Invoking the `fit` function will train the model with the data provided (that is, the data we saved in S3 through our EMR/Spark preparation):

```
INFO:sagemaker:Creating training-job with name:
xgboost-2019-04-27-20-39-02-968
2019-04-27 20:39:03 Starting - Starting the training job...
2019-04-27 20:39:05 Starting - Launching requested ML
instances......
...
train-error:0.169668#011validation-error:0.169047
2019-04-27 20:49:02 Uploading - Uploading generated training model
2019-04-27 20:49:02 Completed - Training job completed
Billable seconds: 480
```

The logs will show the some details about the training and validation error being optimized by XGBoost, as well as the status of the job and training costs.

Applying and evaluating the model

The following steps will show you how to use `sagemaker` to create batch predictions so you can evaluate the model.

In order to obtain predictions, we can use a batch transform job:

```
transformer = sagemaker_model.transformer(instance_count=1,
                                   instance_type='ml.m4.2xlarge',
                                   output_path=s3_output_location)
transformer.transform(s3_test_data,
                   content_type='text/csv',
                   split_type='Line')
transformer.wait()
```

For every file in the input s3 directory, the batch transform job will produce a file with the scores:

```
aws s3 ls s3://mastering-ml-aws/chapter4/sagemaker/output/xgboost/ | head
```

The preceding command generates the following output:

```
2019-04-28 01:29:58 361031 part-00000-19e45462-84f7-46ac-87bf-d53059e0c60c-
c000.csv.out
2019-04-28 01:29:58 361045 part-00001-19e45462-84f7-46ac-87bf-d53059e0c60c-
c000.csv.out
```

We can then load this single-column CSV file into a `pandas` dataframe:

```
import pandas as pd

scores_df = pd.read_csv(output_path + \
    'part-00000-19e45462-84f7-46ac-87bf-d53059e0c60c-c000.csv.out',
    header=None,
    names=['score'])
```

These scores represent probabilities (derived via logistic regression). If we had set the objective to binary: hinge, we would get actual predictions instead. Choosing which kind to use depends on the type of application. In our case, it seems useful to gather probabilities, as any indication of a particular user being more likely to perform clicks would help to improve the marketing targeting.

One of the advantages of SageMaker XGBoost is that it provides a serialization in S3 of a compatible XGBoost model with Python's standard serialization library (pickle). As an example, we will take a portion of our test data in S3 and run the model to get scores. With this, we can compute the area under the ROC curve by performing the following steps:

1. Locate the model tarball in s3:

```
aws s3 ls --recursive s3://mastering-ml-
aws/chapter4/sagemaker/output/xgboost/ | grep model
```

The output looks as follows:

```
chapter4/sagemaker/output/xgboost/xgboost-2019-04-27-20-39-02-968/o
utput/model.tar.gz
```

Copy the model from S3 to our local directory and uncompress the tarball:

```
aws s3 cp s3://mastering-ml-
aws/chapter4/sagemaker/output/xgboost/xgboost-2019-04-27-20-39-02-9
68/output/model.tar.gz /tmp/model.tar.gz
tar xvf model.tar.gz
```

Here is the output of the preceding command, showing the name of the file uncompressed from the tarball:

```
xgboost-model
```

3. Once the model is locally downloaded and untared, we can load the model in memory via the `pickle` serialization library:

```
import xgboost
import pickle as pkl

model_local = pkl.load(open('xgboost-model', 'rb'))
```

4. Define the names of our columns (`f0` to `f99` for the features, and `click` as the label) and load the validation data from S3:

```
column_names = ['click'] + ['f' + str(i) for i in range(0, 100)]
validation_df = pd.read_csv(s3_validation_data + \
                            'part-00000-25f35551-
ffff-41d8-82a9-75f429553035-c000.csv',
                            header=None,
                            names=column_names)
```

5. To create predictions with `xgboost`, we need to assemble a matrix from our `pandas` dataframe. Select all columns except the first one (which is the label), and then construct a DMatrix. Call the predict method from the `xgboost` model to get the scores for every row:

```
import xgboost
matrix = xgboost.DMatrix(validation_df[column_names[1:]])
validation_df['score'] = model_local.predict(matrix)
```

In the following screenshot, the reader can see how the dataframe looks:

	click	f0	f1	f2	f3	f4	f5	f6	f7	f8	...	f91	f92	f93	f94	f95	f96	f97	f98	f99	score
0	1	0.0	0.0	0.0	0.0	1.0	0.0	0.0	0.0	0.0	...	0.0	0.0	0.0	0.0	0.0	0.0	0.0	0.0	0.0	0.226555
1	0	0.0	0.0	0.0	0.0	0.0	0.0	0.0	0.0	0.0	...	0.0	0.0	0.0	0.0	0.0	0.0	0.0	0.0	0.0	0.167860
2	0	0.0	0.0	0.0	0.0	0.0	0.0	0.0	0.0	0.0	...	0.0	0.0	0.0	0.0	0.0	0.0	0.0	0.0	0.0	0.512123
3	1	0.0	0.0	0.0	0.0	0.0	0.0	0.0	0.0	0.0	...	0.0	0.0	0.0	0.0	0.0	0.0	0.0	0.0	0.0	0.512123
4	1	0.0	0.0	0.0	0.0	0.0	0.0	0.0	0.0	0.0	...	0.0	0.0	0.0	0.0	0.0	0.0	0.0	0.0	0.0	0.141251

6. Given the `click` column and the `score` column, we can construct the ROC AUC:

```
from sklearn.metrics import roc_auc_score
roc_auc_score(validation_df['click'], validation_df['score'])
```

For our sample, we get a AUC value of 0.67, which is comparable to the value we got with Spark's random forests.

In this chapter, we did not focus on building the most optimal model for our dataset. Instead, we focused on providing simple and popular transformations and tree models you can use to classify large volumes of data.

Summary

In this chapter, we covered the basic theoretical concepts for understanding tree ensembles and showed ways to train and evaluate these models in EMR, through Apache Spark, as well as through the SageMaker XGBoost service. Decision tree ensembles are one of the most popular classifiers, for many reasons:

- They are able to find complex patterns in relatively short training time and with few resources. The XGBoost library is known as the most popular classifier among Kaggle competition winners (these are competitions held to find the best model for an open dataset).
- It's possible to understand why the classifier is predicting a given value. Following the decision tree paths or just looking at the feature importance are quick ways to understand the rationale behind the decisions made by tree ensembles.
- Implementations of distributed training are available through Apache Spark and XGBoost.

In the next chapter, we will look into how to use machine learning to cluster customers based on their behavioral patterns.

Exercises

1. What is the main difference between random forests and gradient-boosted trees?
2. Explain why the Gini Impurity may be interpreted as the misclassification rate.
3. Explain why it is necessary to perform feature encoding for categorical features.
4. In this chapter, we provided two ways to do feature encoding. Find one other way to encode categorical features.
5. Explain why the accuracy metric we used in Chapter 2, *Classifying Twitter Feeds with Naive Bayes*, is not suitable for predicting clicks on our dataset.
6. Find other objectives we can use for the XGBoost algorithm. When would you use each objective?

5
Customer Segmentation Using Clustering Algorithms

This chapter will introduce the main clustering algorithms by exploring how to apply them to customer segmentation based on their behavioral patterns. In particular, we will demonstrate how Apache Spark and Amazon SageMaker can seamlessly interoperate to perform clustering. Throughout this chapter, we will be using the **Kaggle Dataset E-Commerce** data from **Fabien Daniel**, which can be downloaded from `https://www.kaggle.com/fabiendaniel/customer-segmentation/data`.

Let's take a look at the topics we will be covering:

- Understanding how clustering algorithms work
- Clustering with **Apache Spark** on **Elastic MapReduce** (EMR)
- Clustering using **SageMaker** through Spark integration

Understanding How Clustering Algorithms Work

Cluster analysis, or clustering, is a process of grouping a set of observations based on their similarities. The idea is that the observations in a cluster are more similar to one another than the observations from other clusters. Hence, the outcome of this algorithm is a set of clusters that can identify the patterns in the dataset and arrange the data into different clusters.

Clustering algorithms are referred to as **unsupervised learning algorithms**. Unsupervised learning does not depend on predicting ground truth and is designed to discover the natural patterns in the data. Since there is no ground truth provided, it is difficult to compare different unsupervised learning models. Unsupervised learning is generally used for exploratory analysis and dimensionality reduction. Clustering is an example of exploratory analysis. In this task, you are looking for patterns and structure in the dataset.

This is different than the algorithms we have been studying so far in the book. **Naive Bayes**, **linear regression**, and **decision trees** algorithms are all examples of supervised learning. There is an assumption that each dataset has a set of observations and an event class associated with those observations. Hence, the data is already grouped based on the actual outcome event for each observation. However, not every dataset has labeled outcomes associated with each event. For example, consider a dataset where you have information regarding each transaction on an e-commerce website:

SKU	Item name	Customer ID	Country
12423	iPhone	10	USA
12423	iPhone	11	USA
12423	iPhone	12	USA
11011	Samsung S9	13	UK
11011	Samsung S9	10	USA
11011	Samsung S9	14	UK

This dataset is a list of transactions but does not have any class variable that informs us regarding what kind of users buy specific products. Hence, if the task is to identify patterns from this dataset, we cannot use any algorithms that can predict a specific event. That is where clustering algorithms come into the picture. We want to explore whether we can find trends in the transactions on the website based on the dataset. Let's look at a simple example. Consider that the dataset only had one feature: **Item name**. We will discover that the data can be arranged in three clusters, namely, iPhone, Samsung S9, and Pixel 2. Similarly, if we consider that the only feature to cluster on is **Country**, the data can be clustered into two clusters: USA and UK. Once you generate the clusters, you can analyze the statistics in each cluster to understand the type of audience buying certain things.

However, in most of your experiences, you will have to cluster the data based on more than one feature. There are many clustering algorithms that you can deploy in clustering the data into clusters. The following diagram shows an example of how clusters would look for the dataset:

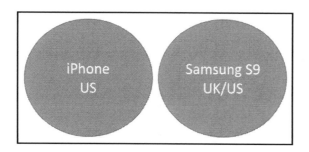

Clustering helps us get an outcome where we can group the data into two clusters and understand the patterns in each cluster. We may be able to cluster the customers into users who buy a certain kind of phone. By analyzing the clusters, we can learn the patterns of which users buy an iPhone or Samsung S9 phone.

In this chapter, we will study two common clustering approaches:

- k-means clustering
- Hierarchical clustering

k-means clustering

The **k-means clustering** algorithm aims to cluster a dataset into k clusters by selecting k centroids in the dataset. Each record is evaluated based on its distance to the centroid and assigned a cluster. Centroids are observations that are at the center of each cluster. To define k-means clustering formally, we are optimizing the **Within-Cluster Sum of the Square** *(WCSS)* distance of observations. Hence, the most optimal clustering would ensure that each cluster has all the observations close to its centroid, and as far away from the other centroids as possible.

There are two important parameters in k-means clustering. Firstly, we need to discover the centroids in our dataset. One of the popular methodologies for selecting centroids is called **Random partitioning**. This methodology uses a technique called **Expectation Maximization (EM)** to achieve high-quality clusters. In the first step, we randomly assign a cluster to each observation. Once each observation is assigned to a cluster, we calculate the quality of the cluster using the WCSS methodology:

$$J = \sum_{i=1}^{M} \sum_{k=1}^{K} w_{ik} ||(x_i - \mu_k)||^2$$

J represents the WCSS score for the clusters that are generated where we have *M* observations and have generated *K* clusters. w_{ik} is 1 if the observation *i* belongs to cluster *k*, and 0 if the observation *i* does not belong to cluster *k*. x_i is the observation, while μ_k is the centroid of cluster *k*. The difference between x_i and μ_k represents the distance between the observation and the centroid. Our aim is to minimize the value of *J*.

In the next step, we calculate new centroids again based on the current clusters in the first step. This is the maximization step in the EM algorithm, where we try to step toward more optimal cluster assignments for records. The new centroid values are calculated using the following formula:

$$\mu_k = \frac{\sum_{i=1}^{M} w_{ik} x_i}{\sum_{i=1}^{M} w_{ik}}$$

This represents the fact that we recalculate the centroids based on the mean of the clusters created in the previous steps. Based on the new centroids, we assign each observation in the dataset to a centroid based on their distance to the centroids. Distance is the measure of similarity between two observations. We will discuss the concept of how to calculate distance later in this section. We recalculate the WCSS score for the new clusters and repeat the minimization step again. We repeat these steps until the assignments of the observations in the cluster do not change.

Although the random partition algorithm allows the k-means algorithm to discover centroids with a low WCSS score, they do not guarantee a global optimum solution. This is because the EM algorithm may greedily find a local optimum solution and stop exploring, for a more optimum solution. Also, selecting different random centroids in the first step may lead to different optimal solutions at the end of this algorithm.

To address this issue, there are other algorithms such as the **Forgy algorithm**, where we choose random observations from the dataset as centroids in the first step. This leads to more spread out centroids in the first step, compared to the random partition algorithm.

As we discussed before, we have to calculate the distance between the observations and the centroid of the cluster. There are various methodologies to calculate this distance. The two popular methodologies are the **Euclidean distance** and the **Manhattan distance**.

Euclidean distance

The Euclidean distance between two points is the length of the line connecting them. For the n-dimensional points P and Q, where both the vectors have n values, the Euclidean distance is calculated using this formula:

$$d(P,Q) = \sqrt[2]{\sum_{i=1}^{n}(p_i - q_i)^2}$$

If the values of the data points are categorical values, then $(p_i - q_i)$ is 1 if both the observations have the same values for a feature and 0 if the observations have different values. For continuous variables, we can calculate the normalized distance between the values of the attributions.

Manhattan distance

The **Manhattan distance** is the sum of absolute differences between two data points. For the n-dimensional points P and Q, where both the vectors have n values, we calculate the Manhattan distance using the following formula:

$$d(P,Q) = \sum_{i=1}^{n}\|p_i - q_i\|$$

The Manhattan distance reduces the effects of outliers in the data, and hence, should be used when we have noisy data with a lot of outliers.

Hierarchical clustering

Hierarchical clustering aims to build a hierarchical structure of clusters from the observations. There are two strategies for generating the hierarchy:

- **Agglomerative clustering**: In this approach, we use a bottom-up methodology, where each observation starts as its own cluster and clusters are merged at each stage of generating a hierarchy.
- **Divisive clustering**: In this approach, we use a top-down methodology, where we divide the observations into smaller clusters as we move down the stages of the hierarchy.

Agglomerative clustering

In **agglomerative clustering,** we start with each observation as its own cluster and combine these clusters based on certain criteria so that we end up with one cluster that contains all the observations. Similar to k-means clustering, we use distance metrics such as the Manhattan distance and the Euclidean distance in order to calculate the distance between two observations. We also use **linkage criteria**, which can represent the distance between two clusters. In this section, we study three linkage criteria, namely, **complete-linkage clustering, single-linkage clustering,** and **average-linkage clustering**.

Complete-linkage clustering calculates the distance between two clusters as the maximum distance between observations from two clusters and is represented as follows:

$$d(A, B) = max\{d(a, b) : a \epsilon A, b \epsilon B\}$$

Single-linkage clustering calculates the distance between two clusters as the minimum distance between observations from two clusters and is represented as follows:

$$d(A, B) = min\{d(a, b) : a \epsilon A, b \epsilon B\}$$

Average-linkage clustering calculates the distance between each observation from cluster A with cluster B and normalizes it based on the observations in cluster A and B. This is represented as follows:

$$d(A, B) = \frac{1}{|A| \cdot |B|} \sum_{a \epsilon A} \sum_{b \epsilon B} d(a, b)$$

Thus, in the first step of agglomerative clustering, we use distance methodology to calculate the distance between each observation and merge observations with the smallest distance. For the second step, we calculate the distances between each cluster using linkage criteria based on the methodologies just presented. We run the necessary iterations until we only have one cluster left with all observations in it.

The following diagram shows how agglomerative clustering would work for observations with only one continuous variable:

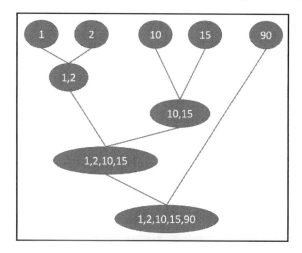

In this example, we have five observations with one continuous feature. In the first iteration, we look at the Euclidean distance between each observation and can deduce that records 1 and 2 are closest to each other. Hence, in the first iteration, we merge the observations 1 and 2. In the second iteration, we discover that the observations 10 and 15 are the closest records and create a new cluster from it. In the third iteration, we observe that the distance between the (1,2) cluster and the (10,15) cluster is smaller than any of those clusters and observation 90. Hence, we create a cluster of (1,2,10,15) in the third iteration. Finally, in the last iteration, we add element 90 to the cluster and terminate the process of agglomerative clustering.

Divisive clustering

Divisive clustering is a top-bottom approach where we first start with a large cluster with all observations and, at iteration, we split the clusters into smaller clusters. The process is similar to using distances and linkage criteria such as agglomerative clustering. The aim is to find an observation or cluster in the larger cluster that has the furthest distance from the rest of the cluster. In each iteration, we look at a cluster and recursively split the larger clusters by finding clusters that have the farthest distance from one another. Finally, the process is stopped when each observation is its own cluster. Divisive clustering uses an exhaustive search to find the perfect split in each cluster, which may be computationally very expensive.

Hierarchical clustering approaches are computationally more expensive than a k-means approach. Hence, even on medium-sized datasets, hierarchical cluster approaches may struggle to generate results compared to a k-means approach. However, since we do not need to start with a random partition at the start of hierarchical clustering, they remove the risks in the k-means approach where a bad random partition may hurt the clustering process.

Clustering with Apache Spark on EMR

In this section, we step through the creation of a clustering model capable of grouping consumer patterns in three distinct clusters. The first step will be to launch an EMR notebook along with a small cluster (a single m5.xlarge node works fine as the dataset we selected is not very large). Simply follow these steps:

1. The first step is to load the dataframe and inspect the dataset:

```
df = spark.read.csv(SRC_PATH + 'data.csv',
                    header=True,
                    inferSchema=True)
```

The following screenshot shows the first few lines of our df dataframe:

	InvoiceNo	StockCode	Description	Quantity	InvoiceDate	UnitPrice	CustomerID	Country
0	536365	85123A	WHITE HANGING HEART T-LIGHT HOLDER	6	12/1/2010 8:26	2.55	17850.0	United Kingdom
1	536365	71053	WHITE METAL LANTERN	6	12/1/2010 8:26	3.39	17850.0	United Kingdom
2	536365	84406B	CREAM CUPID HEARTS COAT HANGER	8	12/1/2010 8:26	2.75	17850.0	United Kingdom
3	536365	84029G	KNITTED UNION FLAG HOT WATER BOTTLE	6	12/1/2010 8:26	3.39	17850.0	United Kingdom
4	536365	84029E	RED WOOLLY HOTTIE WHITE HEART.	6	12/1/2010 8:26	3.39	17850.0	United Kingdom

As you see, the dataset involves transactions of products bought by different customers at different times and in different locations. We attempt to cluster these customer transactions using k-means by looking at three factors:

- The product (represented by the StockCode column)
- The country where the product was bought
- The total amount spent by the customer across all products

Note that this last factor is not directly available in the dataset, but it seems like an intuitively valuable feature (whether the client is a big spender or not). Oftentimes, during our feature preparation, we need to find aggregate values and plug them into our dataset.

2. On this occasion, we first find the total amount spent by each customer by multiplying the `Quantity` and `UnitPrice` columns on a new column:

```
df = df.selectExpr("*",
                   "Quantity * UnitPrice as TotalBought")
```

The following screenshot shows the first few lines of our modified `df` dataframe:

	InvoiceNo	StockCode	Description	Quantity	InvoiceDate	UnitPrice	CustomerID	Country	TotalBought
0	536365	85123A	WHITE HANGING HEART T-LIGHT HOLDER	6	12/1/2010 8:26	2.55	17850	United Kingdom	15.30
1	536365	71053	WHITE METAL LANTERN	6	12/1/2010 8:26	3.39	17850	United Kingdom	20.34
2	536365	84406B	CREAM CUPID HEARTS COAT HANGER	8	12/1/2010 8:26	2.75	17850	United Kingdom	22.00
3	536365	84029G	KNITTED UNION FLAG HOT WATER BOTTLE	6	12/1/2010 8:26	3.39	17850	United Kingdom	20.34
4	536365	84029E	RED WOOLLY HOTTIE WHITE HEART.	6	12/1/2010 8:26	3.39	17850	United Kingdom	20.34

3. Then, we proceed to aggregate the `TotalBought` column by a customer:

```
customer_df = df.select("CustomerID","TotalBought")
    .groupBy("CustomerID")
    .sum("TotalBought")
    .withColumnRenamed('sum(TotalBought)','SumTotalBought')
```

The following screenshot shows the first few lines of the `customer_df` dataframe:

	CustomerID	SumTotalBought
0	17420	598.83
1	16861	151.65
2	16503	1421.43
3	15727	5178.96
4	17389	31300.08

4. We can then join back this new column back to our original dataset based on the customer:

```
from pyspark.sql.functions import *
joined_df = df.join(customer_df, 'CustomerId')
```

The following screenshot shows the first few lines of the `joined_df` dataframe:

	CustomerID	InvoiceNo	StockCode	Description	Quantity	InvoiceDate	UnitPrice	Country	TotalBought	SumTotalBought
0	17850	536365	85123A	WHITE HANGING HEART T-LIGHT HOLDER	6	12/1/2010 8:26	2.55	United Kingdom	15.30	5288.63
1	17850	536365	71053	WHITE METAL LANTERN	6	12/1/2010 8:26	3.39	United Kingdom	20.34	5288.63
2	17850	536365	84406B	CREAM CUPID HEARTS COAT HANGER	8	12/1/2010 8:26	2.75	United Kingdom	22.00	5288.63
3	17850	536365	84029G	KNITTED UNION FLAG HOT WATER BOTTLE	6	12/1/2010 8:26	3.39	United Kingdom	20.34	5288.63

Note that two of the features that we are interested in using for clustering (**Country** and **StockCode**) are categorical. Hence, we need to find a way to encode those two numbers, similar to what we did in the previous chapter. String indexing these features would not be suitable in this case, as k-means works by computing distances between data points. Distances between artificial indices assigned to string values do not convey a lot of information. Instead, we apply one hot encoding to these features so that the vector distances represent something meaningful (note that two data points coinciding on most vector components have a cosine or Euclidean distance closer to 0).

Our pipeline will consist of two one hot encoding steps (for **Country** and **Product**), and a column that represents whether a customer is a big, normal, or small spender. To determine this, we discretize the `SumTotalBought` column into three values using a `QuantileDiscretizer`, which will result in three buckets depending on the quantile each customer falls into. We use the vector assembler to compile a vector of features. Given that the k-means algorithm works by computing distances, we normalize the feature vector so that the third feature (spender bucker) does not have a higher influence on the distance, as it has larger absolute values in the vector component. Finally, our pipeline will run the k-means estimator.

1. In the following code block, we define the stages of our pipeline and fit a model:

```
from pyspark.ml import Pipeline
from pyspark.ml.clustering import KMeans
from pyspark.ml.feature import Normalizer
from pyspark.ml.feature import OneHotEncoder
from pyspark.ml.feature import QuantileDiscretizer
from pyspark.ml.feature import StringIndexer
from pyspark.ml.feature import VectorAssembler
```

```
stages = [
    StringIndexer(inputCol='StockCode',
                  outputCol="stock_code_index",
                  handleInvalid='keep'),
    OneHotEncoder(inputCol='stock_code_index',
                  outputCol='stock_code_encoded'),
    StringIndexer(inputCol='Country',
                  outputCol='country_index',
                  handleInvalid='keep'),
    OneHotEncoder(inputCol='country_index',
                  outputCol='country_encoded'),
    QuantileDiscretizer(numBuckets=3,
                        inputCol='SumTotalBought',
                        outputCol='total_bought_index'),
    VectorAssembler(inputCols=['stock_code_encoded',
                               'country_encoded',
                               'total_bought_index'],
                    outputCol='features_raw'),
    Normalizer(inputCol="features_raw",
               outputCol="features", p=1.0),
    KMeans(featuresCol='features').setK(3).setSeed(42) ]

pipeline = Pipeline(stages=stages)
model = pipeline.fit(joined_df)
```

2. Once we have a model, we apply that model to our dataset to obtain the clusters each transaction falls into:

```
df_with_clusters = model.transform(joined_df).cache()
```

The following screenshot shows the first lines of the `df_with_clusters` dataframe:

TotalBought	SumTotalBought	stock_code_index	stock_code_encoded	country_index	country_encoded	total_bought_index	features_raw	features	prediction
15.30	5288.63	0.0	(1.0, 0.0, 0.0, 0.0, 0.0, 0.0, 0.0, 0.0, 0.0, ...	0.0	(1.0, 0.0, 0.0, 0.0, 0.0, 0.0, 0.0, 0.0, 0.0, ...	2.0	(1.0, 0.0, 0.0, 0.0, 0.0, 0.0, 0.0, 0.0, 0.0, ...	(0.25, 0.0, 0.0, 0.0, 0.0, 0.0, 0.0, 0.0, 0.0,...	0
20.34	5288.63	403.0	(0.0, 0.0, 0.0, 0.0, 0.0, 0.0, 0.0, 0.0, 0.0, ...	0.0	(1.0, 0.0, 0.0, 0.0, 0.0, 0.0, 0.0, ...	2.0	(0.0, 0.0, 0.0, 0.0, 0.0, 0.0, 0.0, 0.0, 0.0, ...	(0.0, 0.0, 0.0, 0.0, 0.0, 0.0, 0.0, ...	0
22.00	5288.63	452.0	(0.0, 0.0, 0.0, 0.0, 0.0, 0.0, 0.0, 0.0, 0.0, ...	0.0	(1.0, 0.0, 0.0, 0.0, 0.0, 0.0, 0.0, ...	2.0	(0.0, 0.0, 0.0, 0.0, 0.0, 0.0, 0.0, 0.0, 0.0, ...	(0.0, 0.0, 0.0, 0.0, 0.0, 0.0, 0.0, ...	0

3. Note the new **prediction** column, which holds the value of cluster each row belongs to. We evaluate how well the clusters were formed by using the silhouette metric, which measures how similar data points are within their cluster compared to other clusters:

```
from pyspark.ml.evaluation import ClusteringEvaluator

evaluator = ClusteringEvaluator()
silhouette = evaluator.evaluate(df_with_clusters)
```

In this example, we got a value of 0.35, which is average as a clustering score (ideally it's near 1.0, but at least it's positive). One main reason for not having a larger value is because we did not reduce the dimensionality of our vectors. Typically, before clustering, we apply some transformation for reducing the cardinality of the feature vector, such as **principal component analysis (PCA)**. We didn't include such a step in this example for simplicity.

4. We can now examine each cluster to have a sense of how the data was clustered. The first thing to look at is the size of each cluster. As we can see in the following, the clusters vary in size, where one cluster captures more than half of the data points:

```
df_with_clusters
.groupBy("prediction")
.count()
.toPandas()
.plot(kind='pie',x='prediction', y='count')
```

The following diagram shows the relative sizes of the different clusters:

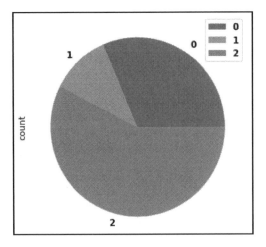

5. If we look at the countries contained on each cluster, we can see that two clusters just contain data points from the UK, and the third cluster only contains points from the rest of the countries. We first inspect the counts for cluster 0:

```
df_with_clusters \
.where(df_with_clusters.prediction==0) \
.groupBy("Country") \
.count() \
.orderBy("count", ascending=False) \
.show()


+--------------+------+
| Country      | count|
+--------------+------+
|United Kingdom|234097|
+--------------+------+
```

Similarly, the count for cluster 1 is displayed:

```
df_with_clusters \
.where(df_with_clusters.prediction==1) \
.groupBy("Country") \
.count() \
.orderBy("count", ascending=False) \
.show()


+--------------+------+
| Country .    | count|
+--------------+------+
|United Kingdom|127781|
+--------------+------+
```

Finally, the count for cluster 2 is shown:

```
df_with_clusters \
.where(df_with_clusters.prediction==2) \
.groupBy("Country") \
.count() \
.orderBy("count", ascending=False) \
.show()


+--------------+-----+
| Country      |count|
+--------------+-----+
| Germany      | 9495|
| France       | 8491|
```

```
.
.
.
| USA            | 291 |
+---------------+-----+
```

6. An interesting observation is that the different clusters seem to have very different spending profiles:

```
pandas_df = df_with_clusters \
    .limit(5000) \
    .select('CustomerID','InvoiceNo','StockCode',
            'Description','Quantity','InvoiceDate',
            'UnitPrice','Country','TotalBought',
            'SumTotalBought','prediction') \
    .toPandas()

pandas_df.groupby('prediction') \
.describe()['SumTotalBought']['mean'] \
.plot(kind='bar',
      title = 'Mean total amount bought per cluster')
```

The preceding `plot()` command produces the following diagram:

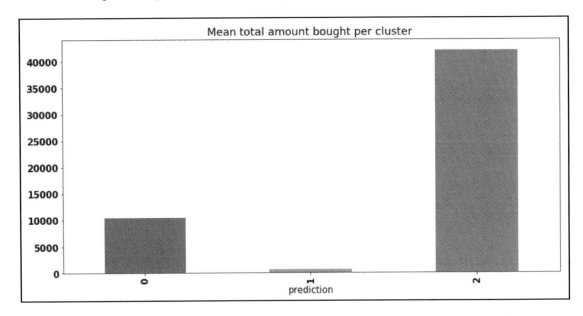

7. To have a sense of how each cluster classifies the products, we look at the product description field of the different clusters. A nice visual representation is to use a word cloud with the words that appear on the product descriptions of each cluster. Using the Python `wordcloud` library, we can create a function that strips out the words of the products and constructs a wordcloud:

```python
import itertools
import re
from functools import reduce
import matplotlib.pyplot as plt
from wordcloud import WordCloud, STOPWORDS

def plot_word_cloud(description_column):
    list_of_word_sets = description_column \
            .apply(str.split) \
            .tolist()
    text = list(itertools.chain(*list_of_word_sets))
    text = map(lambda x: re.sub(r'[^A-Z]', r'', x), text)
    text = reduce(lambda x, y: x + ' ' + y, text)
    wordcloud = WordCloud(
        width=3000,
        height=2000,
        background_color='black',
        stopwords=STOPWORDS,
        collocations=False).generate(str(text))
    fig = plt.figure(
        figsize=(10, 5),
        facecolor='k',
        edgecolor='k')
    plt.imshow(wordcloud, interpolation='bilinear')
    plt.axis('off')
    plt.tight_layout(pad=0)
    plt.show()
```

8. We call this function on each cluster and obtain the following:

```python
plot_word_cloud(pandas_df[pandas_df.prediction==0].Description)
```

The resulting word cloud for cluster 0 is as follows:

9. Take a look at the following code:

```
plot_word_cloud(pandas_df[pandas_df.prediction==1].Description)
```

The resulting word cloud for cluster 1 is as follows:

Take a look at the following code:

```
plot_word_cloud(pandas_df[pandas_df.prediction==2].Description)
```

The resulting word cloud for cluster 2 is as follows:

We can see in the word clouds that, despite some very common words, the relative importance of a few words such as *Christmas* or *retrospot* comes out with a higher weight on one of the clusters.

Clustering with Spark and SageMaker on EMR

In this section, we will show how **Spark** and **SageMaker** can work together seamlessly through code integration.

In the previous chapter, regarding decision trees, we performed the data preparation in Apache Spark through **EMR** and uploaded the prepared data in S3 to then open a SageMaker notebook instance using the `SageMaker` Python library to perform the training. There is an alternative way of doing the same thing, which, on many occasions, is more convenient, using the `sagemaker_pyspark` library. This library allows us to perform the training stage through SageMaker services just by adding a special stage to our pipeline. To do this, we will define a pipeline identical to the one we wrote in the previous section, with the difference being the last stage.

Instead of including Apache Spark's implementation of KMeans, we will use KMeansSageMakerEstimator:

1. Firstly, we will import all the necessary dependencies:

```
from pyspark.ml import Pipeline
from pyspark.ml.clustering import KMeans
from pyspark.ml.feature import Normalizer
from pyspark.ml.feature import OneHotEncoder
from pyspark.ml.feature import QuantileDiscretizer
from pyspark.ml.feature import StringIndexer
from pyspark.ml.feature import VectorAssembler
from sagemaker_pyspark import IAMRole
from sagemaker_pyspark.algorithms import KMeansSageMakerEstimator
```

2. Next, we start by defining the IAM role to use and the full pipeline:

```
role = 'arn:aws:iam::095585830284:role/EMR_EC2_DefaultRole'

kmeans = KMeansSageMakerEstimator(
    sagemakerRole=IAMRole(role),
    trainingInstanceType="ml.m4.xlarge",
    trainingInstanceCount=1,
    endpointInstanceType="ml.m4.xlarge",
    endpointInitialInstanceCount=1)
kmeans.setK(3)
kmeans.setFeatureDim(3722)

stages = [
    StringIndexer(inputCol='StockCode',
outputCol="stock_code_index", handleInvalid='keep'),
    OneHotEncoder(inputCol='stock_code_index',
outputCol='stock_code_encoded'),
    StringIndexer(inputCol='Country', outputCol='country_index',
handleInvalid='keep'),
    OneHotEncoder(inputCol='country_index',
outputCol='country_encoded'),
    QuantileDiscretizer(numBuckets=3,
inputCol='SumTotalBought',outputCol='total_bought_index'),
    VectorAssembler(inputCols=['stock_code_encoded',
'country_encoded', 'total_bought_index'],
                    outputCol='features_raw'),
    Normalizer(inputCol="features_raw",
                outputCol="features", p=1.0),
                kmeans ]

pipeline = Pipeline(stages=stages)
model = pipeline.fit(joined_df)
```

`KMeansSageMakerEstimator` implements the estimator interface from Apache Spark, so it is included as any other estimator or transformer on our pipelines. Through the `KMeansSageMakerEstimator` constructor, we define the amount and type of machines to use as well as the IAM role. We explain the purpose of the role in the next subsection, *Understanding the purpose of the IAM Role*. Additionally, we set the number of clusters we want to create (value of *k*) as well as the length of the vectors we'll be using for training (which we find by examining the output rows from the last section).

Let's look at what happens under the hood when we call `fit()` on the pipeline. The first part of the pipeline works exactly the same as before, whereby the different stages launch Spark jobs that run a series of transformations to the dataset by appending columns (for example, the encoded vectors or discretized features). The last stage, being a SageMaker estimator, works in a slightly different way. Instead of using the EMR cluster resources to compute and train the clustering model, it saves the data in S3 and makes an API call to the SageMaker KMeans service pointing to that S3 temporary location. The SageMaker service, in turn, spins up EC2 servers to perform the training and creates both a SageMaker model and endpoint. Once the training is complete, the `KMeansSageMakerEstimator` stores a reference to the newly created endpoint that is used each time the model's `transfom()` method is called.

You can find the models and endopoints created by `KMeansSageMakerEstimator` by inspecting the SageMaker AWS console at `https://console.aws.amazon.com/sagemaker/`.

Now, follow these steps:

1. Let's examine what happens when we call the `transform()` method of the pipeline:

```
df_with_clusters = model.transform(joined_df)
```

The first series of transformations (the data preparation stages) will run on the EMR cluster through Spark jobs. As the final transformation is a SageMaker model, it relies on the SageMaker endpoint to obtain the predictions (in our case, the cluster assignment).

> You should remember to delete the endpoint (for example using the console) once it's no longer required.

2. Then, run the following code:

```
df_with_clusters.show(5)
```

Take a look at the following screenshot:

```
---------+-------------+---------------+------------------+--------------------+--------------------+------------------+---------------+
_encoded|country_index|country_encoded|total_bought_index|        features_raw|            features|distance_to_cluster|closest_cluster|
---------+-------------+---------------+------------------+--------------------+--------------------+------------------+---------------+
,[1.0])|          0.0|  (37,[0],[1.0])|              2.0|(3722,[0,3684,372...|(3722,[0,3684,372...|0.26693078875541687|            2.0|
,[1.0])|          0.0|  (37,[0],[1.0])|              2.0|(3722,[403,3684,3...|(3722,[403,3684,3...| 0.2682397961616516|            2.0|
,[1.0])|          0.0|  (37,[0],[1.0])|              2.0|(3722,[452,3684,3...|(3722,[452,3684,3...|  0.268250435590744|            2.0|
,[1.0])|          0.0|  (37,[0],[1.0])|              2.0|(3722,[288,3684,3...|(3722,[288,3684,3...| 0.268185555934906|            2.0|
,[1.0])|          0.0|  (37,[0],[1.0])|              2.0|(3722,[281,3684,3...|(3722,[281,3684,3...|0.2680809795856476|            2.0|
---------+-------------+---------------+------------------+--------------------+--------------------+------------------+---------------+
```

(The image has been truncated to show just the last few columns.)

Note how the two columns were added by the `distance_to_cluster` and `closest_cluster` pipelines.

3. By instructing the cluster evaluator to use this column, we can evaluate the clustering ability:

```
evaluator = ClusteringEvaluator()
evaluator.setPredictionCol("closest_cluster")
silhouette = evaluator.evaluate(df_with_clusters)
```

The silhouette value we get is almost the same as the one using Spark's algorithm.

Understanding the purpose of the IAM role

SageMaker is a managed service on AWS that manages the hardware responsible for training and inference. In order for SageMaker to perform such tasks on your behalf, you need to allow it through IAM configuration. For example, if you're running on EMR, the EC2 instances (that is, the computers) in the cluster are running with a specific role. This role can be found by going to the cluster page on the EMR console: `https://console.aws.amazon.com/elasticmapreduce/`.

The following screenshot shows the cluster details, including the security and access information:

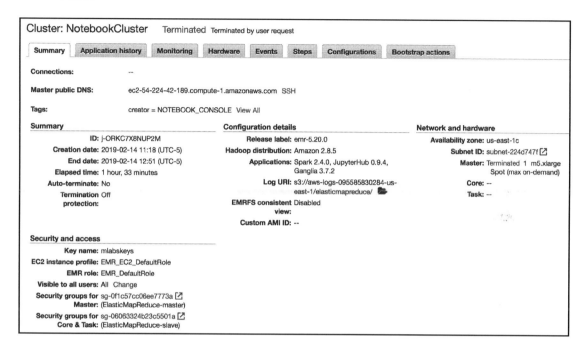

The role under **EC2 instance profile** in the previous screenshot is the one we are using, that is, EMR_EC2_DefaultRole.

We then go to the IAM console at `https://console.aws.amazon.com/iam/home` to edit the permissions of that role to grant access to SageMaker resources, as well as allow the role to be assumed:

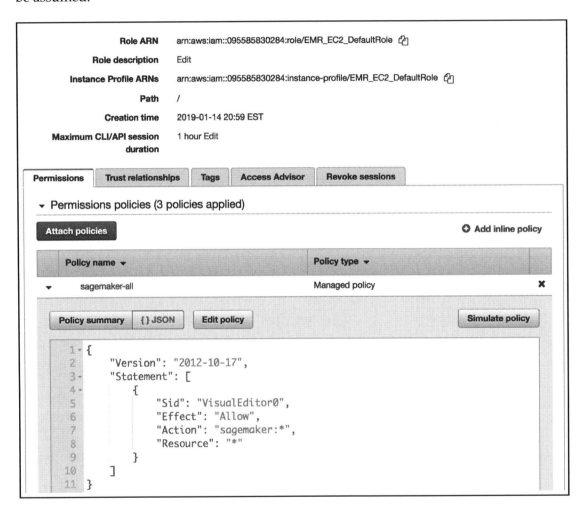

In the **Trust relationships** section, we click on the **Edit trust relationship** button to open the dialog that will allow us to add the settings:

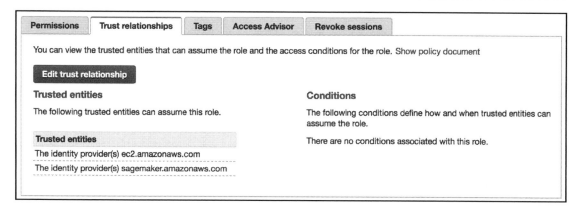

You can edit and allow the role to be assumed as follows:

```
Edit Trust Relationship

You can customize trust relationships by editing the following access control policy document.

Policy Document
 1 {
 2     "Version": "2008-10-17",
 3     "Statement": [
 4       {
 5         "Sid": "",
 6         "Effect": "Allow",
 7         "Principal": {
 8           "Service": "ec2.amazonaws.com"
 9         },
10         "Action": "sts:AssumeRole"
11       },
12       {
13         "Effect": "Allow",
14         "Principal": {
15           "Service": "sagemaker.amazonaws.com"
16         },
17         "Action": "sts:AssumeRole"
18       }
19     ]
20 }
```

Cancel   Update Trust Policy

The previous changes are required to allow our EMR cluster to talk to SageMaker and enable the kind of integration described in this section.

Summary

In this chapter, we studied the difference between supervised and unsupervised learning and looked at situations when unsupervised learning is applied. We studied the exploratory analysis application of unsupervised learning, where clustering approaches are used. We studied the k-means clustering and hierarchical clustering approaches in detail and looked at examples of how they are applied.

We also looked at how clustering approaches can be implemented on Apache Spark on AWS clusters. In our experience, clustering tasks are generally done on larger datasets, and, hence, taking the setup of the cluster into account for such tasks is important. We discussed these nuances in this chapter.

As a data scientist, there have been many situations where we analyze data with the sole purpose of extracting value from the data. You should consider clustering approaches in these cases as it will help you to understand the inherent structure in your data. Once you discover the patterns in your data, you can identify events and categories by which your data is arranged. Once you have established your clusters, you can also evaluate any new observation based on which cluster it may belong to and predict that the observation will exhibit similar behavior to other observations in the cluster.

In the next chapter, we will cover a very interesting problem: how to make recommendations through machine learning by finding products that similar users find relevant.

Exercises

1. What are the situations where you would apply the k-means algorithm compared to hierarchical clustering?
2. What is the difference between a regular Spark estimator and an estimator that calls SageMaker?
3. For a dataset that takes too long to train, why would it not be a good idea to launch such a job using a SageMaker estimator?
4. Research and establish other alternative metrics for cluster evaluation.
5. Why is string indexing not a good idea when encoding features for k-means?

6
Analyzing Visitor Patterns to Make Recommendations

This chapter will focus on the problem of finding similar visitors based on the theme park attractions they attend, to make improved marketing recommendations. Collaborative filtering methods will be introduced with examples showing how to train and obtain custom recommendations both in Apache Spark (EMR) and through the AWS SageMaker built-in algorithms. Many companies leverage the kinds of algorithms we describe in this chapter to improve the engagement of their customers by recommending products that have a proven record of being relevant to similar customers.

We will cover the following topics in this chapter:

- Making theme park attraction recommendations through Flickr data
- Finding recommendations through Apache Spark's Alternating Least Squares method
- Recommending attractions through SageMaker Factorization Machines

Making theme park attraction recommendations through Flickr data

Throughout this chapter, we will make use of the dataset from `https://sites.google.com/site/limkwanhui/datacode`, which consists of Flickr data from users who take photos at different locations, these photos are then mapped to known theme park attractions. Flickr is an image-hosting service. Let's assume Flickr wants to create a plug-in on their mobile app that, as users take photos on the different attractions, identifies user preferences and provides recommendations on other attractions that might be of interest to them.

Let's also suppose that the number of photos a user takes on a particular attraction is an indicator of their interest in the attraction. Our goal is to analyze a dataset with triples of the *user ID, attraction, number of photos taken* form so that given an arbitrary set of attractions visited by a user, the model is able to recommend new attractions that similar users found interesting.

Collaborative filtering

Collaborative filtering is a process for providing recommendations to users based on their behavior by analyzing the behaviors of a lot of users. We observe the effects of this algorithm in our day-to-day life in a large number of applications. For example, when you are using streaming services, such as Netflix or YouTube, it recommends videos that you may be interested in based on your streaming history. Social networks, such as Twitter and LinkedIn, suggest people for you to follow or connect with based on your current contacts. Services such as Instagram and Facebook curate posts from your friends and tailor your timeline based on the posts that you read or like. As a data scientist, collaborative filtering algorithms are really useful when you are building recommendation systems based on a large amount of user data.

There are various ways in which collaborative filtering can be implemented on a dataset. In this chapter, we will be discussing the memory-based approach and the model-based approach.

Memory-based approach

In the memory-based approach, we generate recommendations in two phases. Consider a situation where we are trying to generate recommendations for a given user based on their interests. In the first phase, we discover users who are similar to the given user based on their interests. We rank all the users based on how similar they are to a given user. In the second phase, we discover the top interests among the group of users that are most similar to a given user. The top interests are ranked based on their similarity to the set of top-ranked users. This ranked list of interests is then presented to the original user as recommendations.

For example, in the process of movie recommendations, we look at the movies a user is interested in or has watched recently and discover other users who have watched similar movies. Based on the top-ranked list of similar users, we look at the movies they have watched recently and rank them based on the similarity to the list of ranked users. Then, the top-ranked movies are then presented as recommendations to the user.

To find a similarity between users, we use functions called similarity measures. Similarity measures are popularly used in search engines to rank a similarity between query terms and documents. In this section, we discuss the cosine similarity measure, which is commonly used in collaborative filtering. We treat each user's interest as a vector. To discover users with similar interests, we calculate the cosine of the angle between two users' interest vector. It can be represented as follows:

$$similarity(u_1, u_2) = cos(\vec{u_1}, \vec{u_2}) = \frac{\vec{u_1} \cdot \vec{u_2}}{||\vec{u_1}|| \cdot ||\vec{u_2}||}$$

Based on the similarity between a given user and all users in the dataset, we select the top k users. We then aggregate the interest vectors of all users to discover the top-ranked interests and recommend it to the user.

Note that memory-based models do not use any modeling algorithms that were discussed in the previous chapters. They only rely on simple arithmetic to generate recommendations for users based on their interests.

Model-based approach

For the model-based approach, we use machine learning techniques to train a model that can predict the probability of each interest being relevant to a given user. Various algorithms, such as Bayesian models or clustering models, can be applied for model-based collaborative filtering. However, in this chapter, we focus on the matrix-factorization-based approach.

Matrix factorization

The matrix factorization approach works by decomposing a matrix of users and the interests of the users. In this methodology, we map the user data and the information about the interests to a set of factors. The score of a user to interest is calculated by taking a dot product of the vector scores for the user and the interest. These factors can be inferred from the user ratings or from the external information about the interests in the algorithm.

For example, consider a matrix where one dimension represents the users and the other dimension represents the movies the users have rated:

	Avengers	Jumanji	Spiderman
User 1	4		4
User 2	1	5	2
User n	5	2	4

The values in the matrix are the ratings provided by the users. The matrix factorization methodology maps the movies into shorter vectors that represent concepts, such as the genre of the movie. These vectors are known as latent factors. We map the movies to genres and also map what genres users are interested in based on how they rate movies in each genre. Using this information, we can calculate the similarity between a user and movie based on the dot product (multiplying the interest of the user in genres by the likelihood of the movie to belong to genres) between both the vectors. Thus, the unknown ratings in the matrix can be predicted using the knowledge of known ratings by consolidating the users and interests to less granular items (that is, genres). In our previous example, we assume that we already have a known mapping of movies to genre. However, we cannot make an assumption that we will always have explicit data to generate such mappings to latent factors.

Hence, we explore methodologies that can help us generate such mappings automatically based on the data. Matrix factorization models therefore need to be able to generate a map between users and interests through a latent factors vector. To ensure we can generate a dot product between the latent factors of a user and the item, the length of the latent factors is set to a fixed value. Each interest item, i, is represented by a vector, q_i, and each user, u, is represented by a vector, p_u. The q_i and p_u vectors are both latent factors that are derived from the data. The rating for an item, i, for a user, u, is represented as follows:

$$r_{ui} = q_i^T \cdot p_u$$

In general, if we already have a partial set of ratings from users to interests, we can use that to model ratings between other users and interests. We use optimization techniques to calculate this. Our objective is to predict the values of p_u and q_i. Hence, we do that by minimizing the regularized error when predicting these vectors by using the known ratings. This is represented in the following formula:

$$min_{q_i, p_u} \sum_{(u,i)\epsilon K} (r_{ui} - q_i^T p_u)^2 + \lambda(||q_i||^2 + ||p_u||^2)$$

Here, k is a set of (u, i) where the rating, r_{ui}, is known. Now, let's look at study two approaches for minimizing the preceding equation.

Stochastic gradient descent

We studied the stochastic gradient-descent algorithm in Chapter 3, *Predicting House Value with Regression Algorithms* regarding linear regression. A similar methodology is used to minimize the function to predict the correct latent factors for each user and interest. We use an iterative approach, where during each iteration, we calculate the error of predicting q_i and p_u based on all the known ratings:

$$e_{ui} = r_{ui} - q_i^T \cdot p_u$$

Based on the magnitude of error, we update the values of q_i and p_u in the opposite direction of the error:

$$q_i = q_i + \gamma(e_{ui} \cdot p_u - \lambda \cdot q_i)$$

$$p_u = p_u + \gamma(e_{ui} \cdot q_i - \lambda \cdot p_u)$$

We stop the iterations after the values of q_i and p_u converge. Stochastic gradient descent is also used in algorithms such as **Factorization Machines** (**FMs**), which uses it to compute values of vectors. FMs are a variant of **support vector machine** (**SVM**) models that can be applied in a collaborative filtering framework. We do not explain support vector machines or FMs in detail in this book, but encourage you to understand how they work.

Alternating Least Squares

One of the challenges of minimizing the optimization function to predict the values of both q_i and p_u is that the equation is not convex. This is because we are trying to optimize two values at the same time. However, if we used a constant for one of the values, or q_i or p_u, we can solve the equation optimally for the other variable. Hence, in the Alternating Least Squares technique, we alternatively set the values of q_i and p_u as constant while optimizing for the other vector.

Hence, in the first step, we set base values for both the vectors. Assuming that one of the values is constant, we use linear programming to optimize the other vector. In the next step, we set the value of the optimized vector as constant and optimize for the other variable. We will not explain how linear programming is used to optimize for quadratic questions as it is an entire field of study and not in the scope of this book. This methodology optimizes each vector until convergence.

The advantage of stochastic gradient descent is that it is faster than the ALS method, as it depends on predicting the values of both the vectors in each step while modifying the vectors based on the proportion of errors. However, in the ALS methodology, the system calculates the values of each vector independently, and hence leads to better optimization. Moreover, when the matrix is dense, the gradient descent methodology has to learn from each set of data, making it less efficient than the ALS methodology.

Finding recommendations through Apache Spark's ALS

In this section, we will go through the process of creating recommendations in Apache Spark using **Alternating Least Squares (ALS)**.

Data gathering and exploration

The first step is to download the data from `https://sites.google.com/site/limkwanhui/datacode`. We will be using the `poiList-sigir17` dataset with photos taken by users at different theme park attractions (identified as points of interest by Flickr). There are following two datasets we're interested in:

- The list of points of interests, which captures the names and other properties of each attraction:

```
poi_df = spark.read.csv(SRC_PATH + 'data-sigir17/poiList-sigir17',
                        header=True, inferSchema=True, sep=';')
```

The following screenshot shows the first few lines of the `poi_df` dataframe:

	poiID	poiName	lat	long	rideDuration	theme	theme2	theme3	theme4
0	1	Gadget's Go Coaster	33.810259	-117.918438	1.00	Kiddie	Roller Coaster	None	None
1	2	Astro Orbitor	28.418532	-81.579153	1.50	Spinning Ride	None	None	None
2	3	Mad Tea Party	33.813458	-117.918289	1.50	Family	Spinning Ride	None	None
3	4	Dumbo the Flying Elephant	33.813680	-117.918928	1.67	Family	Spinning Ride	None	None

- The photos taken by Flickr users at different points of interest:

```
visits_path = SRC_PATH+'data-sigir17/userVisits-sigir17'
visits_df = spark.read.csv(visits_path,
                           header=True,
                           inferSchema=True, sep=';')
```

The following screenshot shows a sample of the `visits_df` dataframe:

	id	nsid	takenUnix	poiID	poiTheme	poiFreq	rideDuration	seqID
0	5858403310	10004778@N07	1308262550	6	Ride	1665	120.0	1
1	5857850631	10004778@N07	1308270702	26	Family	18710	900.0	1
2	5858399220	10004778@N07	1308631356	6	Ride	1665	120.0	2
3	8277294024	10004778@N07	1355568624	26	Family	18710	900.0	3
4	9219062165	10004778@N07	1373030964	29	Water	10427	900.0	4

In this dataset, we will be using the `nsid` field (indicating the user taking the photo) and `poiID`, which indicates the actual point of interest or attraction visited while taking the photo. For our purposes, we will ignore the rest of the fields.

Let's do some basic inspection on our dataset. The dataset has about 300,000 rows of data. By taking a sample of 1,000 entries, we can see that there are 36 unique Flickr users:

```
sample_df = visits_df.limit(1000).toPandas()
sample_df.describe()
```

The output of the preceding `describe()` command is as follows:

```
count 1000
 unique 36
 top 10182842@N08
 freq 365
```

This is important, as we need to have enough entries per user to ensure we have enough information about users to make predictions. Furthermore, it's actually more relevant to know whether users visit different attractions. One the nice things about Apache Spark is that one can work on datasets using SQL. Finding the number of distinct attractions users see on average can easily be done with SQL.

In order to work with SQL, we first need to give a table name to the dataset. This is done by registering a temp table:

```
poi_df.createOrReplaceTempView('points')
visits_df.createOrReplaceTempView('visits')
```

Once we register the tables, we can do queries, such as finding the number of unique attractions:

```
spark.sql('select distinct poiID from visits').count()
31
```

Or we can combine SQL with other dataset operations, such as `.describe()`:

```
spark.sql('select nsid,count(distinct poiID) as cnt from visits group by nsid').describe().show()
```

The following screenshot contains the result of the output of the `show()` command:

	summary	nsid	cnt
0	count	8903	8903
1	mean	None	4.86027181848815
2	stddev	None	5.965584836576787
3	min	10000151@N02	1
4	max	99987318@N03	31

The preceding SQL command finds the number of distinct attractions each user visits. The describe dataset operation finds statistics on these users, which tells us that, on average, users visit about five different locations. This is important as we need to have enough attractions per user to be able to correctly identify user patterns.

Similarly, we should look at the number of photos users take at each location, to validate that in fact we can use the number of photos taken as an indicator of the user's interest. We do that through the following command:

```
spark.sql('select nsid,poiID,count(*) from visits group by
nsid,poiID').describe().show()
```

The output of the preceding command is shown by the following screenshot:

	summary	nsid	poiID	count(1)
0	count	43271	43271	43271
1	mean	None	14.920061935245315	7.674678190936193
2	stddev	None	8.437883931275111	52.93100615991835
3	min	10000151@N02	1	1
4	max	99987318@N03	31	4128

The SQL command counts the number of entries for each user and attraction, and then we find a statistical summary using the describe. We can conclude therefore that on average, each user takes about eight pictures at every location they visit.

Training the model

To train our model, we will construct a dataset that computes the number of photos taken by each user at each location:

```
train_df = spark.sql('select hash(nsid) as user_hash_id, poiID, count(*) as
pictures_taken from visits group by 1,2')
```

The following screenshot shows the first few lines of the train_df dataframe:

	user_hash_id	poiID	pictures_taken
0	-1861435726	19	7
1	-1064654977	26	8
2	-636721096	17	1

We hash the user because the ALS trainer just supports numerical values as features.

To train the model, we simply need to construct an instance of ALS and provide the user column, item column (in this case the attraction IDs), and the rating column (in this case, `pictures_takes` is used as a proxy for rating). `coldStartStrategy` is set to drop as we're not interested in making predictions for users or attractions not present in the dataset (that is, predictions for such entries will be dropped rather than returning NaN):

```
from pyspark.ml.recommendation import ALS

recommender = ALS(userCol="user_hash_id",
                  itemCol="poi_hash_id",
                  ratingCol="pictures_taken",
                  coldStartStrategy="drop")

model = recommender.fit(train_df)
```

Getting recommendations

Once we build a model, we can generate predictions for all users in our dataset:

```
recommendations = model.recommendForAllUsers(10)
```

The preceding command will pick the top 10 recommendations for each user. Note that because of how ALS works, it might actually recommend attractions already visited by the user, so we need to discard that for our purposes, as we will see later on.

The recommendations look as follows:

	user_hash_id	recommendations
0	413285690	[(25, 39.260990142822266), (18, 34.83002853393...
1	1005782960	[(29, 6.377601146697998), (25, 6.2345833778381...
2	1410121870	[(25, 12.15351390838623), (29, 11.446855545043...

Each user gets a list of tuples with the recommended attraction as well as the score for the recommendation. In this case, the score represents the estimated number of photos we would expect each user to take at the recommended location. Even though the model just provides the IDs of the attractions, we would like to inspect a few of these recommendations to make sure they are good. In order to do that, we will construct a dictionary of IDs to attraction names (point of interest names) by collecting the result of a query that finds the name of each attraction in the points table:

```
row_list = spark.sql('select distinct p.poiName, p.poiID from visits v join
points p on (p.poiID=v.poiID) ').collect()
id_to_poi_name = dict(map(lambda x: (x.poiID, x.poiName), row_list))
```

The map contains the following entries:

```
{1: 'Test Track',
 10: 'Golden Zephyr',
 19: "Tarzan's Treehouse",
 22: 'Country Bear Jamboree'
 ....
 }
```

For each user, we want to remove the recommendations for already-visited sites and output the recommendations. To do that, we need to process the list of tuples on each row. Apache Spark provides a convenient way to do this by allowing users to create custom SQL functions, or **user-defined functions (UDFs)**. We will define and register a UDF that is capable of extracting the names of each recommended attraction through the use of the preceding map:

```
def poi_names(recommendations, visited_pois):
    visited_set = set([id_to_poi_name[poi] for poi in visited_pois])
    recommended = str([[(id_to_poi_name[poi], weight) \
                      for (poi,weight) in recommendations
                      if id_to_poi_name[poi] not in visited_set])
    return "recommended: %s ; visited: %s "%(recommended, visited_set)

spark.udf.register("poi_names", poi_names)
```

The poi_names function receives the recommendations tuple for a user as well as the attractions visited and then returns a string that contains all recommended attraction names that were not in the set of visited, as well as an enumeration of the visited attractions.

We then register the recommendations as a table so it can be used in our next query:

```
recommendations.createOrReplaceTempView('recommendations')

recommendation_sample = spark.sql('select user_hash_id,
collect_list(poiID), poi_names(max(recommendations), collect_list(poiID))
as recommendation from recommendations r join visits v on (r.user_hash_id =
hash(v.nsid)) group by 1')\
    .sample(fraction=0.1, withReplacement=False) \
    .collect()
```

The preceding query joins the user recommendations table with the visits table and joins by user, collecting all points of interest visited by each user, and through the UDF it outputs the recommended attractions as well as the names of the already-visited attractions. We sample and collect a few instances of the table to inspect. In the companion notebook, we can observe the entries:

```
print(recommendation_sample[0].recommendation)

recommended: [("It's A Small World", 31.352962493896484), ('Walt Disney
World Railroad', 23.464025497436523), ('Pirates of the Caribbean',
21.36219596862793), ('Buzz Lightyear Astro Blasters', 17.21680450439453),
('Haunted Mansion', 15.873616218566895), ('Country Bear Jamboree',
9.63521957397461), ('Astro Orbiter', 9.164801597595215), ('The Great Movie
Ride', 8.167647361755371)] ; visited: {"California Screamin'", 'Sleeping
Beauty Castle Walkthrough', 'Voyage of The Little Mermaid', "Tarzan's
Treehouse", 'Main Street Cinema', 'The Many Adventures of Winnie the Pooh',
'Jungle Cruise', 'Tom Sawyer Island', 'Test Track', 'The Twilight Zone
Tower of Terror'}
```

We can observe that this user visited a number of adventure-like attractions and the model recommended a few more. Here, the reader can inspect a couple more recommendations:

```
print(recommendation_sample[200].recommendation)

recommended: [('Splash Mountain', 0.9785523414611816), ('Sleeping Beauty
Castle Walkthrough', 0.8383632302284241), ("Pinocchio's Daring Journey",
0.7456990480422974), ('Journey Into Imagination With Figment',
0.4501221477985382), ("California Screamin'", 0.44446268677711487), ('Tom
Sawyer Island', 0.41949236392974854), ("It's A Small World",
0.40130260586738586), ('Astro Orbiter', 0.37899214029312134), ('The
Twilight Zone Tower of Terror', 0.3728359639644623)] ; visited: {"Snow
White's Scary Adventures"}

print(recommendation_sample[600].recommendation)

recommended: [('Fantasmic!', 20.900590896606445), ('Pirates of the
Caribbean', 9.25596809387207), ("It's A Small World", 8.825133323669434),
```

```
('Buzz Lightyear Astro Blasters', 5.474684715270996), ('Main Street
Cinema', 5.1001691818237305), ('Country Bear Jamboree',
4.3145904541015625), ("California Screamin'", 3.717888832092285), ("It's A
Small World", 3.6027705669403076), ('The Many Adventures of Winnie the
Pooh', 3.429044246673584)] ; visited: {'Haunted Mansion', 'The Twilight
Zone Tower of Terror', 'Journey Into Imagination With Figment'}
```

Recommending attractions through SageMaker Factorization Machines

FMs are one of the most widely used algorithms for making recommendations when it comes to very sparse input. It is similar to the **stochastic gradient descent (SGD)** algorithm we discussed under the model-based matrix factorization methodology. In this section, we will show how to use AWS' built-in algorithm implementation of FMs to get recommendations for our theme park visitors.

Preparing the dataset for learning

In order to use such an algorithm, we need to prepare our dataset in a different way. We will pose the recommendation problem as a regression problem in which the input are a pair of user and attraction, and the output is the expected level of interest this user will have toward the attraction. The training dataset must have the actual empirical interest (measured by the number of photos taken) for each pair of user and attraction. With this data, the FM model will then be able to predict the interest of an arbitrary attraction for any user. Hence, to obtain recommendations for a user, we just need to find the list of attractions that yields the highest predicted level of interest.

So then how do we encode the user and the attractions in a dataset?

Given that FMs are extremely good at dealing with high-dimensional features, we can one-hot encode our input. Since there are 8,903 users and 31 attractions, our input vector will be of length 8,934 where the first 31 vector components will correspond to the 31 different attractions, and the remaining positions correspond to each user. The vector will always have zeros except for the positions corresponding to the user and attraction, which will have a value of 1. The target feature (label) used in our model will be the level of interest, which we will discretize to a value of 1 to 5 by normalizing the number of pictures taken according to their corresponding quantile.

The following figure shows how such a training dataset could look:

31 attractions					8903 users					interest
a0	a1	a2	...	a30	u0	u1	u2	..	u8902	label
0	1	0		0	0	0	1		0	4.0
0	0	1		0	1	0	0		0	1.0
0	1	0		0	0	0	1		0	3.0
1	0	0		0	0	0	1		0	1.0

As you can imagine, this matrix is extremely sparse, therefore we need to encode our rows using a sparse representation. Like most SageMaker algorithms, we must drop our data in S3 to allow SageMaker to train the data. In past chapters, we used CSV as an input. However, CSV is not a good representation for our dataset; given its sparse nature, it would occupy too much space (with a lot of repeated zeros!). In fact, at the time of writing, SageMaker doesn't even support CSV as an input format. In a sparse representation, each vector must indicate the following three values:

- The size of the vector
- The positions in which we have a value other than 0
- The values at each of these non-zero positions

For example, the sparse representation for the first row in the preceding figure would be the following:

- Vector size = 8934
- Non-zero positions = [1, 33]
- Values at non-sero positions = [1, 1]

The only input format FMs currently supports is called protobuf recordIO. Protobuf, short for **Protocol buffers**, is a language-neutral, platform-neutral extensible mechanism for serializing structured data initially developed by Google. In our case, the structure will be the sparse representation of our matrix. Each record in the protobuf file we store in S3 will have all three items necessary for sparse representation, as well as the target feature (label).

Following, we will go through the process of preparing the dataset and uploading it to S3.

We will start with the Spark dataframe that we used for training in the previous section (`train_df`) and apply a `Pipeline` that does the one-hot encoding as well as normalizing the photos-taken target feature:

```
from pyspark.ml.feature import OneHotEncoder
from pyspark.ml.feature import StringIndexer
from pyspark.ml import Pipeline
from pyspark.ml.feature import QuantileDiscretizer
from pyspark.ml.feature import VectorAssembler

pipeline = Pipeline(stages = [
    StringIndexer(inputCol='user_hash_id',
                    outputCol="user_hash_id_index",
                    handleInvalid='keep'),
    OneHotEncoder(inputCol='user_hash_id_index',
                    outputCol='user_hash_id_encoded'),
    StringIndexer(inputCol='poiID',
                    outputCol='poi_id_indexed',
                    handleInvalid='keep'),
    OneHotEncoder(inputCol='poi_id_indexed',
                    outputCol='poi_id_encoded'),
    QuantileDiscretizer(numBuckets=5,
                        inputCol='pictures_taken',
                        outputCol='interest_level'),
    VectorAssembler(inputCols=['poi_id_encoded', 'user_hash_id_encoded'],
                    outputCol='features'),
])

model = pipeline.fit(train_df)
```

The pipeline is similar to pipelines we've built in the previous chapters, the difference being that we have not included a machine learning algorithm as a final step (since this stage will run through SageMaker's FMs once the dataset is in S3). We first string index the user and attraction (point of interest) features, and then chain them into a one-hot encoder. The quantile discretizer will reduce the photos taken feature into five buckets according to their percentile. We will name this feature `interest_level`. Additionally, we will assemble a vector with these encoded attractions and user vectors.

Next, we transform the training dataset by applying the model:

```
sparse_df = model.transform(train_df)
```

This will produce a dataset:

user_hash_id	poiID	pictures_taken	user_hash_id_index	user_hash_id_encoded	poi_id_indexed	poi_id_encoded	interest_level	features
-1861435726	19	7	279.0	(8903,[279],[1.0])	17.0	(31,[17],[1.0])	3.0	(8934,[17,310],[1...
-1064654977	26	8	181.0	(8903,[181],[1.0])	5.0	(31,[5],[1.0])	3.0	(8934,[5,212],[1...
-636721096	17	1	2187.0	(8903,[2187],[1.0])	4.0	(31,[4],[1.0])	1.0	(8934,[4,2210],[1...

Note how the encoded fields (`user_hash_id_encoded`, `poi_id_encoded`, and features) show the sparse representation of the vectors.

Once we have this encoded dataset, we can split them into testing and training. SageMaker will use the training dataset for fitting and the test dataset for finding the validation errors at each epoch upon training. We need to convert each of these datasets into recordio format and upload them to s3.

If we were working in Scala (the native programming language used by Spark), we could do something like this:

```
sagemaker_train_df.write.format("sagemaker") \
    .option("labelColumnName", "interest_level") \
    .option("featuresColumnName", "features") \
    .save("s3://mastering-ml-aws/chapter6/train-data")
```

Unfortunately, `pyspark` does not support writing a dataframe directly into recordio format at the time of this writing. Instead we will collect all our spark dataframes in memory and convert each row to a sparse vector, and then upload it to S3.

The following `spark_vector_to_sparse_matrix` function does exactly that. It takes a Spark dataframe row and converts it into a sparse `csr_matrix` (from `scipy`, a Python library with scientific utilities). The `upload_matrices_to_s3` function receives a Spark dataset (either training or testing), collects each row, builds a sparse vector with the features, and stacks them into a matrix. Additionally, it builds a target feature vector with all the interest levels. Given this matrix and label vector, we use the utility function `write_spmatrix_to_sparse_tensor`, of the `sagemaker` library to write the data in recordio format. Finally, we upload that object to S3. To do this, let's first import all the necessary dependencies:

```
from scipy.sparse import csr_matrix
import numpy as np
import boto3
import io
import numpy as np
import scipy.sparse as sp
import sagemaker.amazon.common as smac
```

Next, let's define two auxiliary functions: `spark_vector_to_sparse_matrix`, which will take a row and produce a `scipy` sparse matrix, and `upload_matrices_to_s3`, which is responsible for uploading the test or training dataset to s3:

```
def spark_vector_to_sparse_matrix(row):
    vect = row['features']
    return csr_matrix((vect.values, vect.indices, np.array([0,
vect.values.size])),
                        (1, vect.size),
                        dtype=np.float32)

def upload_matrices_to_s3(dataframe, dataset_name):
    features_matrices =
        dataframe.select("features") \
                .rdd.map(spark_vector_to_sparse_matrix).collect()
    interest_levels =
        dataframe.select("interest_level") \
                .rdd.map(lambda r: r['interest_level']).collect()

    interest_level_vector = np.array(interest_levels, dtype=np.float32)
    buffer = io.BytesIO()
    smac.write_spmatrix_to_sparse_tensor(buffer, \
                                        sp.vstack(features_matrices), \
                                        interest_level_vector)
    buffer.seek(0)
    bucket = boto3.resource('s3').Bucket('mastering-ml-aws')
    bucket.Object('chapter6/%s-
data.protobuf'%dataset_name).upload_fileobj(buffer)
```

Finally, we need to upload the training and testing dataset by calling the `upload_matrices_to_s3` method on both variables:

```
upload_matrices_to_s3(sagemaker_train_df, 'train')
upload_matrices_to_s3(sagemaker_test_df, 'test')
```

Training the model

Now that we have the data in S3 in the right format for learning, we can start training our model to get recommendations.

We will instantiate the SageMaker session and define the paths where to read and write the data:

```
import sagemaker
from sagemaker import get_execution_role
import json
import boto3

sess = sagemaker.Session()
role = get_execution_role()
container = sagemaker.amazon.amazon_estimator.get_image_uri('us-east-1',
    "factorization-machines",
    "latest")

s3_train_data = 's3://mastering-ml-aws/chapter6/train-data.protobuf'
s3_test_data = 's3://mastering-ml-aws/chapter6/train-data.protobuf'
s3_output_location = 's3://mastering-ml-aws/chapter6/sagemaker/output/'
```

With the session, we can instantiate the SageMaker estimator by setting the number and type of computers to use. We also specify the hyperparameters. Two important parameters to consider are the feature dim (which is the length of our training vectors) and the predictor type. Since our problem is posed as a regression, we will use regressor. If instead of interest level, we had modeled it as a presence/no presence of interest, we would have used the binary_classifier value:

```
from sagemaker.session import s3_input

recommender = sagemaker.estimator.Estimator(container,
                                            role,
                                            train_instance_count=1,
    train_instance_type='ml.c4.xlarge',
                                            output_path=s3_output_location,
                                            sagemaker_session=sess)

recommender.set_hyperparameters(predictor_type='regressor',
                        feature_dim=8934,
                        epochs=200,
                        mini_batch_size=100,
                        num_factors=128)

recommender.fit({'train': s3_input(s3_train_data), \
                'test': s3_input(s3_test_data)})
```

The logs will show some validation stats and a confirmation for when the model has completed:

```
[02/23/2019 22:01:02 INFO 140697667364672] #test_score (algo-1) : ('rmse',
0.19088356774389661)
2019-02-23 22:01:11 Uploading - Uploading generated training model
 2019-02-23 22:01:11 Completed - Training job completed
```

Getting recommendations

Once the model is fitted, we can launch a predictor web service:

```
predictor = recommender.deploy(instance_type='ml.c5.xlarge',
initial_instance_count=1)
```

This will launch the web service endpoint that hosts the trained model and is now ready to receive requests with predictions. Let's take one user from our recommendations made with Spark's ALS and compare it to the predictions made by SageMaker:

```
print(recommendation_sample[1].user_hash_id)
-525385694
```

We can collect the features of that user:

```
sagemaker_test_df.select('features').where('user_hash_id=-525385694') \
                  .rdd.map(build_request).collect()

[{'data': {'features': {'shape': [8934],
    'keys': [4, 3297],
    'values': [1.0, 1.0]}}}]
```

Here, `build_request` is a convenient function to create a JSON request compatible with how SageMaker expects the sparse-encoded requests:

```
def build_request(row):
    vect = row['features']
    return {'data':{ 'features': {'shape':[int(vect.size)],
                                  'keys':list(map(int,vect.indices)),
                                  'values':list(vect.values)}}}
```

As we know, the user ID position in the vector is 3297 and the attraction position is 4. We can call the service to get a prediction for the service:

```
import json

predictor.content_type = 'application/json'
predictor.predict(json.dumps({'instances': [
    {'data': {'features': {'shape': [8934], 'keys': [4, 3297],
              'values': [1, 1]}}}]}))
```

Here's the output:

```
{'predictions': [{'score': 0.8006305694580078}]}
```

 More details about the formats of the JSON requests and responses can be found here: https://docs.aws.amazon.com/sagemaker/latest/dg/cdf-inference.html.

Since we can ask the predictor for the score for an arbitrary pair of (user, attraction), we'll find the scores of all 31 attractions for the user in question and then sort by score:

```
def predict_poi(poi_position):
    prediction = predictor.predict(
            json.dumps({'instances': [{'data':
                        {'features': {'shape': [8934],
                                      'keys': [poi_position, 3297],
                                      'values': [1, 1]}}}]}))
    return prediction['predictions'][0]['score']

predictions = [(poi_position, predict_poi(poi_position)) for poi_position
in range(0,31)]
predictions.sort(key=lambda x:x[1], reverse=True)
```

Given those scores, we can find the names of the highest-ranking attractions, excluding those already visited:

```
user_visited_pois =
    [id_to_poi_name[x] for x in
set(recommendation_sample[1]['collect_list(poiID)'])]

for (poi_position, score) in predictions[:10]:
  recommended_poi =
id_to_poi_name[int(model.stages[2].labels[poi_position])]
  if recommended_poi not in user_visited_pois:
      print(recommended_poi)
```

The output is as follows:

```
Test Track
 Walt Disney World Railroad
 Main Street Cinema
 Tom Sawyer Island
 Tarzan's Treehouse
 Mark Twain Riverboat
 Sleeping Beauty Castle Walkthrough
 Snow White's Scary Adventures
```

Let's compare this with the recommendations made by Spark:

```
print(recommendation_sample[1].recommendation)
recommended: [("Pinocchio's Daring Journey", 3.278768539428711), ('Tom
Sawyer Island', 2.78713321685791), ('Splash Mountain', 2.114530324935913),
("Tarzan's Treehouse", 2.06896710395813), ('Fantasmic!',
1.9648514986038208), ("Snow White's Scary Adventures", 1.8940000534057617),
('Main Street Cinema', 1.6671074628829956), ('Mark Twain Riverboat',
1.314055323600769), ('Astro Orbiter', 1.3135600090026855)] ; visited: {'The
Many Adventures of Winnie the Pooh', 'Rose & Crown Pub Musician', 'Golden
Zephyr', "It's A Small World"}
```

As the reader might notice, there are many overlapping recommendations. For a more thorough analysis regarding the quality of the model and its predictive power, we can use the evaluation methods discussed in Chapter 3, *Predicting House Value with Regression Algorithms*, as this problem is posed as a regression.

Summary

In this chapter, we studied a new type of machine learning algorithm called collaborative filtering. This algorithm is used in recommendation systems. We looked at memory-based approaches that use similarity measures to find users similar to a given user and discover recommendations based on the collective interests of the top-ranked similar users. We also studied a model-based approach called matrix factorization, that maps users and interests to latent factors and generate recommendations based on these factors. We also studied the implementations of various collaborative filtering approaches in Apache Spark and SageMaker.

In the next chapter, we will focus on a very popular topic: deep learning. We will cover the theory behind this advanced field as well as a few modern applications.

Exercises

1. Find an example of a recommendation system that is not described in this chapter. Evaluate which approach of collaborative filtering would fit that approach.
2. For a movie-recommendation engine, explore how the issue of sparsity of data affects each algorithm listed in this chapter.

Section 3: Deep Learning

3

One of the main innovations in the field of AI and machine learning is the advent of deep learning algorithms. We dedicate this part of the book to deep learning algorithms and explain how readers can implement them using various technologies in AWS. We take a practical approach to explaining deep learning algorithms rather than a theoretical approach, and explain how deep learning works with help of several real-world examples. Readers will learn what deep learning is, the applications of deep learning, and how to implement deep learning systems on AWS.

This section contains the following chapters:

- Chapter 7, *Implementing Deep Learning Algorithms*
- Chapter 8, *Implementing Deep Learning with TensorFlow on AWS*
- Chapter 9, *Image Classification and Detection with SageMaker*

Implementing Deep Learning Algorithms

7

Deep learning is an area of machine learning that has gained significantly in terms of popularity in recent years. Deep learning, which is also referred to as deep structured learning or hierarchical learning refers to using multiple layers of artificial neural networks to train from data. Over the last few years, it has become possible to perform certain tasks, such as image recognition, better than human beings.

We will cover the following topics in this chapter:

- Understanding deep learning
- Applications of deep learning
- Understanding deep neural networks
- Understanding convolutional neural networks

Understanding deep learning

Deep learning algorithms have gained in popularity over the last decade. Technologies such as self-driving cars, speech recognition, and robotics have improved significantly on account of deep learning algorithms. Deep learning has helped researchers to significantly reduce the number of errors when training models to perform such tasks and also surpassed humans in performing certain tasks. However, what is most interesting is that deep learning algorithms are inspired by how human brains work.

Let's take an example of image recognition. We see objects and are able to recognize them based on past experiences of when we saw these objects. However, let's break this process down into what exactly happens. First, light hits the object, enters our eye, and hits the retina. The retina is a sensory membrane that converts this light into nerve signals. This signal is then passed through various layers behind the retina to the brain. Our brain identifies the number of objects that exist in the scene before our eyes. Based on past references, our brain can identify the objects.

There is no one process of us looking at the object and recognizing it. There are various levels of abstractions between when the light enters our eyes and when our brain identifies the object. There is no specific process when our brain stops and decides what features in the signal it is trying to interpret. Such a feature extraction process occurs automatically.

Deep learning algorithms also follow a similar process. Deep learning breaks the tasks of getting the data into the various layers of abstractions, such that each layer interprets the input data, and provides a meaningful output for the next layer of abstraction. For example, in image recognition tasks, the input may be a set of pixels from the image. In the first layer, the pixels can be processed to find edges in the image. In the second layer, this information regarding edges can be processed to detect corners between these edges. In the next layer, these corners and edges can be used to detect objects in the image. And the next layer may predict what each object is. These layers of abstractions do not need to be defined by us, but can train automatically by themselves.

In algorithms such as Naive Bayes and linear regression, we always used hand-crafted features. We already had analysts look at the incoming dataset and define feature sets based on the data. We labeled each category as categorical or continuous. However, in deep learning methodologies, we only require datasets with simple features and use layers of abstractions to create additional abstract features. Hence, in tasks such as image recognition, where the datasets are sets of pixels, traditional algorithms would need help in identifying objects in the images before they can learn how to classify them. We would also have to extract features from the objects, such as color and size before we can feed these features to the classification models. However, for deep learning algorithms, we use pixels of the image as input to the algorithm with labeled objects such that the deep learning models can identify when errors are made and undertake self-correction.

Deep learning algorithms can perform both supervised and unsupervised learning algorithms.

Applications of deep learning

We will present examples of popular deep learning algorithm applications in this section.

Self-driving cars

Self-driving cars have become a mainstay in the auto industry, with every major company investing in building the next generation of self-driving cars. Most companies offer some level of autopilot capabilities in their latest cars. These algorithms are mostly powered by deep learning algorithms. Let's take a look at how self-driving algorithms are developed using deep learning.

The task of the self-driving algorithm is to analyze the conditions on the road and react to them correctly in order to drive the car from the origin to the destination address. The input for this algorithm is the video feed they receive from the cameras fitted on all sides of the car. The output of the algorithm is the signals to the steering wheel, accelerator, and brakes.

This task is extremely complicated since the driver needs to make split-second decisions when dealing with road conditions. The driver not only has to remember which turns to take in order to reach the destination or the speed limits on the road, but also has to monitor the movements of other cars on the road and pedestrians who may cross the roads.

Creating a rules-based algorithm for such a task is very difficult as there are a vast number of permutations that can occur on the road. Moreover, generating any labeled dataset with well-defined features is also difficult since the number of situations that could arise is very hard to label in a comprehensive dataset.

Deep learning algorithms are perfect in such situations because automatically extracting features from the video feed and training the models based on a reward function helps us to abstract the issues in self-driving cars. We can set the input of the deep learning algorithm as the pixels in the video feed and the reward function as our progress toward the destination while obeying all traffic rules. Simulators are used to train these models. Such simulations mimic the actual conditions on the road.

Deep learning algorithms can automatically determine how to generate the layers of abstractions to translate the pixels from the video feed to detecting edges and objects, similar to image recognition models. Once the objects are detected, based on the mistakes and corrections made by the car, we train the models to learn how to output the accelerator, brakes, and steering wheel instructions. Initially, when running the models, self-driving cars make mistakes and crash into objects. However, with sufficient iterations, deep learning models can learn how to avoid such mistakes and drive on a predetermined path. Thus, without extracting the features manually from the video feeds, and without generating any structured datasets, deep learning algorithms can automatically learn to achieve certain objectives.

Learning to play video games using a deep learning algorithm

Another popular example of using deep learning is to train a machine to play computer games. Researchers across the world tested their deep learning algorithms by training models to play 2D platforming titles, such as Super Mario. The input to the model is the pixels on the screen, while the output generated by the model is a sequence of controller instructions that control the characters and finish the objectives in the game.

We do not need to teach deep learning models that this is a video game and that a character named Mario has to jump on platforms to finish the levels. We just have to define a reward function such that if the character moves to the next platform without dying, we reward the deep learning model, and if the character dies, we penalize the model. As mentioned before, the deep learning model automatically divides the problem into multiple levels of abstractions.

The model learns how to detect edges and platforms on the screen automatically. It starts by making random movements with the character and quickly learns how the pixels on the screen are manipulated when different controller buttons are pushed. Based on the movements of the character, the model learns how to move the main character forward. Similar to the self-driving car, it will also automatically learn that touching certain objects on the screen leads to a penalty, and jumping on certain edges on the screen leads to the player falling into pits. Hence, based on these reward functions giving feedback to the model, the model learns how to navigate the obstacles in the level to move the player in the right direction. With further training, it can also learn how to solve puzzles in the game.

Thus, just by providing the screen pixels to the deep learning model, we can train a machine to play video games. You see examples of these implementations everywhere around you. Soon, machines will learn how to solve complex puzzles by thinking rationally based on these machine learning models.

Understanding deep learning algorithms

In the next section, we study one of the most popular deep learning algorithm, called deep neural networks.

Before we look at what deep neural networks are, we will study what neural networks are. Then, we will learn what deep neural network algorithms are and why they are an improvement over neural networks. Finally, we will study convolutional neural networks—which is a variant of neural networks that is used in the field of image recognition – and show how we can automatically learn layers of abstractions from the pixels in the image.

Neural network algorithms

Neural network algorithms are machine learning algorithms that are inspired by biological neural network algorithms. Neural networks mimic how our neurons in our brain work. They have input nodes where the information is fed into the network, and an output layer that transmits a specific action or prediction. Neural networks define a structure in which the information of the machine learning model is stored.

The following screenshot shows a neural network structure:

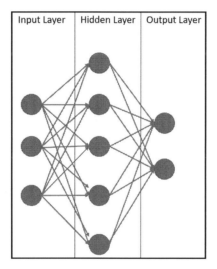

The input features from a dataset are fed into neural network input nodes. For example, if we have a dataset that has features such as temperature, cloud conditions, and wind speed, and our task is to predict whether it will rain on a given day, then such features are fed to the neural networks as input. These features can either be in binary or continuous values. Note that each input feature corresponds to one input node.

The information regarding the model is stored on the edges and the nodes in the hidden layer. There are various algorithms that can be used to train neural networks. Most algorithms iteratively pass input parameters in the neural network and predict the values of output nodes based on the weights in the hidden nodes. Based on the error in prediction, these weights are adjusted to improve the model.

The output nodes correspond to the expected actions or predictions that the neural network algorithms need to make. Our aim is to train the weights in the hidden nodes such that the values of the output nodes are accurate.

Thus, the neural networks are loosely based on biological neurons that can process an input signal and produce an output based on the function of that neuron.

Activation function

Now, let's look at how a neural network algorithm is trained to calculate the weights of each hidden node. Before we begin training a neural network model, we need to define how each hidden node will process the input signal and produce an output. The function that is used to calculate the output of a hidden node based on an input function is called the activation function. Activation functions define the range of output that can be generated by the hidden nodes. In its simplest form, an activation function can be a step function where the node output is either 0 or 1 based on the input. A simple example in our weather dataset is this: if the sky is cloudy, the output of a hidden node might be 1 as a prediction for rain, and if the sky is sunny, the output of the hidden node is 0.

Such a step activation function is defined as follows:

$$f(x) = \begin{cases} 0 \text{ for } x<=0 \\ 1 \text{ for } x>0 \end{cases}$$

Similarly, if we plan to use a logistic or sigmoid step function, the range of the output is from $-\infty$ to ∞.

A logistic step function is defined as follows:

$$f(x) = \frac{1}{1 + e^{-x}}$$

Based on the learning algorithm we are using, we can select activation functions. Most machine learning libraries that support neural network learning also support using various activation functions.

Each edge between nodes is assigned a weight, w_{ij}, such that that link is between neuron i and neuron j.

Backpropagation

Once we have established the weights of the connections in the neural networks and the activation function, a neural network is able to effectively produce an output based on a given input. However, this is an untrained neural network, and an algorithm is needed to modify and adapt a neural network based on the errors it makes when predicting an output.

The weight updates for backpropagation using stochastic gradient descent can be executed using the following equation.

The backpropagation algorithm is one of the popular mechanisms that can achieve this outcome. Backpropagation algorithms define a methodology for how the errors in the output can be propagated through the connections by modifying the values of the connections. The intuition behind the algorithm is very simple. Consider a child touching a very hot pan and learning not to touch pans that are situated on top of a stove. The child makes a mistake, but learns from it and avoids making the same mistake again. Backpropagation algorithms also allow neural networks to make errors. The difference between the predicted output and the expected output can be calculated using formulas, such as mean squared errors. Once we quantify the error, we can use algorithms, such as gradient descent, to determine how to modify the weights of the connections. We also used the algorithm of gradient descent for the linear regression algorithm in Chapter 3, *Predicting House Value with Regression Algorithms*. The backpropagation process is similar to how we learn the coefficients for the linear regression algorithm. However, instead of learning the values of the regressors, we are estimating the value of the weights of the connections in neural networks.

The weight updates for backpropagation using stochastic gradient descent can be done using the following equation:

$$w_{ij}(t + 1) = w_{ij}(t) + \lambda \frac{\partial C}{\partial w_{ij}} + \xi(t)$$

In this equation, λ is the learning rate of the neural network. This is a tunable parameter and defines how quickly the neural network can adapt to the training dataset. The weight, $w_{ij}(t+1)$, is calculated based on the previous weight of the connection. The value of change in the weight is determined by the learning rate, which is the difference between the error, the previous weight, and a stochastic term.

We iterate over the training data by passing it through the neural network and modifying the weights of the connections during each iteration. The weights are modified such that the error rates reduce with each iteration. Although stochastic gradient descent does not achieve a global maxima, it is effective in training a neural network to reduce errors. We terminate the iteration when the error is below a certain acceptable value, or it converges such that the improvements in accuracy are minimal.

Neural networks can be used to train supervised learning as well as unsupervised learning.

Introduction to deep neural networks

A **deep neural network (DNN)** is a variant of neural networks where we use more than one hidden layer. The data has to pass through more than one hidden layer for a network to qualify as a deep neural network. This adds complexity to the neural network model as it drastically increases the connections in the network, and thus the learning time.

A representation of a deep neural network is shown here:

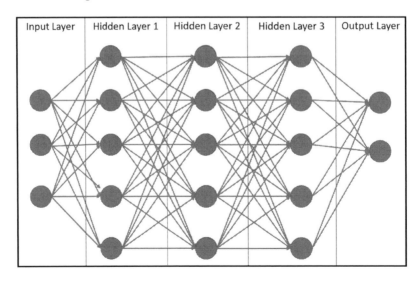

However, having additional hidden layers also allows the network to pass the input data through multiple layers of pattern recognition. Each hidden layer gets the input from the previous hidden layers. Hence, they can recognize more complex patterns than the previous layers. This happens as the previous layers aggregate, and recombines the features from the previous layers. This is called the feature hierarchy. The features that are deeper in the DNN can recognize more complex patterns. Hence, DNN is more capable of handling datasets with complex patterns. Moreover, since the hidden layers automatically generate these layers of abstractions, domain expertise is not required for feature extraction. For example, in image recognition, we do not need to label the edges of objects in the image since initial layers can learn to identify edges, while deeper layers learn to identify the objects that may be generated by those edges.

Deep learning and DNN are popular buzzwords that data scientists hear about in the industry. For most applications, such as self-driving cars or robotics, DNN is synonymous with artificial intelligence. Due to the advances in GPU architectures, which suit the generation of these DNN structures, such algorithms are not able to process large datasets in order to train highly accurate machine learning algorithms.

Understanding convolutional neural networks

In this section, we will take a look at a variant of DNNs, where the structure of the network is modified for image recognition tasks.

In the neural networks that we've discussed in this chapter so far, we've seen that all the input layers are one dimensional. However, images are two-dimensional. To capture how images are fed to a neural network for training, we have to modify the structure of the input layer. Traditional algorithms require humans to label the edges of the objects in the image. **Convolutional neural networks (CNNs)** can automatically detect the objects in the image with enough training and, based on the labels of the image, they can learn how to identify objects in the images without explicitly labeling the edges in the image.

CNNs require a preprocessing phase where the image has to be prepared into a specific data structure that is used as an input for feed-forward DNNs. The first task in the preprocessing phase is to break the picture down into smaller images, such that we do not lose any information from the image. The inspiration for a CNN comes from the organization of the visual cortex in humans. Our neurons respond to visuals that are seen in a specific field of vision. This is called the local receptive field. These local receptive fields overlap with each other. Similarly, in CNN, we take an image as an input and represent overlapping subsections of an image as local receptive fields.

The following diagram shows how a sliding window is used to generate feature maps from an image using the concept of local receptive fields:

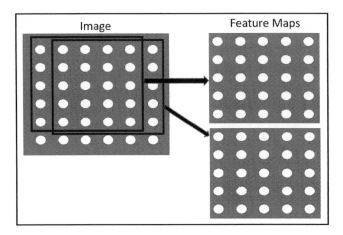

The advantage of using this methodology is that it eliminates the issues of size and position of an object in an image. For example, imagine there is a cat in the image. Based on our training examples, we have labeled images with pictures of cats. Using local receptive fields, we detect that cat and label the feature map as having a picture of a cat in the image. In a new image, irrespective of the location of the cat in the image, we will find a feature map that has an image of a cat, since we create multiple sub-images using this sliding window approach. This layer of feature maps generated from the image is called the convolutional layer.

We can also generate multiple feature maps from the same set of pixels by applying various filters to the process. For example, we can apply color filters to the pixels and generate three feature maps from the same set of pixels. As a data scientist, you would have to design the CNNs based on the amount of information that you want to extract from the image, as well as the amount of processing power that we can use when generating these networks.

Once the convolution layers are generated, we create condensed feature maps from the image by using a process called pooling. This helps us to represent the feature maps in smaller feature maps. There are two popular pooling processes that can be applied when condensing a feature map. In a max-pooling approach, reduce the dimensionality of the feature map by only selecting the maximum value from each grid.

The following screenshot shows how max-pooling takes the maximum value from each feature map and reduces the dimensionality of the feature map from a matrix of 4x4 to 2x2:

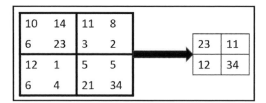

Another type of pooling is called average pooling, which is where we select the average of the values in a grid when pooling the data. The following diagram shows how average pooling works:

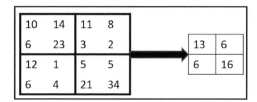

Max-pooling is generally preferred over average pooling as it acts as a noise suppressant and removes the non-dominant features when reducing the dimensionality of a feature map. Similar to a convolutional layer, a pooling layer can also use overlapping windows to create a smaller feature map. Note that these decisions can be made based on the level of detail you want to capture from an image.

Another component of a CNN is the convolution layer. When we design a CNN, a set of images might determine what feature maps we extract from the image. However, based on the application, we would want to extract different features from the images. For example, if our image recognition software is detecting charts generated by a seismometer (a device that detects earthquakes), our feature maps would have black and white graphs, where our algorithm needs to be sensitive to detecting the edges in time-series. In such cases, we can design a convolution kernel that can translate certain patterns in a feature graph into another feature graph that can annotate such patterns. Similarly, if you are processing colored images with objects, creating three feature maps for each color, detecting edges, and then merging the feature maps, is helpful. Thus, convolutional layers help scientists who design such neural networks to adapt them to specific applications. We are not going to explain the details of how convolution layers can be set up, as most libraries allow you to use predesigned CNNs to apply to your applications.

Thus, using local receptive fields, convolution layers, and pooling, we construct the following structure to flatten an image into input for a DNN:

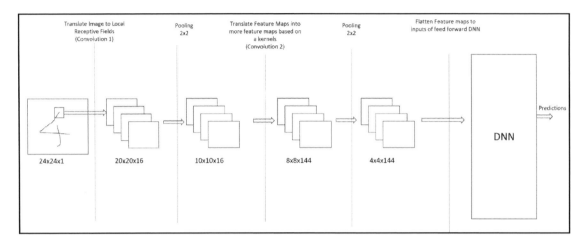

An image is translated into feature maps using the first layer of convolution by employing the local perceptive fields methodology. Then, we reduce the dimensions of the feature maps by pooling the data, so as to reduce the dimensionality of feature maps from 20x20 to 10x10. In the next phase, we translate the pooled feature maps into more feature maps based on a kernel we might have selected. These kernels may translate the feature maps that detect straight lines or intersections. We then pool the output of the convolution layer into 4x4 feature maps. At this point, the original image is translated into information that is specific to the task of a DNN. These feature maps represent the spatial components of the images too. The DNN then trains based on this data and learns to predict output based on what the feature maps may represent.

Summary

In this chapter, we explained what deep learning means and how it is applied in real-world applications. We also studied applications, such as self-driving cars and a video game bot, and how they can automatically learn how to perform tasks using deep learning. We explained what neural networks are and how DNNs are an improved version of them. We also studied a variant of DNNs, called CNNs and presented the various components of a CNN.

Our aim in this chapter was to provide you with information about deep learning algorithms so that you could understand how they can be applied in the real world. Although we did not dive deep into the mathematics of deep learning, or provide all details on concepts such as activation function, we hope that you gained a working knowledge in the field of deep learning. For those curious minds out there, there is a vast amount of ongoing research in this field and we implore you to learn more about the algorithms that you are interested in.

In the next chapter, we will look at how deep learning can be implemented using popular technologies, such as TensorFlow and MXNet. This knowledge will help you to implement a large array of deep learning algorithms.

Exercises

1. If you own a smartphone, you have a lot of apps on your phone that employ deep learning. Explore which apps on your phone use one of the algorithms listed in this chapter and examine how to design such an algorithm.
2. List the various components of CNN and design a CNN that would detect the features of a human face.

8
Implementing Deep Learning with TensorFlow on AWS

TensorFlow is a very popular deep learning framework that can be used to train deep neural networks, such as those described in the previous chapter.

In this chapter, we will cover the following topics:

- About TensorFlow
- TensorFlow as a general machine learning library
- Training and serving the TensorFlow model through SageMaker
- Creating a custom neural net with TensorFlow

About TensorFlow

TensorFlow is a library for deep learning, first released by Google in 2015. Initially, it included a core library that allowed users to work with tensors (multidimensional arrays) in symbolic form, thus enabling low-level neural network design and training at high performance. Nowadays, it's a fully fledged deep learning library that allows data scientists to build models for complex problems, such as image recognition, using high-level primitives. You can also use TensorFlow for solving standard machine learning problems, such as the ones we've been considering in the past chapters. TensorFlow has similar abstractions to the ones we have been using in `scikit-learn`, Apache Spark, and SageMaker. For example, it allows the user to create classification models or regression models using high-level abstractions, such as estimators, predictors, and evaluators.

TensorFlow as a general machine learning library

In this section we will show how we use TensorFlow to create a regression model for the house estimation problem of Chapter 3, *Predicting House Value with Regression Algorithms*. To get started, we will first launch a SageMaker notebook and choose the TensorFlow kernel (conda_tensorflow_p36), which has all the necessary TensorFlow dependencies needed for this section:

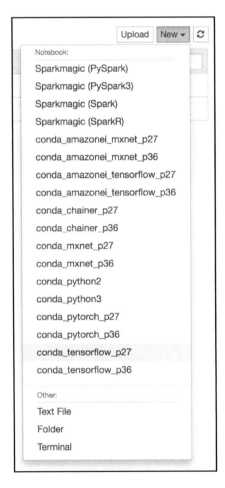

Now, let's consider the estimation problem from Chapter 3, *Predicting House Value with Regression Algorithms*. Recall that we had a set of indicators (age of the house, distance to nearest center, and so on) to estimate the median value of the house (expressed in the medv column, which is our target feature), as shown in the following screenshot:

	ID	crim	zn	indus	chas	nox	rm	age	dis	rad	tax	ptratio	black	lstat	medv
270	418	25.94060	0.0	18.10	0	0.679	5.304	89.1	1.6475	24	666	20.2	127.36	26.64	10.4
205	309	0.49298	0.0	9.90	0	0.544	6.635	82.5	3.3175	4	304	18.4	396.90	4.54	22.8
161	235	0.44791	0.0	6.20	1	0.507	6.726	66.5	3.6519	8	307	17.4	360.20	8.05	29.0

In Chapter 3, *Predicting House Value with Regression Algorithms*, we identified 11 learning features to use for predicting the target feature (medv):

```
training_features = ['crim', 'zn', 'indus', 'chas', 'nox',
'rm', 'age', 'dis', 'tax', 'ptratio', 'lstat']

label = 'medv'
```

With this information, we define a TensorFlow linear regressor capable of solving our regression problem with a pre-built neural net:

```
tf_regressor = tf.estimator.LinearRegressor(
    feature_columns=[tf.feature_column.numeric_column('inputs',
                                shape=(11,))])
```

For the regressor, we decided to create a single-feature input, which assembles the rest of the features into a vector of numbers that will represent the input layer. It is also possible to create one named feature per training feature (as we did in Chapter 3, *Predicting House Value with Regression Algorithms*), but we'll just have a single vector feature to simplify the prediction service discussed at the end of the section.

To construct a regressor, we need to pass in the TensorFlow feature columns, which can be of several different kinds. The tf.feature_column package provides functions to construct different kinds of columns, depending on the encoding being used by the model (for example, categorical, bucketized, and so on.). The feature columns inform the model on the expected format of the data being submitted as input. In our case, we will just tell the model to expect vector rows of length 11.

To construct the actual data to be passed into the model, we need to create a matrix. The `pandas` library has a convenient method, `as_matrix()`, so we'll slice the training features and build a matrix:

```
training_df[training_features].as_matrix()
```

Similarly, we'll create the vector of features:

```
training_df[label].as_matrix()
```

Once we have these two things, we can start plugging the data into the model. TensorFlow expects the data to be fed by defining a function that knows how to source the data into tensors (the building blocks of TensorFlow that represents a multidimensional array).

The following is the code block for plugging in the data:

```
training_input_fn = tf.estimator.inputs.numpy_input_fn(
    x={'inputs': training_df[training_features].as_matrix()},
    y=training_df[label].as_matrix(),
    shuffle=False,
    batch_size=1,
    num_epochs=100,
    queue_capacity=1000,
    num_threads=1)
```

The `tf.estimator.inputs.numpy_input_fn` utility is able to construct such a function by providing the training matrix and target feature vectors. It will also create partitions of the data for running through the network a number of epochs. It also allows the user to pick the size of the batch (recall the mini-batch method mentioned in Chapter 3, *Predicting House Value with Regression Algorithms*, for stochastic gradient descent) and other data feeding parameters. In essence, the underlying regressor's neural network relies on the `training_input_fn` function for creating the input tensors at each stage of the algorithm.

Likewise, we create a similar function for feeding the testing data, in preparation for model evaluation:

```
test_input_fn = tf.estimator.inputs.numpy_input_fn(
    x={'inputs': test_df[training_features].as_matrix()},
    y=test_df[label].as_matrix(),
    shuffle=False,
    batch_size=1)
```

To train the model, we call the usual `fit()` method, providing the function we created for sourcing the data:

```
tf_regressor.train(input_fn=training_input_fn, steps=50000)
```

The `steps` argument is a limit we can impose on the number of total steps. A step, here, is one gradient descent update for one batch. Hence, each epoch runs a number of steps.

Once it completes the training, TensorFlow will output the loss metric in the `final` epoch:

```
INFO:tensorflow:Loss for final step: 1.1741621.
```

We can then evaluate the accuracy of our model by running the test dataset (by providing the test dataset sourcing function):

```
tf_regressor.evaluate(input_fn=test_input_fn)
```

The preceding code generates the following output:

```
{'average_loss': 37.858795,
 'label/mean': 22.91492,
 'loss': 37.858795,
 'prediction/mean': 21.380392,
 'global_step': 26600}
```

The average loss depends on the units of the target feature, so let's look at building a scatter plot like the one we created in Chapter 3, *Predicting House Value with Regression Algorithms*, to compare actual versus predicted house values. To do that, we first need to obtain `predictions`.

We simply call the `predict()` function to get `predictions`, again providing the test dataset sourcing function:

```
predictions = tf_regressor.predict(input_fn=test_input_fn)
```

The `predictions` returned a value that is actually a Python generator of single-value vectors, so we can obtain a list of `predictions` by constructing the list-through-list comprehension:

```
predicted_values = [prediction['predictions'][0] for prediction in
predictions]
```

We can thus examine `predicted_values`:

```
predicted_values[:5]
```

The preceding code generates the following output:

```
[22.076485, 23.075985, 17.803957, 20.629128, 28.749748]
```

We can plug in the predicted values as a column to our original `pandas` test dataframe:

```
test_df['prediction'] = predicted_values
```

This allows us to use the pandas plotting method to create the chart:

```
test_df.plot(kind='scatter', x=label, y='prediction')
```

We can see the result in the following screenshot:

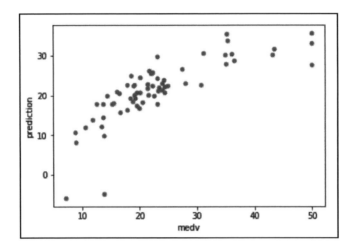

Note that there is a clear correlation. To improve the performance, we would have to tune our regression model, the size of the batches, steps, epochs, and so on.

Training and serving the TensorFlow model through SageMaker

Instead of training the model in a notebook instance, we train the model using the SageMaker infrastructure. In previous chapters, we used built-in estimators, such as BlazingText, XGBoost, and **Factorization Machines (FMs)**. In this section, we will show how we can build our own TensorFlow models and train them through SageMaker, much like we did with these pre-built models. To do this, we just have to teach SageMaker how our TensorFlow model should be constructed and comply with some conventions regarding the format, location, and structure of the data. Through a Python script, we specify all of this.

SageMaker will rely on this Python script to perform the training within SageMaker training instances:

```
import sagemaker
from sagemaker import get_execution_role
import json
import boto3
from sagemaker.tensorflow import TensorFlow

sess = sagemaker.Session()
role = get_execution_role()
tf_estimator = TensorFlow(entry_point='tf_train.py', role=role,
                          train_instance_count=1,
train_instance_type='ml.m5.large',
                          framework_version='1.12', py_version='py3')
tf_estimator.fit('s3://mastering-ml-aws/chapter8/train-data/')
```

The first few lines in the preceding code block are the usual imports and session creation necessary for getting started with SageMaker. The next important thing is the creation of a TensorFlow estimator. Note how we provide the constructor with a Python script, TensorFlow version, and Python version, as well as the usual parameters for instance number and type.

Upon calling the `tf_estimator.fit(training_data_s3_path)` function, SageMaker will do the following tasks:

1. Launch an EC2 instance (server).
2. Download the S3 data to a local directory.
3. Call the `tf_train.py` Python script to train the model. The Python script is expected to store the model on a certain local directory of the EC2 instance.
4. Package the stored model in a `.tar.gz` file and upload it to S3. Additionally, it will create an Amazon container and SageMaker model identifier.

Hence, the training happens on a SageMaker managed server, but the model it produces is a SageMaker compatible model, which can be used to serve predictions or run batch transform jobs, like the ones we worked with in previous chapters.

Let's take a look at the `tf_train.py` Python script, which is responsible for the model training and saving the model.

This Python script must receive some information from the SageMaker container. In particular, it must receive the following:

- The local directory where SageMaker has downloaded the data (from S3)
- The location where the Python script needs to store the trained model
- Other hyperparameters needed by the model (we will not dive into this yet and work with just fixed values, but we will show in Chapter 14, *Optimizing Models in Spark and SageMaker*, how these can be used for hyperparameter tuning)

Take a look at the following code:

```python
import pandas as pd
import argparse
import os
import tensorflow as tf

if __name__ == '__main__':
    parser = argparse.ArgumentParser()
    parser.add_argument('--epochs', type=int, default=100)
    parser.add_argument('--batch_size', type=int, default=1)
    parser.add_argument('--steps', type=int, default=12000)
    parser.add_argument('--model_dir', type=str)
    parser.add_argument('--local_model_dir', type=str,
default=os.environ.get('SM_MODEL_DIR'))
    parser.add_argument('--train', type=str,
default=os.environ.get('SM_CHANNEL_TRAINING'))

    args, _ = parser.parse_known_args()
    housing_df = pd.read_csv(args.train + '/train.csv')
    training_features = ['crim', 'zn', 'indus', 'chas', 'nox',
                         'rm', 'age', 'dis', 'tax', 'ptratio', 'lstat']
    label = 'medv'
    tf_regressor = tf.estimator.LinearRegressor(
        feature_columns=[tf.feature_column.numeric_column('inputs',
                                    shape=(11,))])
    training_input_fn = tf.estimator.inputs.numpy_input_fn(
        x={'inputs': housing_df[training_features].as_matrix()},
        y=housing_df[label].as_matrix(),
        shuffle=False,
        batch_size=args.batch_size,
        num_epochs=args.epochs,
        queue_capacity=1000,
        num_threads=1)
    tf_regressor.train(input_fn=training_input_fn, steps=args.steps)


    def serving_input_fn():
```

```
feature_spec = tf.placeholder(tf.float32, shape=[1, 11])
return tf.estimator.export.build_parsing_serving_input_receiver_fn(
    {'input': feature_spec})()
```

```
    tf_regressor.export_savedmodel(export_dir_base=args.local_model_dir +
'/export/Servo',
serving_input_receiver_fn=serving_input_fn)
```

The first part of the script is just setting up an argument parser. Since SageMaker calls this script as a black box, it needs to be able to inject such arguments to the script. With these arguments, it can train the TensorFlow model. You might notice that the training is exactly the same as what we did in the previous section. The only new part is saving the model and the definition of a new kind of function (`serving_input_fn`). This function has a similar purpose to the ones we used for training and testing, but instead, it will be used at the serving time (that is, each time a prediction request is made to the service). It is responsible for defining the necessary transformation from an input tensor placeholder to the features expected by the model. The `tf.estimator.export.build_parsing_serving_input_receiver_fn` utility can conveniently build a function for such purposes. It builds a function that expects `tf.Example` (a `protobuf`-serialized dictionary of features) fed into a string placeholder, so that it can parse such examples into feature tensors. In our case, we just have a single vector as input, so the transformation is straightforward. The last line in our script saves the model into the location requested by SageMaker through the `local_model_dir` argument. In order for the deserialization and unpacking to work, the convention is to save the model in a `/export/Servo` subdirectory.

Once we run the `fit()` command, we can deploy the model as usual:

```
predictor = tf_estimator.deploy(instance_type='ml.m5.large',
initial_instance_count=1)
```

For this example, we used a non-GPU instance type, but these are largely recommended for serious serving and training. We will dive into this in *Chapter 15, Tuning Clusters for Machine Learning.*

The `deploy()` command will launch a container capable of serving the model we constructed. However, constructing the payload to send to such service is not as trivial as the examples in the previous chapter, as we need to construct `tf.Example`.

At prediction time we want to obtain the price given a specific feature vector. Suppose we want to find the price for these features:

```
features_vector = [0.00632, 18.0, 2.31, 0.0, 0.538, 6.575, 65.2, 4.09,
296.0, 15.3, 4.98]
```

The first step is to construct a `tf.train.Example` instance, which in our case consists of a single feature called `inputs` with the floating point values of `features_vector`:

```
model_input = tf.train.Example(features=tf.train.Features(

    feature={"inputs":
tf.train.Feature(float_list=tf.train.FloatList(value=features_vector))}))
```

The next step is to serialize the `model_input` `protobuf` message using `SerializeToString`:

```
model_input = model_input.SerializeToString()
```

Since this is really a string of bytes, we need to further encode `model_input` so that it can be sent in the payload as a string without special characters. We use `base64` encoding to do such a thing:

```
encoded = base64.b64encode(model_input).decode()
```

Lastly, we call our `predictor` service by assembling a JSON request:

```
predictor.predict('{"inputs":[{"b64":"%s"}]}' % encoded)
```

Note there is a special convention used for sending base64, encoded `protobuf` examples by creating a dictionary keyed with `b64`. The output decoded from JSON is a dictionary with the following prediction:

```
{'outputs': [[24.7537]]}
```

> The `inputs` and `outputs` payload JSON keys are part of the contract for SageMaker and should not be confused with the name of our single feature, `inputs`, which can be an arbitrary string.

Creating a custom neural net with TensorFlow

In the previous section, *Training and serving the TensorFlow model through SageMaker*, we used the high-level library of TensorFlow to construct a regression model using a `LinearRegressor`. In this section, we will show how we can construct an actual neural network using the Keras library from TensorFlow. Keras facilitates the design of neural networks by hiding some of the complexity behind the core (low-level) TensorFlow library.

In this chapter, we will use the ubiquitous MNIST dataset, which consists of a series of images of handwritten digits along with the real label (values between 0 and 1). The MNIST dataset can be downloaded from `https://www.kaggle.com/c/digit-recognizer/data`.

The dataset comes as a CSV with 784 columns corresponding to each of the pixels in the 28 x 28 image. The values for each column represent the strength of the pixel in a gray scale from 0 to 255. It also has an additional column for the label with a value between 0 and 9, corresponding to the actual digit.

Let's download the dataset and do our usual splitting into testing and training using `pandas` and `scikit-learn`:

```
import pandas as pd
from sklearn.model_selection import train_test_split

mnist_df = pd.read_csv('mnist/train.csv')
train_df, test_df = train_test_split(mnist_df, shuffle=False)
```

We can inspect the dataset through `train.head()`:

	label	pixel0	pixel1	pixel2	pixel3	pixel4	pixel5	pixel6	pixel7	pixel8	...	pixel774	pixel775	pixel776	pixel777	pixel778	pixel779	pixel780	pixel781
0	1	0	0	0	0	0	0	0	0	0	...	0	0	0	0	0	0	0	0
1	0	0	0	0	0	0	0	0	0	0	...	0	0	0	0	0	0	0	0
2	1	0	0	0	0	0	0	0	0	0	...	0	0	0	0	0	0	0	0

As we can see, the columns are labeled `pixelX`, where x is a number between 0 and 783. Let's define the names of these columns in distinct variables:

```
pixel_columns = ['pixel' + str(i) for i in range(0, 784)]
label_column = 'label'
```

Each row in this dataset becomes a training example and thus represent the input layer of our network. On the other end of the network, we will have 10 nodes, each representing the probability of each digit given each input vector. For our example, we will just use one middle layer.

The following diagram depicts our network structure:

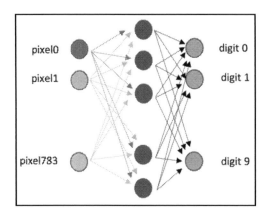

To define such a network in Keras is very simple:

```
import tensorflow as tf
from tensorflow import keras

model = keras.Sequential([
    keras.layers.InputLayer(input_shape=(784,), batch_size=5),
    keras.layers.Dense(256, activation=tf.nn.relu),
    keras.layers.Dense(10, activation=tf.nn.softmax)
])
```

Note how easy it is to define such a model. It consists of three layers:

- An input layer, where each vector is of size 784, and each gradient descent update will feed a mini-batch of five examples
- A middle dense layer (meaning each node will connect to every other node in the next layer) with a **Rectified Linear Unit (ReLU)** activation function on each node
- An output layer of size 10 using a softmax activation function (as we want a probability distribution over the digits)

In addition to defining the network through a sequence of layers, TensorFlow will need to compile the model. This basically entails providing the kind of optimization method to use, the `loss` function, and the required metrics:

```
model.compile(optimizer='adam',
              loss='sparse_categorical_crossentropy',
              metrics=['accuracy'])
```

The next stage will be to fit the model with our data. In order to feed the dataset into TensorFlow, we need to create `numpy` matrices, where each row is a training instance and each column represents a node in the input layer. Conveniently, the `pandas` method `dataframe.as_matrix()` does exactly that, so we will slice the dataset to include the training columns and construct such a matrix. Additionally, we will normalize the matrix to have each grayscale value between 0 and 1:

```
import numpy as np

vectorized_normalization_fn = np.vectorize(lambda x: x / 255.0)
normalized_matrix =
      vectorized_normalization_fn(train_df
[pixel_columns].as_matrix())
```

Likewise, we obtain the `labels` vector by transforming the `pandas` series into a vector of digits:

```
labels = train_df[label_column].as_matrix()
```

Now that we have our training matrix and labels, we are ready to fit our model. We do this by simply calling `fit()` and providing the labeled training data:

```
model.fit(normalized_matrix, labels, epochs=3)
```

The training will end with the loss and accuracy metrics on the training dataset:

```
Epoch 3/3
31500/31500 [==============================] - 16s 511us/sample - loss:
0.0703 - acc: 0.9775
```

In order to determine whether our model is overfitting (that is, it just learns how to classify the images in our training dataset but fails to generalize over new images), we need to test our model in the testing dataset. For this, we will perform the same transformations we made on our training dataset, but for the test dataset.

The `evaluate()` function of our model will provide accuracy evaluation metrics:

```
normalized_test_matrix =
vectorized_normalization_fn(test_df[pixel_columns].as_matrix())
test_labels = test_df[label_column].as_matrix()
_, test_acc = model.evaluate(normalized_test_matrix, test_labels)

print('Accuracy on test dataset:', test_acc)
```

The preceding code generates the following output:

```
Accuracy on test dataset: 0.97
```

Note that our simple model is, in fact, fairly accurate. Let's examine a few images in the testing dataset to see how the prediction matches the actual digit. For doing this, we will plot the images and compare them to the predicted digit by performing the following steps:

1. First, we will define a function that obtains the predicted label for a particular row (`index`) on our testing dataset matrix:

```
def predict_digit(index):
    predictions = model.predict(normalized_test_matrix[index:index
+ 1])
    return np.argmax(predictions, axis=1)[0]
```

`model.predict()` will obtain the predictions given a matrix of features. In this case, we just need one single row, so we slice our matrix into a single row to obtain the prediction for just the index in question. The predictions will be a vector of 10 components, each representing the strength of each digit. We use the `argmax` function to find the digit that maximizes the strength (that is, finding the most probable digit).

2. Next, we define a function, `show_image()`, which, given an index, will plot the image:

```
from IPython.display import display
from PIL import Image

def show_image(index):
    print("predicted digit: %d" % predict_digit(index))
    print("digit image:")
    vectorized_denormalization_fn = np.vectorize(lambda x:
np.uint8(x * 255.0))
    img_matrix = normalized_test_matrix[index].reshape(28, 28)
    img_matrix = vectorized_denormalization_fn(img_matrix)
    img = Image.fromarray(img_matrix, mode='L')
    display(img)
```

We rely on the `PIL` library to perform the plotting. In order to plot the image, we need to denormalize our values back to the 0-255 range and reshape the 784 pixels into a 28x28 image.

Let's examine a few instances in the following screenshots:

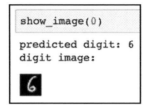

And the second instance:

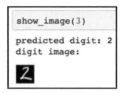

The following images were not able to be recognized correctly by the model:

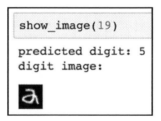

And the second instance:

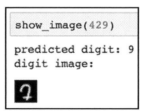

You may probably agree that even a human could make similar mistakes.

So, how can we build a service on top of our `model`?

One simple way to do this is to create an `estimator` instance from our `model`:

```
estimator = tf.keras.estimator.model_to_estimator(model)
```

Recall that `LinearRegressor` we used in the previous section was also an `estimator` instance, so the same process for training, serializing, and serving the model would apply starting from this `estimator` instance.

Summary

In this chapter, we went through the process of creating two different TensorFlow models: one using the high-level library of estimators, and the other using Keras to build a custom neural network. In the process, we also showed how SageMaker can seamlessly handle the training and serving of TensorFlow models.

In the next chapter, *Image Classification and Detection with SageMaker,* we will show how to use deep learning out-of-the-box on AWS to detect and recognize images.

Exercises

The following are the questions for this chapter:

- What is the difference between an epoch, batch, and step?
- How would you design a network that would be able to provide recommendations for the theme park dataset considered in Chapter 6, *Analyzing Visitor Patterns to Make Recommendations*?
- How would you build a network that is capable of classifying the ads in Chapter 5, *Customer Segmentation Using Clustering Algorithms*, as clicks/not-clicks?

9
Image Classification and Detection with SageMaker

We have studied a type of deep learning algorithm called a **Convolutional Neural Network (CNN)**, which is capable of classifying images. However, implementing such an algorithm in practice is extremely complex and requires a lot of expertise. Amazon SageMaker offers features that allow you to train machine learning models such as image classification algorithms using deep learning capabilities.

We'll cover the following topics in this chapter:

- Introducing Amazon SageMaker for image classification
- Training a deep learning model using Amazon SageMaker
- Classifying images using Amazon SageMaker

Introducing Amazon SageMaker for image classification

The field of data science has been revolutionized because of services such as Tensorflow and SageMaker. Complex algorithms, such as Deep learning, were only accessible to large corporations and research labs in the past. However, thanks to services such as SageMaker, anyone who can write code to call these services can train and use sophisticated machine learning algorithms. This has enabled teenagers, with a working knowledge of machine learning, to create applications that can perform complex machine learning tasks. You will have the power to perform machine learning tasks at the same level as the world's top scientists by accessing state-of-the-art machine learning models in SageMaker marketplace.

Amazon SageMaker offers a large number of algorithms that data scientists can use to train their machine learning models, and it also offers tools to generate predictions on a batch of test data or create an endpoint to use the model as a service. When we work on smaller test datasets, we can use Python machine learning libraries, such as `scikit-learn`. However, when we are working on a larger dataset, we have to rely on frameworks, such as Apache Spark, and use the libraries, such as `MLLib`.

Amazon offers a suite of machine learning libraries in SageMaker where we can use pre-tuned models from various vendors to train our machine learning models. Hence, when you are working on a problem, you can search the Amazon SageMaker marketplace to find algorithms that are already available. If there are multiple algorithms and models available from different vendors, you can choose between algorithms based on their pricing models and accuracy.

The SageMaker marketplace can be used to select models offered by vendors other than Amazon. Hence, if you need a specialized algorithm that is tuned to functions in the field of genetic engineering or a specialized version of an image classification algorithm, such as **Construction-worker Detector**, you can select one of the pre-trained models and directly get predictions.

Amazon SageMaker also offers jobs to tune parameters of the algorithms that are available in the marketplace so that they can be adapted to your cluster size and applications. Such jobs are called **Hyperparameter-tuning Jobs**. You can provide various values of parameters to check an algorithm. Amazon SageMaker can then automatically train to select what tuning parameters would work best for your application. You can also set the values of these parameters manually.

In this chapter, we'll present how to use Amazon SageMaker using an example of an image classifier. This algorithm learns from a labeled set of images and then detects objects in the testing dataset by assigning a probability of the existence of each object in the test image. For this test, we use a publicly available dataset called `Caltech265` (`http://www.vision.caltech.edu/Image_Datasets/Caltech256/`). This dataset contains 30,608 images. The dataset is labeled with 256 objects.

 Please download the following dataset files to your AWS S3 bucket: `http://data.mxnet.io/data/caltech-256/caltech-256-60-train.rec` and `http://data.mxnet.io/data/caltech-256-60-val.rec`

For the purpose of our experiment, we'll store the training data files in the AWS bucket under the `image-classification-full-training/train` folder. This file contains 15,420 image files that are resized to 224 x 224 pixels.

Training a deep learning model using Amazon SageMaker

In this section, we will show how to train image classification models using this dataset. Similarly, download the `validation` file to the AWS bucket under the `image-classification-full-training/validation` folder.

In `Chapter 7`, *Implementing Deep Learning Algorithms*, we studied an algorithm called a CNN, which uses deep neural networks to build an object detection model. This model trains on labeled images and learns how to identify objects in an image using various layers of deep neural networks. Building this deep learning model from scratch is difficult. Amazon SageMaker offers an easy way to train image classification algorithms using your own dataset and then deploys that model to detect objects in images. We'll provide a code example of training a model using the `caltech256` dataset and then we'll test it on image files in the next section, *Classifying images using Amazon SageMaker*.

Similar to Chapter 8, *Implementing Deep Learning with TensorFlow on AWS*, you will have to start a new SageMaker instance and use Jupyter Notebooks to start the test. Amazon SageMaker already offers a large amount of example code for you to get started. To access these examples, please refer to the **SageMaker Examples** tab:

The code that we use in this chapter is also a modification of the image classification example provided by SageMaker. You can create a new notebook with the kernel of `conda_python3`:

> In chapters such as Chapter 5, *Customer Segmentation Using Clustering Algorithms*, and Chapter 6, *Analyzing Visitor Patterns to Make Recommendations*, we used the high-level `sagemaker` Python library provided by Amazon. Here, we have chosen to show how to use the SageMaker generic client from the `boto3` library. This library provides a declarative interface that more closely resembles the API behind SageMaker. Hopefully, you the reader can grasp the lower-level calls made to the API through the examples in this chapter.

We provide a code example here on how to use the boto3 client to create an image classification model using Amazon Sagemaker.

1. Initialize the role and the image-classification image that we want to use in SageMaker, then specify the name of our bucket:

```
import boto3
import re
from sagemaker import get_execution_role
from sagemaker.amazon.amazon_estimator import get_image_uri

role = get_execution_role()

bucket='mastering-ml-aws'

training_image = get_image_uri(boto3.Session().region_name, 'image-
classification')
```

The training image called **image-classification** is a Docker image of the image-classification algorithm. Amazon SageMaker provides a large variety of such images, which you can use to train your classifiers. Each image has its own tuning parameters, which you can also provide when training that algorithm.

2. We will declare these tuning parameters, in the following code block:

```
# Define Parameters

num_layers = "18"
image_shape = "3,224,224"
num_training_samples = "15420"
num_classes = "257"
mini_batch_size =  "64"
epochs = "2"
learning_rate = "0.01"
```

An image classification algorithm uses deep neural networks; these parameters will be familiar to you as we studied them in Chapter 7, *Implementing Deep Learning Algorithms*.

We define the number of hidden layers that will be used by the deep learning algorithm. We also have to specify the number of channels and the size of each image. We define the number of training images and the number of classes (object types). The number of epochs defines the number of times we will iterate over the training dataset. The accuracy of the deep learning classifier increases with the number of iterations we have over the dataset. The learning rate defines the number of changes the deep learning algorithm is allowed to make to the weights.

We would recommend that you run this algorithm with different parameters to observe the effects on evaluation and training time.

3. Once we define the parameters, we initialize the boto3 client for S3, where we have stored our training and validation files.

```python
import time
import boto3
from time import gmtime, strftime


# caltech-256
s3_train_key = "image-classification-full-training/train"
s3_validation_key = "image-classification-full-training/validation"
s3_train = 's3://{}/{}/'.format(bucket, s3_train_key)
s3_validation = 's3://{}/{}/'.format(bucket, s3_validation_key)

s3 = boto3.client('s3')
```

4. We construct a JSON with all the parameters required to train our image classifier:

```python
# create unique job name
job_name_prefix = 'example-imageclassification'
timestamp = time.strftime('-%Y-%m-%d-%H-%M-%S', time.gmtime())
job_name = job_name_prefix + timestamp
training_params = \
{
    # specify the training docker image
    "AlgorithmSpecification": {
        "TrainingImage": training_image,
        "TrainingInputMode": "File"
    },
    "RoleArn": role,
    "OutputDataConfig": {
        "S3OutputPath": 's3://{}/{}/output'.format(bucket,
job_name_prefix)
```

```
    },
    "ResourceConfig": {
        "InstanceCount": 1,
        "InstanceType": "ml.p2.xlarge",
        "VolumeSizeInGB": 50
    },
    "TrainingJobName": job_name,
    "HyperParameters": {
        "image_shape": image_shape,
        "num_layers": str(num_layers),
        "num_training_samples": str(num_training_samples),
        "num_classes": str(num_classes),
        "mini_batch_size": str(mini_batch_size),
        "epochs": str(epochs),
        "learning_rate": str(learning_rate)
    },
    "StoppingCondition": {
        "MaxRuntimeInSeconds": 360000
    },
    "InputDataConfig": [
        {
            "ChannelName": "train",
            "DataSource": {
                "S3DataSource": {
                    "S3DataType": "S3Prefix",
                    "S3Uri": s3_train,
                    "S3DataDistributionType": "FullyReplicated"
                }
            },
            "ContentType": "application/x-recordio",
            "CompressionType": "None"
        },
        {
            "ChannelName": "validation",
            "DataSource": {
                "S3DataSource": {
                    "S3DataType": "S3Prefix",
                    "S3Uri": s3_validation,
                    "S3DataDistributionType": "FullyReplicated"
                }
            },
            "ContentType": "application/x-recordio",
            "CompressionType": "None"
        }
    ]
}
```

There are a lot of things to learn in this JSON. We define the algorithm that we want to use for training in the `AlgorithmSpecification` section. `OutputDataConfig` defines where the model will be stored. `ResourceConfig` defines the instance type to be used for a training job. Note that tasks such as image classification run faster on GPU-based instances on AWS. All the parameters for the algorithm are defined in the `HyperParameters` section. We set the training dataset and the validation dataset under the `InputDataConfig` section of JSON. This JSON configuration will be used in the next code block to set parameters for the training job.

The following code block starts a `sagemaker` training job:

```
# create the Amazon SageMaker training job

sagemaker = boto3.client(service_name='sagemaker')
sagemaker.create_training_job(**training_params)
```

After you start the training job, you can observe its progress of the training job on your Amazon SageMaker dashboard:

This dashboard also shows you statistics for your model, including the CPU and GPU usage, and the memory utilization. You can also observe the training and validation accuracy of the model we're training on this dashboard.

Since we are only using two epochs, the training accuracy of this model is low:

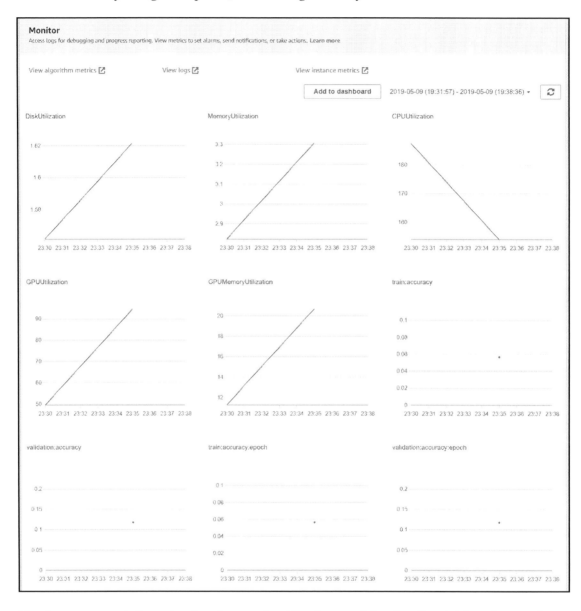

You have successfully trained an image classification model using SageMaker. SageMaker is very easy to use, as you just have to select the algorithm image, select the training dataset, and set the parameters for the algorithm. SageMaker automatically trains the model based on this information and also stores the model on your S3 bucket.

Classifying images using Amazon SageMaker

The SageMaker models that you have trained are now available to be used to predict objects in images. As we discussed at the beginning of the chapter, SageMaker offers a marketplace where you can use many models directly to perform your tasks.

1. Since we trained our own machine learning model, we will have to create a SageMaker model that can be used for prediction. The following code shows how to generate a usable model in Amazon Sagemaker

```
import boto3
from time import gmtime, strftime

sage = boto3.Session().client(service_name='sagemaker')

model_name="example-full-image-classification-model"

info = sage.describe_training_job(TrainingJobName=job_name)
model_data = info['ModelArtifacts']['S3ModelArtifacts']

hosting_image = get_image_uri(boto3.Session().region_name, 'image-
classification')

primary_container = {
    'Image': hosting_image,
    'ModelDataUrl': model_data,
}

create_model_response = sage.create_model(
    ModelName = model_name,
    ExecutionRoleArn = role,
    PrimaryContainer = primary_container)
```

To create a model in SageMaker, we have to specify the model name that was generated in the previous steps. In our example, the model name was set to `example-full-image-classification-model`. We also have to specify the container in which the model will be stored. Since we used the image-classification Docker image to generate this model, we have to specify it as a parameter. This image will help SageMaker read the trained model and define how it can be used for prediction.

The `create_model` function will create the model and return an **Amazon Resource Name (ARN)** for the model. This can be used to call the model to generate predictions.

For testing, we will download the raw images from the `Caltech256` dataset and store them in an `S3` bucket. We will use these images to generate predictions:

```
!wget -r -np -nH --cut-dirs=2 -P /tmp/ -R "index.html*"
http://www.vision.caltech.edu/Image_Datasets/Caltech256/images/008.bathtub/

batch_input = 's3://{}/image-classification-full-
training/test/'.format(bucket)
test_images = '/tmp/images/008.bathtub'

!aws s3 cp $test_images $batch_input --recursive --quiet
```

Once we have downloaded all the images and stored them in an S3 bucket, we specify the parameters for running a batch prediction job. This job will predict the probability of each of the 256 objects being present in an image:

```
timestamp = time.strftime('-%Y-%m-%d-%H-%M-%S', time.gmtime())
batch_job_name = "image-classification-model" + timestamp
request = \
{
    "TransformJobName": batch_job_name,
    "ModelName": model_name,
    "MaxConcurrentTransforms": 16,
    "MaxPayloadInMB": 6,
    "BatchStrategy": "SingleRecord",
    "TransformOutput": {
        "S3OutputPath": 's3://{}/{}/output'.format(bucket, batch_job_name)
    },
    "TransformInput": {
        "DataSource": {
            "S3DataSource": {
                "S3DataType": "S3Prefix",
                "S3Uri": batch_input
            }
        },
        "ContentType": "application/x-image",
        "SplitType": "None",
        "CompressionType": "None"
    },
    "TransformResources": {
            "InstanceType": "ml.p2.xlarge",
            "InstanceCount": 1
    }
}

print('Transform job name: {}'.format(batch_job_name))
print('\nInput Data Location: {}'.format(s3_validation))
```

As you might have guessed, we have to specify the model name in the `ModelName` parameter and the input folder in the `TransformInput` parameter. We also have to specify the `output` folder where the predictions are stored. We have to specify the instance type that we are using in the `TransformResources` parameter and the max number of files to process in the `MaxConcurrentTransforms` parameter.

The following code uses the parameters and starts the `create_transform_job`:

```
sagemaker = boto3.client('sagemaker')
sagemaker.create_transform_job(**request)
```

You can monitor your transforms job on the SageMaker dashboard under **Inference** | **Batch Transforms Jobs** section. Once the task is finished, you can access the predictions in the S3 bucket you specified as the `output` folder.

The predictions can be seen in the following format:

```
{
  "prediction": [
      0.0002778972266241908,
      0.05520012229681015,
  ...
    ]
}
```

Since our model had 256 object categories, the output specifies the probability of each object being present in the image. You can run the model on various datasets to check whether your model can predict the objects in the dataset correctly.

SageMaker offers a very easy-to-use service to not only train deep learning models but also to use them in applications to generate predictions. Although the service is very intuitive, SageMaker is expensive when you use the pre-built models on a large dataset to generate predictions. Based on the application being developed, data scientists should always consider the overall cost they would incur when using such services compared to building the same models on their own clusters in Apache Spark.

Summary

In this chapter, we studied how Amazon SageMaker offers various ready-to-use machine learning models to generate predictions, as well as algorithm images that can be used to train your models. Amazon SageMaker generates a layer of abstraction between you and the messy details of setting up your own clusters to train and create your own machine learning model. Amazon SageMaker dashboards also offer a place to store your trained models and monitor your batch-processing jobs for predictions.

You can also train your own machine learning models using your own datasets in SageMaker. We presented an example of training a machine learning model that is capable of performing object detection in images. We demonstrated how this model can then be deployed on SageMaker and used for running batch-prediction jobs. You will be able to use this as a template to work on other algorithms in Amazon SageMaker.

In this book, our aim is to provide you with an understanding of how machine learning algorithms work and how you can utilize powerful tools such as Apache Spark, Tensorflow, and SageMaker to deploy large-scale training and prediction jobs using machine learning.

Exercises

1. For each of the examples provide in previous chapters, find an algorithm in Amazon SageMaker Marketplace that would be applicable to solve that problem.
2. Amazon SageMaker also provides a service to create endpoints to generate predictions. For the preceding example, create an endpoint for the model that we trained and generate predictions for one image.

4
Section 4: Integrating Ready-Made AWS Machine Learning Services

The objective of this section is to introduce readers to various machine learning services that are provided by AWS to perform specific machine learning tasks. As the readers will be well-versed with machine learning by this point in the book, they will learn how to use the tools provided by AWS for machine learning tasks such as image recognition and natural language processing.

This section contains the following chapters:

- Chapter 10, *Working with AWS Comprehend*
- Chapter 11, *Using AWS Rekognition*
- Chapter 12, *Building Conversational Interfaces Using AWS Lex*

10
Working with AWS Comprehend

As a data scientist, knowing how machine learning algorithms work is very important. However, it may not be efficient to build your own machine learning models to perform certain tasks, as it takes a lot of effort and time to design an optimal algorithm. In Chapter 10, *Working with AWS Comprehend*, Chapter 11, *Using AWS Rekognition* and Chapter 12, *Building Conversational Interfaces Using AWS Lex*, we will look at the **machine learning as a service** (**MLaaS**) product that you can access in AWS. These products allow you to use models that are pre-trained in AWS using either the AWS dashboard or API calls.

In this chapter, we will cover the following topics:

- Introducing Amazon Comprehend
- Accessing Amazon Comprehend
- Testing entity recognition using Comprehend
- Testing sentiment analysis using Comprehend
- Implementing text classification using Comprehend APIs

Introducing Amazon Comprehend

Amazon Comprehend is a service available in AWS that offers **natural language processing** (**NLP**) algorithms. NLP is a field in machine learning that analyzes human (natural) languages and can identify various attributes of these languages. In most of our previous chapters, we looked at examples of structured data. The data had predefined features and was organized as rows of observations. However, a natural language dataset is more complicated to process. Such datasets are called **unstructured datasets**, as the structure of the features is not well-defined.

Hence, algorithms are needed to extract structure and information from a text document. For example, a natural language has words that are arranged using a grammatical structure. Natural-language sentences also have keywords, which contain more information regarding places, people, and other details. They also have a context, which is very hard to learn, and the same words may convey different meanings based on how they are arranged.

The field of NLP studies how to process these text documents and extract information from them. NLP not only involves clustering and classifying the documents, but also preprocessing the data to extract important keywords and entity information from the text. Based on the domain of the text documents, different preprocessing is required, as the styles of written documents change. For example, medical and legal texts are written with a lot of jargon and are well-structured. However, if you are using an NLP algorithm to process Twitter data, the text may be composed of poor grammar and hashtags. Hence, based on the domain of the data, you need a separate process to preprocess the data and how the models should be trained. Domain expertise is generally required when training NLP models.

AWS Comprehend provides tools to both train machine learning models and use pre-trained models to perform NLP tasks. It provides real-time dashboards to analyze text data and also provides tools to train machine learning algorithms using their UI.

In this chapter, we will explore four NLP tasks that can be accomplished using AWS Comprehend. We will also suggest when a data scientist should employ ready-to-use tools and when they should invest time in building their own machine learning algorithms.

Accessing AmazonComprehend

`Amazon Comprehend` is available to use on the AWS Console. When you log into the AWS Management Console, search for Amazon Comprehend in the **AWS Services** box. Selecting **Amazon Comprehend** will take you to the **AWS Comprehend** start screen, as shown in the following screenshot:

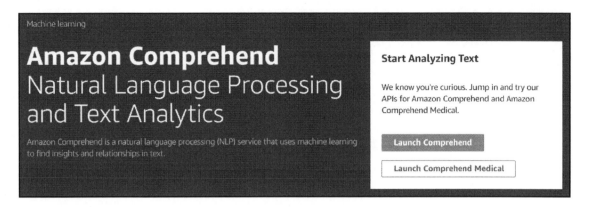

Click on **Launch Comprehend** when you get to this screen, which will take you to the AWS Comprehend dashboard. You should be able to access the algorithms used in the following sections from this page.

Named-entity recognition using Comprehend

Named-entity recognition (NER) is a field in NLP that tags mentions of named entities in unstructured text. Named entities are names of people, places, organizations, and so on. For example, consider the following sentence:

Tim Cook traveled to New York for an Apple store opening.

In this sentence, there are three named entities. Tim Cook is the name of a person, New York is the name of a city (location), and Apple is the name of an organization. Hence, we need an NER model that can detect these entities. Note that Apple is an ambiguous noun, as it can be the name of a company or a fruit. The NER algorithm should understand the context in which the term is used and identify it accordingly.

AWS Comprehend offers a good NER tool that can be used to identify entities. This tool can be used in real-time via their dashboard or using their APIs. AWS Comprehend detects the following entities:

- **Commercial Item**: Brand names
- **Date**: Dates in different formats
- **Event**: Names of concerts, festivals, elections, and so on
- **Location**: Names of cities, countries, and so on

- **Organization**: Names of companies and governmental organizations
- **Person**: Names of people
- **Quantity**: Commonly used units used to quantify a number
- **Title**: Names of movies, books, and so on

To access the AWS dashboard for NER, go to the **Real-time Analysis** tab in the menu. You can then add input text in the text box provided on the page. The following screenshot demonstrated how Amazon Comprehend performs the NER task:

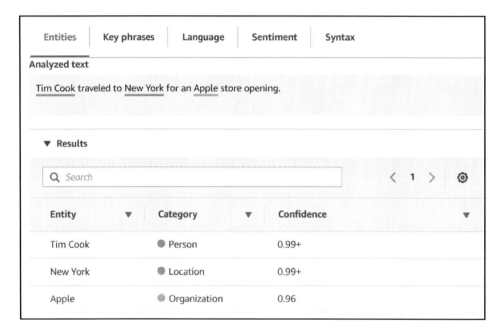

You can see that the NER tool in Amazon Comprehend automatically labels the entities in the sentence. Along with labeling the categories of the entities, it also gives us a confidence score. This score can be used to determine whether we trust the results from the tool.

The NER tool in Amazon Comprehend can also be accessed using the API provided by AWS.

The following code shows how you can call the Comprehend tool to get the entity scores:

```
import boto3
import json

comprehend = boto3.client(service_name='comprehend')
```

```
text = "Tim Cook traveled to New York for an Apple store opening"

print(json.dumps(comprehend.detect_entities(Text=text, LanguageCode='en'),
sort_keys=True, indent=4))
```

You use the `boto3` package, which is an AWS tool package for Python. We first initialize the Comprehend client and then pass our text to the client to get a JSON response with information about the named entities. In the following code block we can see the response we receive from the client:

```
{
    "Entities": [
        {
            "Score": 0.9999027252197266,
            "Type": "PERSON",
            "Text": "Tim Cook",
            "BeginOffset": 0,
            "EndOffset": 8
        },
        {
            "Score": 0.992688775062561,
            "Type": "LOCATION",
            "Text": "New York",
            "BeginOffset": 21,
            "EndOffset": 29
        },
        {
            "Score": 0.9699087738990784,
            "Type": "ORGANIZATION",
            "Text": "Apple",
            "BeginOffset": 37,
            "EndOffset": 42
        }
    ]
}
```

Thus, parsing the JSON can get us information regarding the entities in the text.

You can also train a custom NER algorithm in AWS Comprehend using the **Customization | Custom entity recognition** option in the left-hand side menu. You can add training sample documents and a list of annotations for entities. The algorithm automatically learns how to label these entities in the correct context and updates the existing models.

NER algorithms are applied in various applications. One of their important applications is in the field of News Aggregation. You can automatically generate tags for a document so that users can search for documents based on the entities in them. NER is also useful in the field of recommendation algorithms, where NER is used to detect keywords and we can create a news-recommendation algorithm. We can build a collaborative filtering model that can recommend articles about entities that readers of a current article may also be interested in.

Sentiment analysis using Comprehend

Sentiment analysis algorithms analyze text and categorize it based on the sentiments or opinions in the text. Sentiment analysis detects subjective opinions that are expressed in text. For example, reviews on Amazon Marketplace give a good or a bad review of a product. Using sentiment analysis, we can detect whether a review is positive or negative. We can also recognize emotional nuances in a review, such as whether the reviewer was angry, excited, or neutral about a given product. In this age of social media, we have a large number of avenues to voice our opinions on products, movies, politics, and so on. Data scientists use sentiment analysis algorithms to analyze a large amount of data and extract opinions regarding a certain entity based on unstructured text data.

Amazon Comprehend makes the task of sentiment analysis easy by providing a real-time dashboard to analyze the sentiment in text. You can access the **Sentiment Analysis** dashboard the same way you did for the NER algorithm. We'll provide two examples of how Comprehend can perform sentiment analysis on our data. I looked at two reviews on Amazon that were positive and negative and used Comprehend to perform sentiment analysis on them. Consider the first example, as seen in the following screenshot:

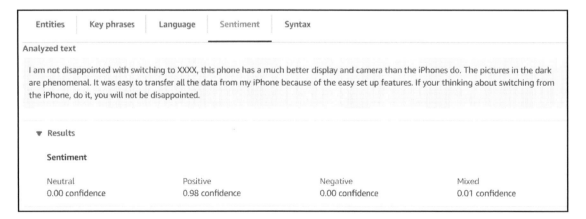

In this example, the reviewer has used words such as disappointed. These terms have negative connotations. However, sentiment analysis algorithms can detect that the user also used a negative before this word and correctly predict that this text has a positive sentiment. Similarly, consider the following example:

Entities	Key phrases	Language	Sentiment	Syntax

Analyzed text

Received the phone. It worked fine for the first 6 weeks,then I lost battery power I turned the phone off at night while charging, did not help. Then every else started to fail.

▼ Results

Sentiment

Neutral	Positive	Negative	Mixed
0.03 confidence	0.03 confidence	0.70 confidence	0.22 confidence

You can see that the reviewer was initially happy regarding the product, but then had issues. Hence, the reviewer was not happy with the product. Hence, the sentiment analysis algorithm correctly predicts that the confidence of the review being negative is 70%. However, it also predicts that there are some mixed sentiments in this review and provides confidence of 22%. We use the soft-max methodology to pixel the sentiment with the highest confidence.

Sentiment analysis can also be accessed using the Amazon API. Here, we provide example code that shows how we can call the sentiment analysis API using the `boto3` Python package:

```
import boto3
import json

comprehend = boto3.client(service_name='comprehend')

text = " It worked fine for the first 6 weeks, then I lost battery power I
turned the phone off at night while charging, did not help. Then every else
started to fail."

print(json.dumps(comprehend.detect_sentiment(Text=text, LanguageCode='en'),
sort_keys=True, indent=4))
```

This API call returns the following JSON with the data regarding the sentiment of the text:

```
{
    "Sentiment": {
        "Sentiment": "NEGATIVE",
        "SentimentScore": {
            "Positive": 0.03148878738284111,
            "Negative": 0.6730570793151855,
            "Neutral": 0.047707948833703995,
            "Mixed": 0.24774616956710815
        }
    }
}
```

You can use the API to classify a large number of reviews to detect what the overall sentiment is for a given product.

Sentiment analysis is a very powerful tool that companies use to analyze social media data to detect the overall sentiment regarding their products and also to determine why users are unhappy with their products. Movie review aggregators, such as Rotten Tomatoes, also use them to detect whether reviews are positive or negative so that they can classify them and generate aggregated scores.

Text classification using Comprehend

Text classification is the process of classifying text documents into categories. Similar to the classification algorithms that we studied in Chapter 2, *Classifying Twitter Feeds with Naive Bayes* to Chapter 6, *Analyzing Visitor Patterns to Make Recommendations*, text classification algorithms also generate models based on labeled training observations. The classification model can then be applied to any observation to predict its class. Moreover, the same algorithms that we studied in the previous chapters, such as Chapter 2, *Classifying Twitter Feeds with Naive Bayes*, Chapter 3, *Predicting House Value with Regression Algorithms*, and Chapter 4, *Predicting User Behavior with Tree-Based Methods*, can also be used for text classification.

Text data is unstructured data. Hence, we need to generate features from text documents so that those features can be used as input for our classification model. For text datasets, features are generally terms in the document. For example, consider the following sentence:

Tim Cook traveled to New York for an Apple store opening.

Let's consider the class of this document as `Technology`. This sentence will be translated into structured data, as follows:

Tim Cook	traveled	to	New York	Apple	Store	Opening	Microsoft	Google	Class
1	1	1	1	1	1	1	0	0	Technology

Each term will be considered a feature in the dataset. Hence, for a large dataset with many documents, the feature set can be as large as the lexicon of that language. The value of the features is set to 0 or 1 based on whether that term exists in that document. As our example contains words such as `Tim Cook` and `New York`, the value of those features for this observation is set to 1. As the terms Microsoft and Google are not present in the sentence, the value of those features is set to 0. The `Class` variable is set to `Technology`.

In this section, we will show a step-by-step methodology on how to train custom classifiers on Comprehend. We'll use a popular text classification dataset called **20 Newsgroups** to generate a machine learning model that can mark a review as positive or negative. The dataset can be downloaded from `https://archive.ics.uci.edu/ml/datasets/Twenty+Newsgroups`.

The dataset can be downloaded as separate text files that are organized into 20 folders. Each folder name represents the category of documents in the folder. The dataset is a publicly available dataset. It contains news articles that are categorized into the following categories:

- `alt.atheism`
- `comp.graphics`
- `comp.os.ms-windows.misc`
- `comp.sys.ibm.pc.hardware`
- `comp.sys.mac.hardware`
- `comp.windows.x`
- `misc.forsale`
- `rec.autos`
- `rec.motorcycles`
- `rec.sport.baseball`
- `rec.sport.hockey`
- `sci.crypt`
- `sci.electronics`

- `sci.med`
- `sci.space`
- `soc.religion.christian`
- `talk.politics.guns`
- `talk.politics.mideast`
- `talk.politics.misc`
- `talk.religion.misc`

You can use the following steps to train the classifier:

1. The first step is to download and preprocess the data into a format that is readable by the Comprehend tools. Comprehend requires the training data to be in the following format in CSV (comma-separated values):

Category	Document

Hence, once you download the dataset, convert the data into the preceding format and upload it to your S3 bucket.

2. You can access the **Custom Classification** tool on the **Comprehend** dashboard, on the left-hand side under the **Customization** tab. To train the model, you have to click on the **Train Classifier** option. Note that Comprehend allows you to train your machine learning models and store them on this dashboard so that you can use them in the future.

When you click on the **Train Classifier** option, you will see the following screenshot:

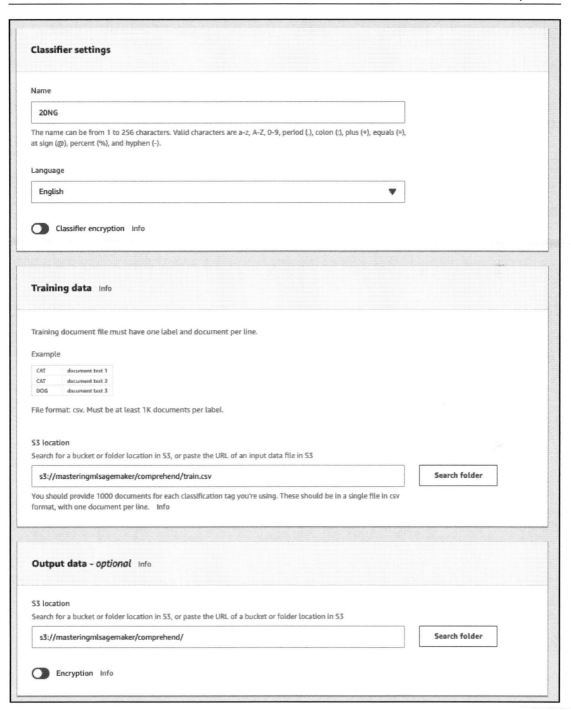

3. Name the classifier and select the language of the documents. Add your S3 location, where the training CSV document is stored. After you select the correct role, you can tag the classifier with relevant values, which can help you to search them in the future. Once you have added all the information, click on **Train classifier**:

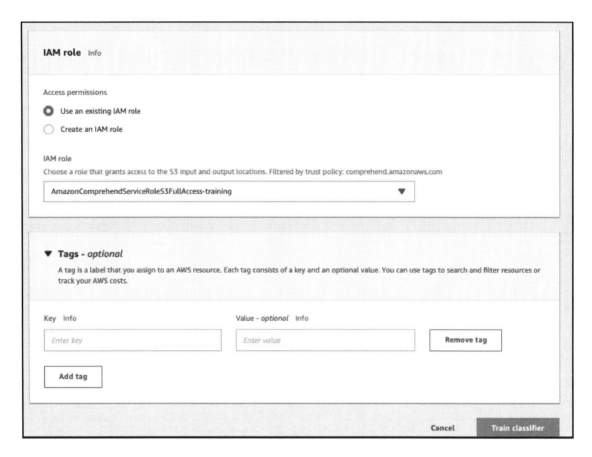

4. You will be taken back to the dashboard screen where you will see that the classifier training is in progress. Once the training is done, the status of the classifier will be marked as **Trained**:

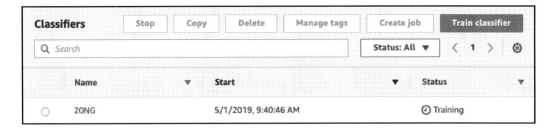

5. You can then click on the classifier to see the evaluation metrics of the model. As you can see, our classification model has an accuracy of 90%:

6. As we now have a classifier that is trained, you can get predictions for any document using this model. We create a `test.csv` file that contains 100 documents to get predictions from this model. We preprocess the data to create a CSV file with one document per line. To start the prediction process, click on the **Create Job** option shown on the preceding screen.

This will take you to another screen, where you can add details on which file you want to use for testing and where the output should be stored:

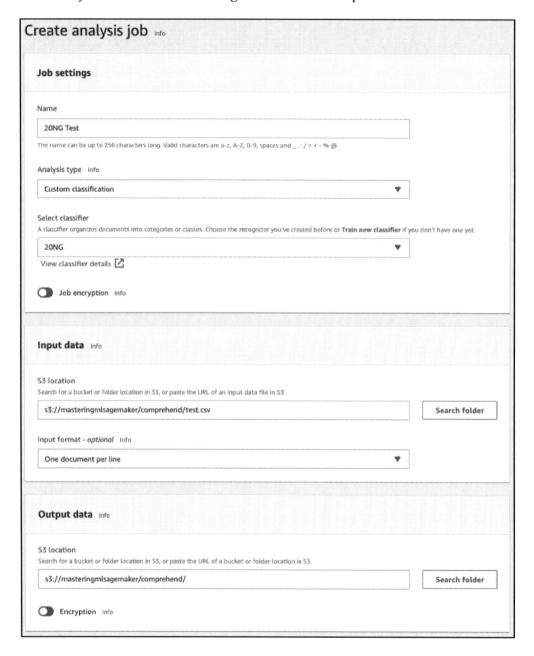

On the **Create analysis job** screen, add the details about the classifier to be used: where the input data is stored (on S3) and an **S3 location** where the output is stored. You can either specify the input data as **one document per line** or **one document per file** and point the input data to the directory that contains all the files. In our example, since the `test.csv` file contains one document on each line, we use that format.

7. Once you click on **Create Job,** it will automatically classify the documents and store the output in the output location. The output is stored in JSON format, where each line of the `output` file contains JSON that gives the analysis of that line.

The following is an example of the output that was generated:

```
{
  "File": "test_2.csv",
  "Line": "0",
  "Classes": [
    {
      "Name": "alt.atheism",
      "Score": 0.8642
    },
    {
      "Name": "comp.graphics",
      "Score": 0.0381
    },
    {
      "Name": "comp.os.ms-windows.misc",
      "Score": 0.0372
    },
    ...
    {
      "Name": "talk.religion.misc",
      "Score": 0.0243
    }
  ]
}
```

Thus, you can see that our model labeled the first line in our input file as `"alt.atheism"` with a confidence score of 86.42%.

You can also create a document classifier and prediction jobs using the Amazon Comprehend APIs:

```
import boto3

client = boto3.client('comprehend')
response = client.create_document_classifier(
    DocumentClassifierName='20NG-test',
    DataAccessRoleArn='Data Access ARN value',
     InputDataConfig={
         'S3Uri': 's3://masteringmlsagemaker/comprehend/train.csv'
     },
     OutputDataConfig={
         'S3Uri': 's3://masteringmlsagemaker/comprehend/'
     },
     LanguageCode='en')
```

Running this function will automatically generate the same classifier that we created in the previous steps. You can access your ARN value from the **Roles** tab on the **My Security Credentials** page. This is the ARN value of the same IAM role we created in step 3. The output data config location will automatically get a confusion metric of the evaluation of the classifier and the response string will be returned as follows:

```
{
    'DocumentClassifierArn': 'string'
}
```

The string will be the Amazon resource name that identifies the classifier. You can also run prediction jobs using the API. The following code can be used to generate the predictions for your input files:

```
import boto3

client = boto3.client('comprehend')
response = client.start_document_classification_job( JobName='Testing
Model', DocumentClassifierArn='<ARN of classifier returned in the previous
step>', InputDataConfig={ 'S3Uri':
's3://masteringmlsagemaker/comprehend/test.csv', 'InputFormat':
'ONE_DOC_PER_LINE' }, OutputDataConfig={ 'S3Uri':
's3://masteringmlsagemaker/comprehend/', }, DataAccessRoleArn='<Data Access
ARN value>')
```

The preceding code will start the exact same classification job that we created on the dashboard. Thus, you can control when you want to use a certain classifier and generate predictions on different datasets as required. The response of the function will be the status of the job. The job will also generate a job ID, that you can ping to check the status of the job using the `describe_document_classification_job()` function.

Thus, we have generated a custom document classifier using Comprehend tools on AWS. These tools will help you to create these classifiers quickly without having to worry about what classification algorithms to select, how to tune the parameters, and so on. Amazon automatically updates the algorithms used by Comprehend based on the expertise of their research teams. However, the main disadvantage is that Comprehend tools can be costly if you are running operations on large datasets, as they charge you per prediction. You can access the pricing information for AWS Comprehend at `https://aws.amazon.com/comprehend/pricing/`.

Summary

In this chapter, we studied how to use a built-in machine learning tool called Comprehend in AWS. We briefly discussed the field of NLP and provided an introduction to its sub-fields, such as NER and sentiment analysis. We also studied how to create a custom document classifier in Comprehend using the dashboard it provides. Moreover, we studied how to access Comprehend's APIs using the `boto3` package in Python.

These tools are fascinating as they will help you to create complex machine learning models quickly and start applying them in your applications. A data scientist who has cursory knowledge in the field of NLP can now train sophisticated machine learning models and use them to make optimal decisions. However, the question most data scientists face is whether the pricing provided by such tools is more economical than building algorithms in-house using Python packages. Note that Comprehend adds a layer of abstraction between data scientists and the machine learning models by making them worry about the underlying cluster configurations. In our experience, we use these tools during the rapid prototyping phases of our projects to evaluate a product. If we decide to move to production, it is easy to calculate the cost differences between using the AWS tools versus building algorithms in-house and maintaining them on our clusters.

We will introduce the Amazon Rekognition in the next chapter. This service is used for image recognition and is an out of the box solution for Object detection and similar applications

Exercise

1. Your task is to perform NER on a large dataset using APIs provided by Amazon Comprehend. Use the annotated NER dataset provided in the Kaggle competition to create a custom entity recognition in Comprehend (`https://www.kaggle.com/abhinavwalia95/chemdner-iob-annotated-chemical-named-etities`).

2. Apply sentiment analysis on the Yelp dataset in Kaggle and then evaluate whether your predictions match the review score (`https://www.kaggle.com/yelp-dataset/yelp-dataset`).

11
Using AWS Rekognition

We have studied deep learning algorithms and how to implement them using SageMaker in Chapter 7, *Implementing Deep Learning Algorithms*, and Chapter 9, *Image Classification and Detection with SageMaker*. You must have realized that training a good **Convolutional Neural Network (CNN)** takes a lot of expertise and resources. Moreover, it also requires a large number of labeled images with objects. Amazon has an out-of-box solution for image recognition, called **Amazon Rekognition**, that offers various tools for image recognition using pretrained image recognition models.

In this chapter, we will cover the following topics:

- Introducing Amazon Rekognition
- Implementing object and scene detection
- Implementing facial analysis

Introducing Amazon Rekognition

Building image recognition models using deep learning is very challenging. Firstly, you need a large, labeled dataset in order to train the deep learning model to perform specific tasks. Secondly, you need knowledge of how to design a network and tune the parameters to get the best accuracy. Finally, training such deep learning models at scale requires expensive GPU-based clusters to train these models.

Amazon Rekognition (https://aws.amazon.com/rekognition/) is a tool offered by AWS featuring image recognition models that are already pretrained for use in your applications. Amazon Rekognition models are based on an analysis of billions of videos and images. Similar to how **Amazon Comprehend** offers NLP models as a service, Rekognition offers various image recognition models that can perform specific tasks. The advantage of using Amazon Rekognition is that you can simply use dashboards and APIs to perform image recognition tasks at high accuracy, without the high-level expertise required to train such machine learning models.

Amazon Rekognition only offers a limited number of models that perform specific tasks. In this section, we'll look at the various tools available in the Amazon Rekognition dashboard. We'll also look at how we can access these features using AWS APIs in Python.

Implementing object and scene detection

Object and scene detection algorithms can recognize various objects in the image and assign confidence to each prediction. This algorithm uses a hierarchy of labels to label objects and returns all the nodes of the leaf when it detects an object. Object detection is a classic application of image recognition. It allows us to identify what is inside an image and label it. For example, consider a newsroom where photographers are submitting hundreds of images and videos every day. You need people to label such images so that if you wish to access an image of a celebrity who was pictured during a car crash, these image libraries can be searchable.

Object detection allows you to automatically label these images so that they can be stored, organized, and retrieved efficiently. One of the key features of an object detection algorithm is that they have to be comprehensive and should be able to detect a large array of objects. Moreover, such algorithms also detect the edges of the object and should be able to return the bounding box for an object. Amazon Rekognition performs both these tasks effectively.

You can access the Amazon Rekognition dashboard using the AWS Console. Just search for Rekognition in the search bar and you will be able to access the demo for Amazon Rekognition. The demo shows you how the tools work, but you would need to use the API if you want to analyze multiple images.

Once, you are on the demo screen, select **Object and Scene detection** to access a demo where you can select a single image and detect the images in the object.

For the purpose of this demo, I have used a screenshot of the Chicago river with ferry boats on the river:

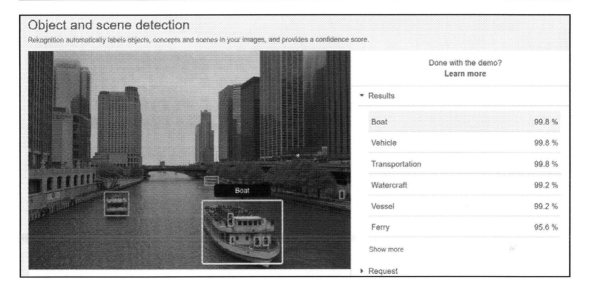

As you can see from the preceding screenshot, the object detection tool returns a ranked list of objects in the image along with the confidence of detection. As we mentioned previously, since the tool uses a hierarchy of categories, it may detect similar categories at the top. For example, it was able to detect the boat in the image. However, it also returned **Vehicle** and **Transportation** categories with the same confidence score. We can also see that the demo shows bounding boxes for each of the objects that it detected in the image.

However, using this tool to perform object detection may be tedious as it only handles one image at a time. So, we can also use an API to access the Amazon Rekognition tool. You need to upload your images to a folder in S3 bucket in order to use object detection on them.

The following Python code can be used to perform the same operation on the image:

```python
import boto3
import json

client = boto3.client('rekognition')
response = client.detect_labels(
                Image={
                    'S3Object':
                            {
                                'Bucket': 'masteringmlsagemaker',
                                'Name':
'ImageRecognition/chicago_boats.JPG'
                            }
                },
```

```
                MaxLabels=5,
                MinConfidence=90
    )

    print(json.dumps(response, sort_keys=True, indent=4))
```

The image has to be in the S3 bucket and you have to specify the bucket name and image name as a parameter of the request function. The response is long, so we only show the format of the first prediction in the response JSON:

```
{
    "LabelModelVersion": "2.0",
    "Labels": [
        {
            "Confidence": 99.86528778076172,
            "Instances": [
                {
                    "BoundingBox": {
                        "Height": 0.29408860206604004,
                        "Left": 0.5391838550567627,
                        "Top": 0.6836633682250977,
                        "Width": 0.25161588191986084
                    },
                    "Confidence": 99.86528778076172
                },
                {
                    "BoundingBox": {
                        "Height": 0.11046414822340012,
                        "Left": 0.23703880608081818,
                        "Top": 0.6440696120262146,
                        "Width": 0.07676628232002258
                    },
                    "Confidence": 99.5784912109375
                },
                {
                    "BoundingBox": {
                        "Height": 0.040305182337760925,
                        "Left": 0.5480409860610962,
                        "Top": 0.5758911967277527,
                        "Width": 0.04315359890460968
                    },
                    "Confidence": 77.51519012451172
                }
            ],
            "Name": "Boat",
            "Parents": [
                {
                    "Name": "Vehicle"
```

```
        },
        {
          "Name": "Transportation"
        }
      ]
    },
  ...
    ]
  }
```

As you can observe from the response, we found three instances of the `Boat` object in the image. The response provides the bounding box for each of the objects found in the image. Moreover, you can observe that the boat in the far right is small, so the confidence in detecting it is much lower than the other two boats in the image. The response also returned the parents of the object in the hierarchy. So, if you have hundreds of images to categorize, you can add them all to an S3 bucket and use this code to iterate through them and detect labels for those objects. Because of tools such as Amazon Rekognition, data scientists now have access to world-class deep learning models that they can apply in the tools that they are building. However, such an object detection algorithm only works for a limited number of objects. For example, we tried the algorithm on x-ray images of cancer in this tool and it was not able to return any results. If you are working on a very specialized product where you are trying to detect medical images of tumors or images from a space telescope, you would need to train your own models based on a large number of labeled images.

Implementing facial analysis

Amazon Rekognition also offers a powerful tool for performing facial analysis on images. It can predict interesting attributes such as age and gender based on looking at the image. It can also detect features such as a smile or whether the person is wearing glasses from this model. Such models would be trained by analyzing a lot of labeled facial images and training an image recognition model to recognize these features. The CNN models that we studied in `Chapter 7`, *Implementing Deep Learning Algorithms*, would be a good fit for such applications as it can automatically generate feature maps using local receptive fields methodology from the image and detect boxes that would contain evidence of these facial features.

The facial analysis demo can be accessed in the same way as the object detection demo. In order to test the model, we picked the picture of Mona Lisa by Leonardo Da Vinci. One of the long-standing mysteries about the image is whether the lady in the image is smiling or not.

In the following screenshot, we can see how the facial analysis demo provides features of the face from the image:

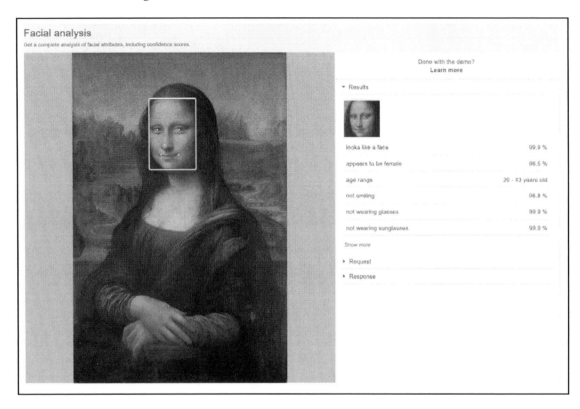

The facial analysis model does predict that there is a face in the image and creates a correct box around it. It correctly predicted that the image is female and predicts an age range for that person. It predicted that the person in the image is not smiling. It also correctly predicted that the person is not wearing any glasses.

You can also access this same information using an API call.

With the following Python code, you can perform the same task of facial analysis as in the preceding demo:

```python
import boto3
import json

client = boto3.client('rekognition')
response = client.detect_faces(
    Image={
```

```
        'S3Object': {
            'Bucket': 'masteringmlsagemaker',
            'Name': 'ImageRecognition/monalisa.jpg'
        }
    },
    Attributes=['ALL']
)

print(json.dumps(response, sort_keys=True, indent=4))
```

You have to store your image on an S3 bucket and provide the bucket and image name to the API call. You can also specify what attributes you need to be returned, or specify All in case you need all the attributes.

The response of this call is in JSON format and looks as follows:

```
{
    "FaceDetails": [
        {
            "BoundingBox": {
                "Width": 0.22473210096359253,
                "Height": 0.21790461242198944,
                "Left": 0.35767847299575806,
                "Top": 0.13709242641925812
            },
            "AgeRange": {
                "Low": 26,
                "High": 43
            },
            "Smile": {
                "Value": false,
                "Confidence": 96.82086944580078
            },
            "Gender": {
                "Value": "Female",
                "Confidence": 96.50946044921875
            },
            "Emotions": [
                {
                    "Type": "CALM",
                    "Confidence": 34.63209533691406
                },
                {
                    "Type": "SAD",
                    "Confidence": 40.639801025390625
                }
            ],
            "Landmarks": [
```

```
        {
            "Type": "eyeLeft",
            "X": 0.39933907985687256,
            "Y": 0.23376932740211487
        },
        {
            "Type": "eyeRight",
            "X": 0.49918869137763977,
            "Y": 0.23316724598407745
        },
        "Confidence": 99.99974060058594
    }
  ]
}
```

We have edited this response to maintain brevity. However, you can observe that you can see information about `Age`, `Gender`, and `Smile` as we saw in the demo. However, it also identifies emotions on the face such as sadness and calm. It also locates landmarks on the face such as the eyes, nose, and lips.

Such tools are used in current smartphones where a smile can trigger a photo. It is used in consumer surveys in restaurants to gauge the demographics of people in the restaurant and whether they are happy with the service.

Other Rekognition services

Amazon Rekognition also offers other image recognition services. You can use the API as in the examples in this chapter to access these services. We will list some of the services and their applications here.

Image moderation

We can use Rekognition to monitor images and check whether the content is suggestive or unsafe. Such techniques are used to moderate live video services, such as Twitch or Facebook Live, where **Artificial Intelligence (AI)** can automatically detect unsafe content. As services such as YouTube or Instagram see an unimaginable amount of data being uploaded on them every day, using such AI techniques can help to lower the cost of moderating the platform.

The following screenshot shows how the image moderation tool can detect suggestive themes in the image and automatically label them:

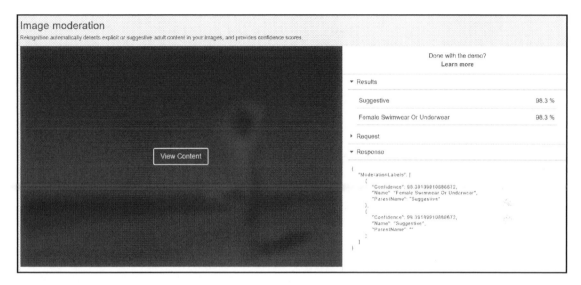

Celebrity recognition

Recognition can also be used to detect celebrities in pictures or videos automatically. This can be done by an image recognition model learning from labeled images and videos. Deep learning algorithms can automatically extract facial features and then compare them to predict who the celebrity may be. For example, many of the movies and TV shows on services such as Amazon Prime can show the names of actors on the screen using this technique. Manually labeling these scenes with the names of actors may be a very tedious task; however, deep learning algorithms can do this automatically.

In the following example, Amazon Rekognition detects an image of Jeff Bezos and labels it correctly:

Face comparison

Celebrity recognition technology can be further extended to do facial comparisons and detect faces that are similar. For example, your Facebook account automatically matches the faces in an image you upload with your friends and tags the images automatically. They use such image recognition algorithms to train models for each face and run those models on your uploaded images to detect whether your friends are in that picture. Amazon Rekognition also offers a feature called **face comparison** that compares faces between two images and detects whether the same people appear in both pictures.

In the following screenshot, we can observe that the face comparison algorithm can automatically match the faces in two images and detect which faces are similar to each other:

Amazon Rekognition also offers another tool that can detect text in a picture. This model is similar to what we built in `Chapter 8`, *Implementing Deep Learning with TensorFlow on AWS*, where our model was able to detect numbers. This tool is also very useful for reading text in the real world. Applications such as Google Translate can analyze camera images and can translate them to your native language. Self-driving cars can also use this technology to read road signs and react accordingly.

The following screenshot shows how Amazon Rekognition can detect text inside an image:

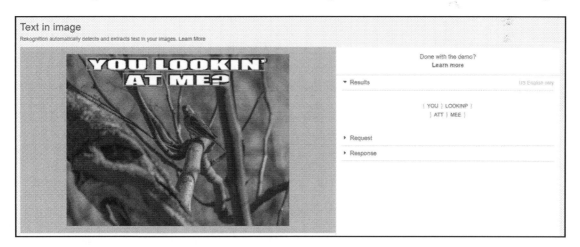

Recognition does not do an accurate job with this image, but is able to box and recreate the text in this image.

We have not given code examples for these services in this section. The API calls are similar to what we discussed in the first two tools presented in this section. We encourage you to try the API calls for these services and test how they work.

Summary

Amazon Rekognition allows data scientists to access high-quality image recognition algorithms using API calls. One of the biggest obstacles in using deep learning is generating large datasets and running expensive GPU-based clusters to train the models. AWS Rekognition makes it easier for users to access these features without the prerequisite expertise required to train such models. The application developers can concentrate on building functionality without having to spend a lot of time on deep learning tasks. In this chapter, we studied various tools that are available in Amazon Rekognition and also learned how to make API calls and read the response JSON. Moreover, we also studied various applications where these tools can be useful.

In the next chapter, we will demonstrate how you can build automated chat bots using a service called Amazon Lex.

Exercise

1. Create an app using Python where you can pass a photo of a group and detect what the mood of the room was at that time. Provide details on what your code detected based on the facial analysis tools and how you summarized the results to find the mood in the photo.
2. Create a tool that would recognize the actors in a movie clip. Provide the time at which the actors appeared on the screen.

12
Building Conversational Interfaces Using AWS Lex

One of the most popular applications of machine learning is chatbots; they can talk to you like a human being and understand your instructions. These chatbots use **natural language processing (NLP)** to decipher instructions and return a query or answer based on your questions. Amazon offers a service called **Lex** (it is a short form of **Alexa**), where you can build sophisticated chatbots that can perform various tasks.

In this chapter, we will cover the following topics:

- Introducing Amazon Lex
- Building custom chatbot using Amazon Lex

Introducing Amazon Lex

Amazon Lex (`https://aws.amazon.com/lex/`) offers services that can be used to create conversational bots. Conversational bots use various machine learning technologies such as **speech recognition**, **NLP**, and **deep learning**. Due to advances in these fields in recent years, conversational bots have become a mainstay in our everyday life. Millions of people use Amazon Alexa, Google Assistant, Siri, or Cortana as a conversational device to perform various tasks. These devices can perform simple tasks, such as tell you the weather, call an Uber for you, order a pizza, and control your lighting. Many businesses offer chatbots for customer support. For example, Verizon FIOS, which is an internet provider, offers a chatbot that can perform tasks such as pointing you to the correct troubleshooting documentation or resetting your router based on a chat with you. Many companies also use such conversational bots to make robocalls (automated calls), where it is very hard for a person to tell whether the caller on the other side is not a real human being.

Building such conversational bots from scratch is not easy. As we studied in `Chapter 10`, *Working with AWS Comprehend,* natural language does not follow a rigid grammatical structure and we have multiple ways to convey the same meaning. So, a conversational bot needs to be able to decipher the relevant data from a natural language query and respond with the most likely answer. Devices such as Amazon Echo can understand the query in different formats and discover what is the most relevant information that can be presented to the user. Firstly, such devices need to understand the speech and convert it into text that the machine can understand. Secondly, they need to trigger the correct skill that can answer that question and present the user input to that skill. Once the skill generates the answer, it has to be translated back to speech using text-to-speech transformers. All these steps require dedicated and high-quality deep learning models to perform these tasks. For example, Amazon uses a deep learning model to determine the pauses between words in their text-to-speech transformers.

Although building such conversational bots may sound like a daunting task, Amazon also offers services where you utilize their models to generate such tasks. This service is called Amazon Lex and you access it using the AWS console.

Building a custom chatbot using Amazon Lex

In this section, we will build a simple custom conversational bot using Amazon Lex. To access the Amazon Lex dashboard, simply go to the AWS console and search for this service. Once you reach the dashboard, you will have an option to create a new bot. You can build separate bots that can handle specific tasks. In this example, we provide the following steps to create a bot that the user can ask to order food from a specific restaurant at a specified time:

1. To get started, click on the **Create bot** option on the dashboard. You will be able to access the following screenshot:

You will have to specify the bot name on this screen and the voice that you want to select when testing the bot. You can also specify when the session times out so that a person who has left the order incomplete and left their machine are not at risk of someone else continuing their chat session. We are creating a custom bot in this example. However, you can also access sample bots to test the service and see how those bots were created.

2. When you click on the **Create** button, you will be taken to the next screen where you have to enter information regarding how your bot works. Firstly, you will have to specify how your specific bot is triggered in the chat screen. In our case, there are various ways in which a user can let the chat window know that they are hungry, so you should add samples of what queries should trigger your bot. Such queries are called **utterances** in Amazon Lex. We added the following utterances that would trigger our bot:

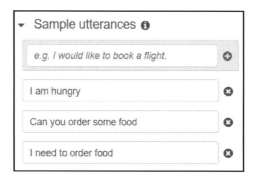

3. Amazon Lex will use machine learning to expand the list of utterances, so that if a user asks a question such as `Can you order some food`, our bot will still be triggered, as the utterance is similar to the one we specified.

4. Once we specify what will trigger our bot, we have to specify what happens when the bot starts. You can either use the Lambda function on AWS that can perform a specific task, or use the dashboard to design the chat. Since designing lambda functions is not in the scope of this book, we will use the dashboard to ask the user what they would like to order. The following screen options show how we can add information that we expect from the users:

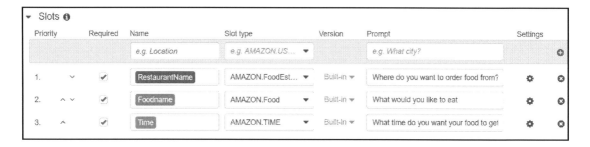

5. We define three variables that we would like our chatbot to get inputs on. For example, we would want to know the name of the restaurant they want to order from, what they want to order, and the time they want their food to be ready. Amazon Lex offers pre-built slots (variable types) that you can select when getting the inputs. For example, the **AMAZON.Food** slot type will try to ensure that the value of the variable is a type of food, while the **AMAZON.Time** variable type will ensure that the time added is a valid time.

6. Once our bot has information for all the variables that are required, you have to specify how the bot will respond. In our case, to keep it simple, we will just tell the user that we have ordered the food (please note that this code does not really order food). If you were building a real application that orders food, you can also invoke a lambda function that can run custom code with the variable names. The following screenshot shows how you can add the information about how the bot responds, along with a confirmation screen:

7. If the user confirms, you can provide a thank you message to the user using the following **Fulfillment** option:

8. Once you are done filling out the form, you can build your bot using the **build** option on the screen. If you made any errors on the screen, the build will prompt you to fix them. Finally, once you have built your bot successfully, you can test it by selecting the **Test Chatbot** option on the right-hand side. The following screen shows how our chatbot works. As you can see, we were able to chat with our chatbot and (pretend to) order food from it, as shown in the following screenshot:

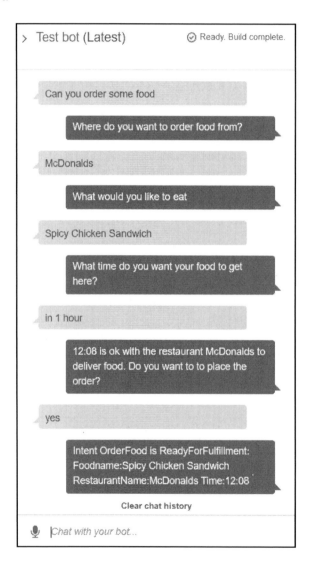

Amazon Lex makes creating chatbots very accessible to everyone by adding a layer of abstraction between the actual machine learning models and the users. You can concentrate on building a bot that best fits your needs, without worrying about the algorithms behind the scenes. As Amazon Lex is a service, AWS charges you based on the calls you make to their machine learning models.

Moreover, Amazon Lex models can be exported to the Alexa Skills kit easily using the **Export** option in the **Actions** drop-down menu for each bot. So, by using Amazon Lex, you can design chatbots in a matter of minutes and publish them to be used by Alexa. Amazon Lex also has APIs that you can use to build the bots, so that you can update or edit your utterances or slots using your code. Please refer to the boto3 API (`https://boto3.amazonaws.com/v1/documentation/api/latest/reference/services/lex-models.html`) documentation to learn how to use the API. The calls to APIs use codes similar to the examples we presented in `Chapter 10`, *Working with AWS Comprehend*, and `Chapter 11`, *Using AWS Rekognition*.

Summary

Amazon Lex makes building conversational bots easier and more accessible for everyone. Conversational bots use a lot of machine learning models to provide users with quick answers to their queries. Amazon Lex provides a graphical interface where you can specify what utterances your bot should respond to, slots of information it should collect, and confirmation questions that your bot should ask the user. Such tools can be tested directly on the dashboard, as we demonstrated in the previous section.

As data scientists need to build applications that wow the customers, using tools such as Amazon Comprehend, Rekognition, and Lex is a good way to build these prototypes rapidly. However, these services may prove to be expensive when used on a large scale. In such cases, we always work on building our own models using frameworks such as Apache Spark or SageMaker.

In the next chapter, we will study how to set up new AWS clusters, and examine the nuances of how to select the correct cluster for your task.

Exercises

1. Create a chatbot that provides you with the status of a flight based on the information provided by the user.
2. Create a chatbot that can answer various weather-related questions.

Section 5: Optimizing and Deploying Models through AWS

5

After mastering the use of various tools regarding machine learning on AWS, one important step that the readers have to master is optimizing these models and deploying them to production. In this part of the book, we discuss how machine learning models trained using AWS tools can be optimized and made ready to be deployed in production environments

This section contains the following chapters:

13
Creating Clusters on AWS

One of the key problems in machine learning is understanding how to scale and parallelize the learning across multiple machines. Whether you are training deep learning models, which are very heavy on hardware usage, or just launching machines for creating predictions it is essential that we select the appropriate hardware configuration, both for const considerations and runtime performance reasons.

In this chapter, we will cover the following topics:

- Choosing your instance types
- Distributed deep learning

Choosing your instance types

In the `Chapter 4`, *Predicting User Behavior with Tree-Based Methods,* and other chapters, we had to launch EMR clusters and SageMaker instances (servers) for learning and model serving. In this section, we discuss the characteristics of the different instance types. In this chapter, you can find all supported instance types AWS provides at `https://aws.amazon.com/ec2/instance-types/`.

Depending on the task at hand, we should use different instance types. For example, we may require an instance type with GPUs rather than CPUs for deep learning. When launching a large iterative **Extract, Transform, and Load** (ETL) job (that is, a data transformation job) on Apache Spark, we might need large amounts of memory. To make it easier for the users, AWS has classified the instances into families that are catered for different use cases. Additionally, AWS constantly provides newer hardware configurations for each family. These are called **generations**. Typically, a new generation provides improved performance over the previous generation. However, older generations are usually still available. In turn, each family has machines of different sizes in terms of compute and memory capabilities.

The most commonly used families are as follows:

- Compute optimized (C-family)
- Memory optimized (M-family)
- Accelerated computing (P-family)
- Storage optimized (I-family)
- General purpose (R-family)

There are other families for each optimization objective, but in the previous list, we list the most commonly used family for each. Each family may have a different configuration. The following table shows a few configurations for the C and M families. Each configuration has a different price. For example, the fifth generation, xlarge, and C-family machine costs $0.085 at the time of this writing on the **us-east-1** region of AWS. As you can see, at a given price level, the user can choose to pay for a configuration that has more memory power and less compute power or vice versa. The **Memory (GB)** column in the following table shows values in gigabytes and the vCPUs are units of processing power in virtual machines, as measured by AWS. The prices shown in the table are just reference prices that correspond to the Virginia data center region on AWS as priced in March, 2019. Currently, AWS charges for the use of the instances for each second the machine is up (that is, even though the price is shown as an hourly amount, a machine can be launched for 120 seconds and the user would only need to pay the corresponding fraction of the hourly price):

Model	vCPU	Memory (GB)	On-demand price (us-east-1 region)
c5.large	2	4	$0.085 per hour
c5.xlarge	4	8	$0.17 per hour
c5.2xlarge	8	16	$0.34 per hour
c5.4xlarge	16	32	$0.68 per hour

m5.large	2	8	$0.096 per hour
m5.xlarge	4	16	$0.192 per hour
m5.2xlarge	8	32	$0.384 per hour

The price for a given configuration can change due to a number of factors, namely, the following:

- The region (data center) of the machine
- Whether the instance is requested as spot or on-demand
- The use of reserved pricing

On-demand versus spot instance pricing

On-demand is the most flexible way to request machines from the cloud. Prices for on-demand instances are fixed and once you launch the machine, it is guaranteed to remain up (unless an error occurs or AWS is experimenting capacity issues, which is extremely rare). On the other hand, spot pricing is based on auctions. AWS has a set of excess capacity machines that are auctioned, typically at a lower price than on-demand. To obtain such machines, at launch time, the user needs to specify how much he or she is willing to spend on such an instance. If the current market price is below the bid value, the machine is successfully provisioned. As soon as the market price exceeds the bid, the machine can be taken away from the user. So, if you use spot pricing, you need to know that the machine can go down at any moment. That said, based on our experience, spot pricing can be reliably for large scale (thousands of machines) production workloads successfully. It is important to choose the bid price and machine configuration adequately and be ready to change these every so often upon the changes in the spot market prices.

In the following link, you can inspect the market value of each instance type in different regions and availability zones (these are distinct isolated data centers within a region) at `https://console.aws.amazon.com/ec2sp/v1/spot/home?region=us-east-1#`:

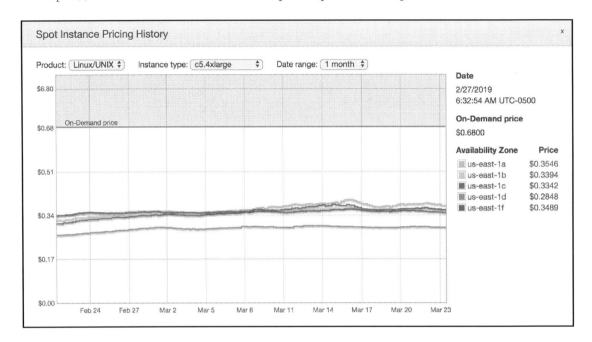

The preceding diagram shows the market price for **c5.4xlarge** machines between March and February, 2019. The reader might observe that the region **us-east-1d** seems to have a lower market price than the rest of the regions. This means that whenever possible, you could request spot instances on that region at a lower bid price.

Currently, SageMaker does not support spot pricing, and only on-demand instances are allowed. Additionally, there is a different price chart for SageMaker-supported instances, which can be found via the following link: `https://aws.amazon.com/sagemaker/pricing/`. There are different prices for the different things you can do with SakeMaker (notebooks, training jobs, batch transform jobs, endpoints, and so on.).

As for **Elastic MapReduce (EMR)**, it does support spot instances. However, there is a minor additional cost added to the raw instance type cost when launched through EMR.

Reserved pricing

Costs can be reduced if you have an accurate estimate of you compute needs ahead. In that case, you can pay AWS upfront and get significant discounts for on-demand instances. For example, if you plan to spend USD 1,000 on m5.xlarge machines over the course of a year, you can opt to pay upfront the USD 1,000 amount and obtain a 40% saving. The more you pay upfront, the larger the savings rate.

Details can be found in the following link: `https://aws.amazon.com/ec2/pricing/reserved-instances/pricing/`.

Amazon Machine Images (AMIs)

Machines can be launched outside EMR or SageMaker directly via the **Elastic Compute** service (`https://aws.amazon.com/ec2`). This is useful when you want to handle the deployment of your own application on the AWS cloud or want to custom-configure the packages that you have available on the instance. When you launch an instance through EC2, you can select an AMI and the machine will come up with all the libraries and packages necessary for your application. You can create your own AMI from a running instance for re-use at a later time or through Docker specs. However, AWS provides several pre-backed AMIs that are very useful for deep learning. We highly encourage you to take a look at the available AMIs via this link: `https://aws.amazon.com/machine-learning/amis/`. These AMIs include the most common machine learning packages (such as TensorFlow, Anaconda, and scikit-learn) installed in a way that ensures compatibility between the different library versions (typically, a tricky task). These **Deep Learning AMIs** are typically referred to as **DLAMIs**.

Deep learning hardware

Most of the instance types in AWS are based on CPUs. CPU instances are typically optimal for performing various sequential tasks. However, the accelerated computing instance types (for example, the P or G families) are based on **graphical processing units (GPUs)**. These kinds of instances, which were originally popular on gaming consoles, turned out to be ideal for deep learning. GPUs are characterized by having more cores than CPUs, but with less processing power. Thus, GPUs are capable of fast parallel processing of simpler instructions.

In particular, GPUs allow for the very fast and parallel multiplication of matrices. Recall from Chapter 7, *Implementing Deep Learning Algorithms*, that deep learning involves multiplying the weights by the signals on different layer inputs, much like a vector dot-product. In fact, matrix multiplications involve doing several dot products between several columns and rows simultaneously. Matrix multiplication is usually the main bottleneck in deep learning, and GPUs are extremely good at performing such operations as there is an opportunity to perform tons of calculations in parallel.

In the following table, we can see typical machine configurations used for deep learning and their relevant characteristics. The number of GPUs and networking performance are especially important when it comes to distributing the deep learning workloads, as we will discuss in the following sections:

Model	GPUs	vCPU	Mem (GiB)	GPU Mem (GiB)	Networking performance
p3.2xlarge	1	8	61	16	Up to 10 gigabits
p3.8xlarge	4	32	244	64	10 gigabits
p3.16xlarge	8	64	488	128	25 gigabits

Elastic Inference Acceleration

In 2018, AWS announced a new feature that allows us to combine regular instances attached through GPU-based accelerator devices via a network at a fraction of the having a GPU instance. Details can be found at `https:/ /docs.aws.amazon.com/sagemaker/latest/dg/ei.htm`.

Distributed deep learning

Let's explore the **distributed deep learning** concept next.

Model versus data parallelization

When are training large amounts of data, or when the network structure is huge, we usually need to distribute the training across different machines/threads so that learning can be performed in parallel. This parallelization may happen within a single machine with several GPUs or across several machines synchronizing through a network. The two main strategies for distributing deep learning workloads are data parallelization and model parallelization.

In data parallelization, we run a number of mini-batches in parallel using the same weights (that is, the same model). This implies synchronizing the weights of the different mini-batches upon a series of runs. One strategy for combining the weights of the different parallel runs is to average the weights resulting of each parallel mini-batch. An efficient way to average out the gradients of each machine or thread is to use algorithms such as **AllReduce** that allow combining the gradients in a distributed fashion without the need of a central combiner. Other alternatives involve hosting a parameter server that acts as a central location for synchronizing weights.

Model parallelism, on the other hand, involves having different threads or machines processing the same mini-batch in parallel while distributing the actual processing. The algorithm being run needs to be able to distribute the work in different threads. This typically works well on machines with multiple GPUs that share a high-speed bus, because model parallelization typically only requires synchronizing the outputs of each layer after each forward pass. However, this synchronization might involve more or less data than the weights synchronization in data parallelism, depending on the structure of the network.

Distributed TensorFlow

TensorFlow natively supports data parallelization on a single machine with more than one GPU, using **AllReduce**. The algorithms for distributing the learning through TensorFlow is an active area of development within TensorFlow.

For example, we can launch a notebook instance with more than one GPU:

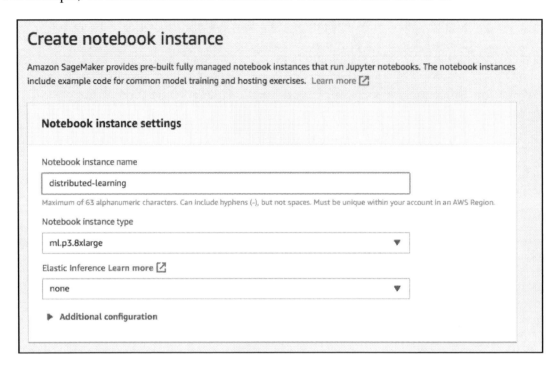

In this example, we have a four-GPU machine. Let's examine how we would change the code to our regressor estimator that we considered in Chapter 8, *Implementing Deep Learning with TensorFlow on AWS*. Recall we used LinearRegressor for solving our house value estimation. To enable the distributed learning across GPUs, we need to define a distribution strategy.

The simplest is MirroredStrategy, which uses the AllReduce technique. This strategy is instantiated and submitted to the regressor as an input, as we show in the following code block:

```
distribution = tf.contrib.distribute.MirroredStrategy(num_gpus=4)
config = tf.estimator.RunConfig(train_distribute=distribution)

tf_regressor = tf.estimator.LinearRegressor(
  config=config,
  optimizer=tf.train.GradientDescentOptimizer(learning_rate=0.0000001),
  feature_columns=[tf.feature_column.numeric_column('inputs',
                              shape=(11,))],
)
```

Currently, the distribution strategy supports `GradientDescentOptimizer` that accepts a learning rate as input. Also, the way to provide the input functions needs to change slightly compared to what we did in `Chapter 8`, *Implementing Deep Learning with TensorFlow on AWS*. In distributed processing, the input function needs to return `tf.Dataset` that we create from tensors obtained through the `pandas as_matrix()` function:

```
def training_input_fn():
    return tf.data.Dataset.from_tensor_slices(
            ({'inputs': training_df[training_features].as_matrix()},
             training_df[label].as_matrix())).repeat(50).batch(1)
```

The training is done in the same way as we did in `Chapter 8`, *Implementing Deep Learning with TensorFlow on AWS*:

```
tf_regressor.train(input_fn=training_input_fn)
```

In the `train_distributed_tensorflow.ipynb` notebook, you can see the full example. In this particular toy example, the distributed learning is not justifiable. However, it should serve the reader as a reference, as there is currently not much documentation and or many examples available regarding how to successfully perform the training on a multi-CPU environment.

Distributed learning through Apache Spark

In previous chapters, we showed how to use Apache Spark for distributed machine learning though the Spark ML library. However, if you want to combine Apache Spark with deep learning libraries such as TensorFlow, it is possible to obtain significant benefits.

Data parallelization

In this scheme, the same mini-batches run in parallel throughout the Spark executors (in a map-like transformation) and the weights are averaged (in a reduce-like operation). Tools such as SparkFlow (`https://github.com/lifeomic/sparkflow`) allow us to define a simple TensorFlow model (such as the one we developed in `Chapter 8`, *Implementing Deep Learning with TensorFlow on AWS*) and perform parallel training by making the Spark driver act as a parameter server. Through this library, we can work with pipeline abstractions (estimators and transformers) that work as smart wrappers of TensorFlow graphs. Similarly, BigDL (`https://bigdl-project.github.io`) allows us to distribute deep learning training using `allreduce` **stochastic gradient descent (SGD)** implementations.

Model parallelization

At the time of this chapter writing, there is no native library that allows us to do model parallelization with TensorFlow through Apache Spark. However, Apache Spark does come with an implementation of a **multilayer perceptron classifier** (**MLPC**) (`https://spark.apache.org/docs/latest/ml-classification-regression.html#multilayer-perceptron-classifier`) that implements model parallelization through Apache Spark. This implementation is relatively simplistic compared to the power of libraries such as TensorFlow. For example, the network structure and the activation functions are fixed. You can only define the number of layers and a few other parameters. That said, it is a good way to get started with distributed deep learning, as your data pipelines are already in Spark.

Distributed hyperparameter tuning

By having a Spark cluster, it is possible to train variants of the same neural network on different machines. Each of these variants could be different hyperparameters, or even slightly different network structures. For example, you might want to switch the activation functions on a particular layer. If we can predefine all these combinations of neural networks beforehand, a simple `map()` transformation can be performed through Spark. Each parallel training job can return the generated model, as well as the loss metric. Libraries such as `sparkdl` (`https://github.com/databricks/spark-deep-learning`) come with good tools for performing such tasks (especially if you're working with images). We'll cover hyperparameter tuning in more detail in `Chapter 15`, *Tuning Clusters for Machine Learning*.

Distributed predictions at scale

Once we have a serialized model, it is possible to make predictions in parallel by sending the model to the different executors and applying it to the data distributed by Spark. The `sparkdl` library, for example, implements a Keras transformer that makes distributed predictions, given a Keras model such as the one we developed in `Chapter 8`, *Implementing Deep Learning with TensorFlow on AWS*.

Parallelization in SageMaker

Many of the use cases identified in the previous section can also easily be addressed just by using **SageMaker**. With SageMaker, we can launch several instances performing parallel training variants of different models. Many of SageMaker's built-in algorithms are designed to perform model parallelization, which is why we usually specify the number (and type) of machines to be used for training. Additionally, it comes with advanced parameter-tuning capabilities that we'll explore in Chapter 15, *Tuning Clusters for Machine Learning*. Lastly, the distributed predictions are done through batch transform jobs such as the ones we showed in Chapter 4, *Predicting User Behavior with Tree-Based Methods*.

Summary

In this chapter, we covered the basic considerations regarding how to choose the kinds of machines for the training clusters. These involve making tradeoffs between costs, memory sizes, compute power, and provisioning limitations. As for deep learning, we provided a concrete example on how to run distributed TensorFlow on SageMaker notebooks and some guidelines on how to further distribute your deep learning pipelines through Apache Spark on EMR. In the next chapter, *Optimizing Models in Spark and SageMaker*, we will dive into the problem of tuning our models for optimal performance from the standpoint of model accuracy.

14
Optimizing Models in Spark and SageMaker

The models that are trained on AWS can be further optimized by modifying the training directives or hyperparameters. In this chapter, we will discuss various techniques that our readers can use to improve the performance of their algorithms.

In this chapter, we will cover the following topics:

- The importance of model optimization
- Automatic hyperparameter tuning
- Hyperparameter tuning in Apache Spark and SageMaker

The importance of model optimization

Very few algorithms produce optimized models on a first attempt. This is because the algorithm might need some parameter tuning from the data scientist to improve their accuracy or performance. For example, the learning rate we mentioned in `Chapter 7`, *Implementing Deep Learning Algorithms*, for deep neural networks needs to be manually tuned. A low learning rate may lead the algorithm to take longer (and hence be more expensive if we're running on a cloud), whereas a high learning rate might miss the optimal set of weights. Likewise, a tree with more levels may take more time to train, but could create a model with better predictive capabilities (though it could also cause the tree to overfit). These parameters that direct the learning of the algorithms are called **hyperparameters**, and contrary to the model parameters (for example, the weights of a network), these are not learned throughout the training process. Some hyperparameters are not just used to optimize or tune the model, but also to define or constrain the problem. For example, the number of clusters is also considered a hyperparameter, though it's not really about optimization here, but rather is used to define the problem being solved.

It is not trivial to adjust these hyperparameters for best performance, and in many cases it requires understanding the data at hand, as well as how the underlying algorithm works. So why not learn these hyperparameters? Many data scientists use algorithms that tweak the values of these hyperparameters to see whether they produce more accurate results. The problem with this approach is that we could be finding the hyperparameters that are optimal on the testing dataset, and we might think our model has a better accuracy when we're just overfitting the testing dataset. For this reason, we typically split the dataset into three partitions: the training dataset, which is used for training the model, the validation dataset, which is used to perform parameter tuning, and the testing dataset, which is just used to assess the final accuracy of the model once the parameter tuning is complete.

Automatic hyperparameter tuning

The simplest way to perform hyperparameter tuning is called grid search. We define different values we would like to try for each hyperparameter. For example, if we are training trees, we may want to try depths of 5, 10, and 15. At the same time, we'd like to see whether the best impurity measure is information gain or gini. This creates a total of six combinations that have to be tested for accuracy. As you might be anticipating, the number of combinations will grow exponentially with the number of hyperparameters to consider. For this reason, other techniques are used to avoid testing all possible combinations. A simple approach is to randomize the combinations be tried. Some combinations will be missed, but some variations will be tested without an inductive bias.

AWS SageMaker provides a service for hyperparameter tuning that is smart in choosing the hyperparameters to test. In both grid search and randomization, each training run doesn't use information about the accuracy obtained in previous runs. SageMaker uses a technique called **Bayesian optimization** that is able to select the next set of hyperparameter combinations to test based on the accuracy values of previously tested combinations. The main idea behind this algorithm is to construct a probability distribution over the hyperparameter space. Each time we obtain the accuracy of a given combination, the probability distribution is adjusted to reflect the new information. A successful optimization will exploit information of known combinations that yielded good accuracy, as well as sufficient exploration of new combinations that could lead to potential improvements. You will appreciate that this is an extremely hard problem to solve, as each training run is slow and probably expensive. We usually can't afford to test too many combinations.

Hyperparameter tuning in Apache Spark

Recall our regression problem from `Chapter 3`, *Predicting House Value with Regression Algorithms*, in which we constructed a linear regression to estimate the value of houses. At that point, we used a few arbitrary values for our hyperparameters.

In the following code block, we will show how Apache Spark can test 18 different hyperparameter combinations for `elasticNetParam`, `regParam`, and `solver`:

```
from pyspark.ml.tuning import CrossValidator, ParamGridBuilder
from pyspark.ml import Pipeline

linear = LinearRegression(featuresCol="features", labelCol="medv")
param_grid = ParamGridBuilder() \
  .addGrid(linear.elasticNetParam, [0.01, 0.02, 0.05]) \
  .addGrid(linear.solver, ['normal', 'l-bfgs']) \
  .addGrid(linear.regParam, [0.4, 0.5, 0.6]).build()

pipeline = Pipeline(stages=[vector_assembler, linear])
crossval = CrossValidator(estimator=pipeline,
                          estimatorParamMaps=param_grid,
                          evaluator=evaluator,
                          numFolds=10)
optimized_model = crossval.fit(housing_df)
```

We will start by constructing our classifier as usual, without providing any hyperparameters. We store the regressor in the `linear` variable. Next, we define the different values to test for each hyperparameter by defining a parameter grid. The functional reference to the methods that set the values is passed to a `ParamGridBuilder` which is responsible for keeping the combinations to test out.

As usual, we can define our pipeline with any preprocessing stages (in this case, we use a vector assembler). `CrossValidator` takes the pipeline, parameter grid, and evaluator. Recall that the evaluator was used to obtain a specific score using a test dataset:

```
evaluator = RegressionEvaluator(labelCol="medv",
predictionCol="prediction", metricName="r2")
```

In this case, we will be using the R2 metric as we did in `Chapter 3`, *Predicting House Value with Regression Algorithms*. `CrossValidator`, upon the call to `fit()`, will run all combinations and find the hyperparameter that achieves the highest R2 value.

Once it completes, we can inspect the underlying best model by accessing it through the `optimized_model.bestModel` reference. Through it, we can show the actual set of hyperparameters used in the best model found:

```
[(k.name, v) for (k, v) in
optimized_model.bestModel.stages[1].extractParamMap().items()]
```

The output of the above statement is as follows:

```
[('epsilon', 1.35),
('featuresCol', 'features'),
('predictionCol', 'prediction'),
('loss', 'squaredError'),
('elasticNetParam', 0.02),
('regParam', 0.6),
('maxIter', 100),
('labelCol', 'medv'),
('tol', 1e-06),
('standardization', True),
('aggregationDepth', 2),
('fitIntercept', True),
('solver', 'l-bfgs')]
```

However, more interesting than the actual parameters used is to see the accuracy changes across the different combinations tested. The `optimized_model.avgMetrics` values will show the accuracy values for all 18 combinations of hyperparameters:

```
[0.60228046689935, 0.6022857524897973, ... 0.6034106428627964,
0.6034118340373834]
```

We can use the `optimized_model`, returned by `CrossValidator`, to obtain predictions using the best model, as it is also a transformer:

```
_, test_df = housing_df.randomSplit([0.8, 0.2], seed=17)
evaluator.evaluate(optimized_model.transform(test_df))
```

In this case, we obtain an R2 of 0.72, which is slightly better than what we got with our arbitrary set of hyperparameters in Chapter 3, *Predicting House Value with Regression Algorithms.*

Hyperparameter tuning in SageMaker

As we mentioned in the previous section, *Automatic hyperparameter tuning*, SageMaker has a library for smart parameter tuning using Bayesian Optimization. In this section, we will show how we can further tune the model we created in Chapter 4, *Predicting User Behavior with Tree-based Methods*. Recall from that chapter that we posed a binary classification problem for trying to predict whether a user would click on an advertisement. We had used an xgboost model, but at that point we hadn't performed any parameter tuning.

We will start by creating the SageMaker session and choosing the xgboost:

```
import boto3
import sagemaker
from sagemaker import get_execution_role

sess = sagemaker.Session()
role = get_execution_role()
container = sagemaker.amazon.amazon_estimator.get_image_uri('us-east-1',
"xgboost", "latest")

s3_validation_data = 's3://mastering-ml-aws/chapter4/test-vector-csv/'
s3_train_data = 's3://mastering-ml-aws/chapter4/training-vector-csv/'
s3_output_location = 's3://mastering-ml-aws/chapter14/output/'
```

Next, we define the estimator just as we did in Chapter 4, *Predicting User Behavior with Tree-Based Methods*:

```
sagemaker_model = sagemaker.estimator.Estimator(container,
                                                role,
                                                train_instance_count=1,
train_instance_type='ml.c4.4xlarge',
                                                train_volume_size=30,
                                                train_max_run=360000,
                                                input_mode='File',
output_path=s3_output_location,
                                                sagemaker_session=sess)

sagemaker_model.set_hyperparameters(objective='binary:logistic',
                                    max_depth=5,
                                    eta=0.2,
                                    gamma=4,
                                    min_child_weight=6,
                                    subsample=0.7,
                                    silent=0,
                                    num_round=50)
```

As we always do with SageMaker service calls, we define the location and format of the input data for training and validation:

```
train_data = sagemaker.session.s3_input(s3_train_data,
distribution='FullyReplicated',
                                        content_type='text/csv',
s3_data_type='S3Prefix')

validation_data = sagemaker.session.s3_input(s3_validation_data,
distribution='FullyReplicated',
                                        content_type='text/csv',
s3_data_type='S3Prefix')

data_channels = {'train': train_data, 'validation': validation_data}
```

With the base estimator defined and the input data determined, we can now construct a training job that will take this estimator, and run a series of training jobs varying the hyperparameters:

```
from sagemaker.tuner import HyperparameterTuner,
ContinuousParameter,IntegerParameter

tree_tuner = HyperparameterTuner
(estimator=sagemaker_model,
                        objective_metric_name='validation:auc',
max_jobs=10,
max_parallel_jobs=3,
hyperparameter_ranges={'lambda':
ContinuousParameter(0, 1000),
                                                'max_depth':
IntegerParameter(3,7),
'eta':ContinuousParameter(0.1, 0.5)})


tree_tuner.fit(inputs=data_channels, logs=True)
```

 SageMaker: Creating hyperparameter tuning job with name:
`xgboost-190407-1532`

The first step is to create an instance of `HyperparameterTuner` in which we set the following:

- The base estimator upon which the hyperparameters will be varied.
- The objective metric, which will be used to find the best possible combination of hyperparameters. Since we're dealing with a binary classification problem, using the area under the curve metric on the validation data is a good choice.
- The different ranges we'd like to test for each hyperparameter. These ranges can be specified for parameters that vary continuously using `ContinuousParameter`, or discretely using `IntegerParameter` or `CategoricalParameter`.
- The number of jobs to run, as well as the maximum amount of jobs to run in parallel. There is a trade off here between accuracy and speed. The more parallel jobs you run, the less data about prior job metrics will be used to inform the next set of hyperparameters to try. This leads to a sub-optimal range search. However, it will complete the tuning faster. In this example, we just run 10 jobs. We typically want to run more than that to obtain significant improvements. Here we just present a low value so that the reader can get fast results.

The fitting can be monitored through the AWS console (`https://console.aws.amazon.com/sagemaker/home?region=us-east-1#/hyper-tuning-jobs`) or through methods in the python SDK, we can see the status of the jobs.

Once it's complete, the AWS Console should look like the following screenshot; in it, you can see the different jobs that ran and the different performance metrics that were obtained:

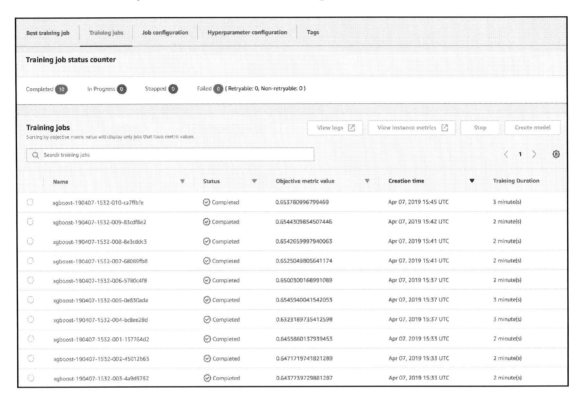

Let us inspect which training job yields the best performance using the SDK. The first thing is to find the name of the best job:

```
tree_tuner.best_training_job()
```

'xgboost-190407-1342-001-5c7e2a26'

Using the methods in the session object, we can show the values of the hyperparameters for the optimal training job:

```
sess.sagemaker_client.describe_training_job(TrainingJobName=tree_tuner.best
_training_job())
```

The output of the previous describe command is as follows:

```
{'TrainingJobName': 'xgboost-190407-1532-005-0e830ada',
 'TrainingJobArn': 'arn:aws:sagemaker:us-east-1:095585830284:training-
job/xgboost-190407-1532-005-0e830ada',
```

```
'TuningJobArn': 'arn:aws:sagemaker:us-east-1:095585830284:hyper-parameter-
tuning-job/xgboost-190407-1532',
 'ModelArtifacts': {'S3ModelArtifacts': 's3://mastering-ml-
aws/chapter14/output/xgboost-190407-1532-005-0e830ada/output/model.tar.gz'}
,
 'TrainingJobStatus': 'Completed',
 'SecondaryStatus': 'Completed',
 'HyperParameters': {'_tuning_objective_metric': 'validation:auc',
 'eta': '0.4630125855085939',
 'gamma': '4',
 'lambda': '29.566673825272677',
 'max_depth': '7',
 'min_child_weight': '6',
 'num_round': '50',
 'objective': 'binary:logistic',
 'silent': '0',
 'subsample': '0.7'},....}
```

Using the `describe_hyper_parameter_tuning_job()` method, we can also get the final value of the optimal AUC metric:

```
sess.sagemaker_client.describe_hyper_parameter_tuning_job(HyperParameterTun
ingJobName='xgboost-190407-1532')
```

The following output is the result of the preceding command:

```
{'HyperParameterTuningJobName': 'xgboost-190407-1532',
 'HyperParameterTuningJobArn': 'arn:aws:sagemaker:us-
east-1:095585830284:hyper-parameter-tuning-job/xgboost-190407-1532',
 'HyperParameterTuningJobConfig': {'Strategy': 'Bayesian',
 'HyperParameterTuningJobObjective': {'Type': 'Maximize',
 'MetricName': 'validation:auc'},
 'ResourceLimits': {'MaxNumberOfTrainingJobs': 10,
 'MaxParallelTrainingJobs': 3},
 ....
 'FinalHyperParameterTuningJobObjectiveMetric': {'MetricName':
'validation:auc',
 'Value': 0.6545940041542053},
 '
 ...}
```

You should explore the full API and Python SDK for a complete set of features and options regarding the automatic tuning. Please check out: `https://github.com/aws/sagemaker-python-sdk` We hope this introduction can help to get started on how to fine-tune the models.

Summary

In this chapter, we covered the importance of model tuning through hyperparameter optimization. We provided examples of doing grid search in Apache Spark, as well as how to use SageMaker's advanced parameter tuning.

In the next chapter we will focus on optimizing the hardware and cluster set up upon which we train and apply models. Both model optimization and hardware optimization are important for successful and cost-effective AI processes.

Exercises

1. Regarding ways to find the best hyperparameters, compare the advantages and disadvantages of grid search, random search, and Bayesian optimization as they apply to hyperparameter tuning.
2. Why do we typically need three splits of data when we do hyperparameter tuning?
3. Which metric do you think would be best for our `xgboost` example: `validation:auc` or `training:auc`?

15
Tuning Clusters for Machine Learning

Many data scientists and machine learning practitioners face the problem of scale when attempting to run ML data pipelines over big data. In this chapter, we will focus primarily on **Elastic MapReduce (EMR)**, which is a very powerful tool for running very large machine learning jobs. There are many ways to configure EMR and not every setup works for every scenario. In this chapter, we will outline the main configurations of EMR and how each configuration works for different objectives. Additionally, we will present AWS Glue as a tool to catalog the results of our big data pipelines.

In this chapter, we will cover the following topics:

- Introduction to the EMR architecture
- Tuning EMR for different applications
- Managing data pipelines with Glue

Introduction to the EMR architecture

In Chapter 4, *Predicting User Behavior with Tree-Based Methods*, we introduced EMR, which is an AWS service that allows us to run and scale Apache Spark, Hadoop, HBase, Presto, Hive, and other big data frameworks. These big data frameworks typically require a cluster of machines running specific software that are correctly configured so that the machines are able to communicate with each other. Let's look at the most commonly used products within EMR.

Apache Hadoop

Many applications, such as Spark and HBase, require Hadoop. The basic installation of Hadoop comes with two main services:

- **Hadoop Distributed Filesystem (HDFS)**: This is a service that allows us to store large amounts of data (for example, files that cannot be stored on a single machine) across many servers. A NameNode server is responsible for indexing which blocks of which file are stored in which server. The blocks of each file are replicated across the cluster so that if a machine goes down, we don't lose any information. DataNode servers are responsible for keeping and serving the data on each machine. Many other EMR services, such as Apache HBase, Presto, and Apache Spark, are able to use HDFS to read and write data. HDFS works well when you are using long-running clusters. For clusters that are launched just for the purpose of a single job (such as a training job), you should consider having the data storage in S3 instead.
- **MapReduce**: This framework was the basis for big data crunching for many years. By allowing users to specify two functions (a map function and a reduce function), many big data workloads were made possible. The map function is responsible for taking chunks of data and transforming them in a one-to-one fashion (for example, take the price of every transaction). The reduce function takes the output of the map function and aggregates it in some way (such as finding the average transaction price per region). MapReduce was designed so that the processing was done on the same machines that we store the HDFS file blocks on, to avoid sending large amounts of data over the network. This data locality principle proved to be very effective for running big data jobs on commodity hardware and with limited network speeds.

EMR allows you to create clusters with three types of nodes:

- **Master node**: This is unique in a cluster and is typically responsible for orchestrating work throughout other nodes in the cluster.
- **Core nodes**: These kinds of nodes will host HDFS blocks and run a DataNode server, hence job tasks running on these nodes may take advantage of data locality.
- **Task nodes**: These nodes do not host HDFS blocks but can run arbitrary job tasks. Tasks running on these nodes will need to read data from filesystems hosted on other machines (for example, core nodes or S3 servers).

Apache Spark

Apache Spark is one of the most popular big data frameworks. It extends the idea of MapReduce by allowing the user to specify additional high-level functions on top of the data. It can perform map and reduce functions but also supports filter, group, join, window functions, and many other operations. Additionally, as we have seen throughout this book, we can use SQL operations to perform ETL and analytics. Apache Spark was designed to cache large amounts of data in-memory to speed up algorithms that require several passes of the data. For example, algorithms that require several iterations of **gradient descent** can run orders of magnitude faster if the datasets are cached in-memory.

Apache Spark also comes with a number of very useful libraries for streaming, graph manipulation, and the machine learning ones that we have used throughout this book. We encourage you to explore these additional libraries as they are extremely high-quality and useful. Spark is unique in that it seamlessly integrates many well-developed libraries together, such as TensorFlow and `scikit-learn`. You can build excellent models with both of these tools, but they do not currently allow us to read and prepare data by parallelizing the work in a cluster like Spark does. In other words, Apache Spark provides the full stack of packages, from data ingestion to model generation. Some people refer to Spark as the operating system for big data. Often, data scientists and engineers use Spark to perform data preparation at scale and then use other tools, such as TensorFlow and SageMaker to build and deploy specialized models. In `Chapter 5`, *Customer Segmentation Using Clustering Algorithms*, we saw how we can smoothly integrate Apache Spark and SageMaker through the use of SageMaker Spark estimators.

Apache Hive

Apache Hive was born as a translator from SQL to MapReduce jobs. You can specify **Data Definition Language** (DDL) and **Data Manipulation Language** (DML) statements and work with SQL as if you were working on a standard database management system using Apache Hive. Many non-technical users that knew SQL could perform analytics at scale when Hive first appeared, which was one of the reasons for its popularity. What happens under the hood with Hive (and with Spark SQL) is that the SQL statement is parsed and a series of MapReduce jobs are constructed on the fly and run on the cluster to perform the declarative operation described by the SQL statement.

Presto

Presto is a product developed by Facebook that also translates SQL into big data workloads but is tailored for interactive analytics. It is extremely fast and is specially optimized for when you have a large fact table and several smaller-dimension tables (such as a transaction and other joined tables, such as a product and clients). AWS provides a serverless alternative based on Presto, called Athena, which is great when your data is on S3. Athena queries are charged based on how much data is scanned. For this reason, it has become extremely popular for big data analytics.

Apache HBase

HBase is a product similar to Google's Bigtable. Conceptually, it can be seen as a huge distributed key-value store. HBase is not as popular anymore due to the appearance of technologies such as AWS DynamoDB, which is serverless and, in our experience, more reliable. However, it can be a cost-effective way to store data when you need to access it through keys. For example, you could use HBase to store a custom model for each user (on the assumption that you have billions of users to justify it).

Yet Another Resource Negotiator

Apache Hadoop also developed **Yet Another Resource Negotiator (YARN)**, which is the fundamental tool with which EMR schedules and coordinates different applications. YARN is effectively the cluster manager behind EMR and is responsible for launching the necessary daemons on different machines. When you configure a cluster through EMR, you can specify the different applications that you want to run. Examples of such applications are Spark, HBase, and Presto. YARN is responsible for launching the necessary processes. In the case of Spark, YARN will launch Spark executors and drivers as needed. Each of these processes reports the necessary memory and CPU code consumption to YARN. That way, YARN can make sure that the cluster load is properly managed and not overloaded.

Tuning EMR for different applications

in this section we will consider the aspects involved in tuning the clusters we use for machine learning. When you launch an EMR cluster, you can specify the different applications you want to run.

The following screenshot shows the applications available in EMR version 5.23.0:

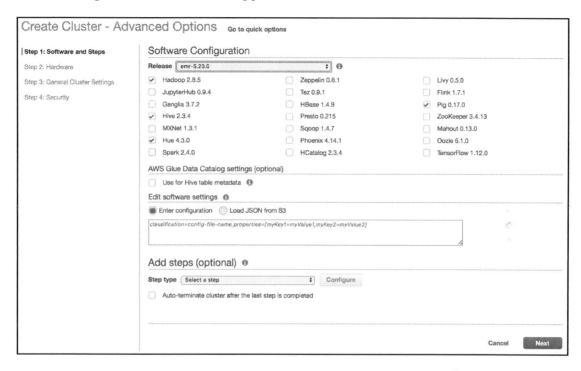

Upon launching an EMR cluster, these are the most relevant items that need to be configured:

- **Applications**: Applications such as Spark).
- **Hardware**: We covered this in `Chapter 10`, *Creating Clusters on AWS*.
- **Use of the Glue Data Catalog**: We'll cover this in the last section of this chapter, *Managing data pipelines with Glue*).
- **Software configuration**: These are properties that we can specify to configure application-specific properties. In the next section, *Configuring application properties*, we'll show how to customize the behavior of Spark through specific properties.
- **Bootstrap actions**: These are user-specific scripts (typically located in S3) that will run on every node of the cluster as it boots up. Bootstrap actions are useful, for example, when you want to install a specific package on all the machines of the cluster upon startup.

- **Steps**: These are the different jobs that the user wants to run once the applications are up. For example, if we want to launch a cluster that runs a training job in Spark and then we want to shut down the cluster, we would specify a Spark job step and check the **auto-terminate cluster after the last step is complete** option. Such a use case is pertinent when we are launching a cluster programmatically (via the AWS API). Scheduled or event-driven AWS Lambda functions can use libraries such as `boto3` to launch clusters programmatically upon the occurrence of an event, or on a regular schedule. More information about AWS Lambda can be found at `https://docs.aws.amazon.com/lambda/`.

Configuring application properties

In the preceding screenshot, you might have noticed that there is a space called **Software Settings** for customizing the configuration of different applications. There are different categories of configurations, named `classifications`, that allow you to override the default configuration of the different applications by changing the values for a chosen set of properties.

In the following code block, we provide a very useful set of properties to configure Spark for two things: maximizing resource allocation and enabling the AWS Glue metastore:

```
classification=spark,properties=[maximizeResourceAllocation=true]
classification=spark-
defaults,properties=[spark.sql.catalogImplementation=hive]
classification=spark-hive-
site,properties=[hive.metastore.connect.retries=50,hive.metastore.client.fa
ctory.class=com.amazonaws.glue.catalog.metastore.AWSGlueDataCatalogHiveClie
ntFactory]
```

Let's look at the effect of each of these configurations.

Maximize Resource Allocation

When you enable `maximizeResourceAllocation`, EMR and Spark will figure out how to configure Spark so as to use all of the available resources (for example, memory and CPU). The alternative is to manually configure properties such as the number of executors, Java heap space for each executor, and the number of cores (that is, threads) for each executor. If you choose to do this manually, you need to take great care not to exceed the available resources of the cluster (and also not to underuse the available hardware). We recommend having this setting always set by default.

The AWS Glue Catalog

AWS Glue provides a service that is known as a Hive metastore. The purpose of this service is to keep track of all the data in our data lake by defining tables that describe the data. A data lake is typically hosted on S3 or HDFS. Any data that lies on these distributed filesystems, and has a tabular format, such as Parquet or CSV, can be added to the metastore. This does not copy or move the data; it is just a way of keeping a catalog of all our data. By configuring the `hive.metastore.client.factory.class` property in the cluster configuration, we allow Spark to use all the tables registered in the Glue Catalog. Additionally, Spark can also create a new table or modify the catalog through Spark SQL statements. In the next section, we will show a concrete example of how Glue is useful.

Managing data pipelines with Glue

Data scientists and data engineers run different jobs to transform, extract, and load data into systems such as S3. For example, we might have a daily job that processes text data and stores a table with the bag-of-words table representation that we saw in Chapter 2, *Classifying Twitter Feeds with Naive Bayes*. We might want to update the table each day to point to the latest available data. Upstream processes can then only rely on the table name to find and process the latest version of the data. If we do not catalog this data properly, it will be very hard to combine the different data sources or even to know where the data is located, which is where AWS Glue metastore comes in. Tables in Glue are grouped into databases. However, tables in different databases can be joined and referenced.

Creating tables with Glue

You can access the Glue console on AWS by going to https://console.aws.amazon.com/ glue/home?region=us-east-1#catalog:tab=databases.

In the console, create a new database, as shown in the following screenshot:

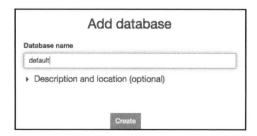

Once the database is created, you can switch to the Athena AWS service and start creating tables from our data in S3 to run queries for analytics. The AWS Athena console can be accessed at `https://console.aws.amazon.com/athena/home`.

Let's create a table in S3 for the Boston house prices dataset that we worked on in `Chapter 3`, *Predicting House Value with Regression Algorithms*.

In the following screenshot we can see how the create table SQL statement will specify the name, format, and fields of the table from our CSV data located in S3:

Note, that the location specifies a folder (not a file). In our case, we have a single `CSV` folder at `s3://mastering-ml-aws/chapter3/linearmodels/train/training-housing.csv`. However, we could have many CSVs on the same folder and all would be linked to the `house_prices` table we just created. Once we create the table, since the data is in S3, we can start querying our table as follows:

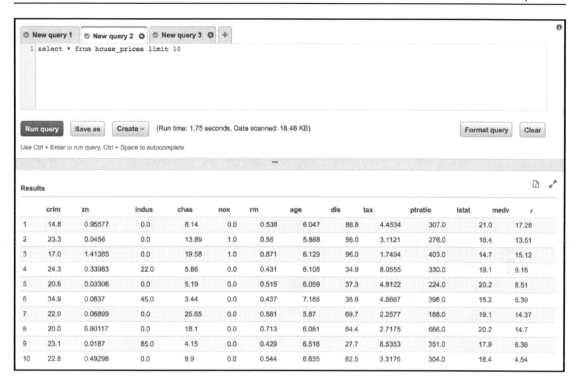

	crim	zn	indus	chas	nox	rm	age	dis	tax	ptratio	lstat	medv	/
1	14.8	0.95577	0.0	8.14	0.0	0.538	6.047	88.8	4.4534	307.0	21.0	17.28	
2	23.3	0.0456	0.0	13.89	1.0	0.55	5.888	56.0	3.1121	276.0	16.4	13.51	
3	17.0	1.41385	0.0	19.58	1.0	0.871	6.129	96.0	1.7494	403.0	14.7	15.12	
4	24.3	0.33983	22.0	5.86	0.0	0.431	6.108	34.9	8.0555	330.0	19.1	9.16	
5	20.6	0.03306	0.0	5.19	0.0	0.515	6.059	37.3	4.8122	224.0	20.2	8.51	
6	34.9	0.0837	45.0	3.44	0.0	0.437	7.185	38.9	4.5667	398.0	15.2	5.39	
7	22.0	0.06899	0.0	25.65	0.0	0.581	5.87	69.7	2.2577	188.0	19.1	14.37	
8	20.0	6.80117	0.0	18.1	0.0	0.713	6.081	84.4	2.7175	666.0	20.2	14.7	
9	23.1	0.0187	85.0	4.15	0.0	0.429	6.516	27.7	8.5353	351.0	17.9	6.36	
10	22.8	0.49298	0.0	9.9	0.0	0.544	6.635	82.5	3.3175	304.0	18.4	4.54	

Note how the data is tabulated correctly. This is because we have told Glue the right format and location of our data. Now we can run ultra-fast analytics using SQL with Presto-as-a-service through Athena.

We just performed a create table operation; however, often, we want to perform alter table commands to switch the underlying data behind a table to a more recent version. It's also very common to perform add-partition operations to incrementally add data to a table (such as new batches or dates). Partitions also help the query engine to filter the data more effectively.

Accessing Glue tables in Spark

Once the table created is in Glue, it will also become available on every EMR Spark cluster (as long as we configure the `hive.metastore.client.factory.class` described in the previous section, *Tuning EMR for different applications*). Let's launch an EMR cluster with the JupyterHub application enabled. The JupyterHub application is an alternative to the EMR notebooks feature we used throughout `Chapter 2`, *Classifying Twitter Feeds with Naive Bayes*, to `Chapter 6`, *Analyzing Visitor Patterns to Make Recommendations*. Consider using `JupyterHub` when you have a team of data scientists reusing the same cluster and running different notebooks. You can learn more on JupyterHub at `https://docs.aws.amazon.com/emr/latest/ReleaseGuide/emr-jupyterhub.html`.

The following screenshot shows our cluster created with the Glue metastore enabled and `JupyterHub` as the application:

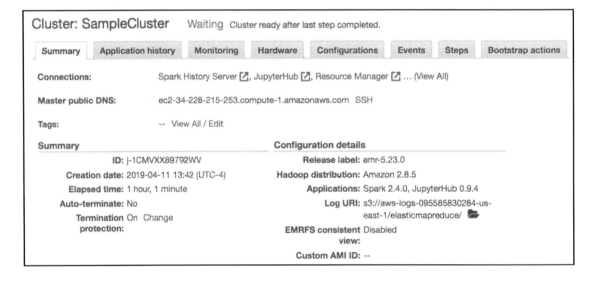

If you click on the `JupyterHub` link, it will take you to an authentication page, such as the following:

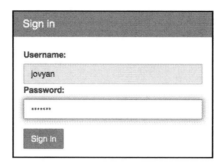

The default configuration of `JupyterHub` has a default user account with a username of `jovyan` and a password of `jupyter` available. The authentication can be customized through the EMR configuration if needed.

Once we authenticate, we can start creating notebooks exactly as we did with EMR notebooks. In this case, we will create a `PySpark3` notebook:

Now, notebooks can use SparkMagic to interleave paragraphs in Python and SQL. Let's look at the following notebook example:

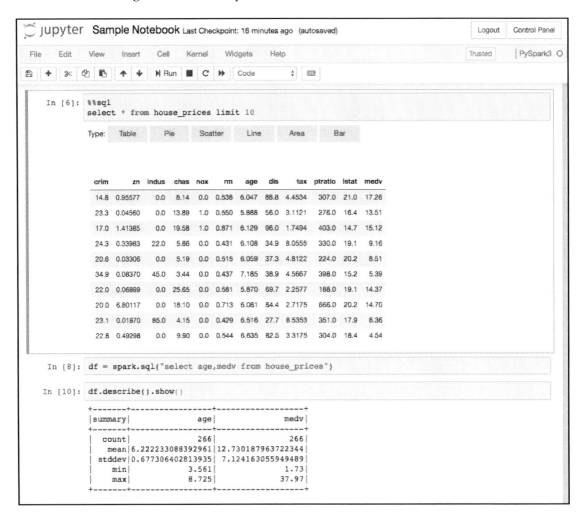

The first paragraph runs a SQL on the table we just created through Glue/Athena through SparkMagic's `%%sql` magic (more on SparkMagic can be found at `https://github.com/jupyter-incubator/sparkmagic`). The second paragraph constructs a Spark DataFrame through a simple SQL statement that selects two fields from our table. The third paragraph runs a Spark job (that is, the describe command) over the Spark DataFrame we constructed. You will appreciate how easy it is to handle, integrate, and process data once we have properly cataloged it in our Glue metastore.

Summary

In this chapter, we looked at the main configuration parameters of EMR and how they can help us run many big data frameworks, such as Spark, Hive, and Presto. We also explored the AWS services of Athena and Glue as a way to catalog the data on our data lake so that we can properly synchronize our data pipelines. Finally, we demonstrated how Glue can also be used in EMR, with smooth integration for `JupyterHub` with SparkMagic.

In the next chapter, *Deploying Models Built in AWS*, we will cover how to deploy machine learning models in different environments.

16
Deploying Models Built in AWS

At this point, we have our models built in AWS and would like to ship them to production. We know that there is a variety of different contexts in which models should be deployed. In some cases, it's as easy as generating a CSV of actions that would be fed to some system. Often we just need to deploy a web service capable of making predictions. However, there are special circumstances in which we need to deploy these models to complex, low-latency, or edge systems. In this chapter, we will look at the different ways to deploy machine learning models to production.

In this chapter, we will cover the following topics:

- SageMaker model deployment
- Apache Spark model deployment

SageMaker model deployment

In Chapter 2, *Classifying Twitter Feeds with Naive Bayes*, we deployed our first model with SageMaker. At that point, we had trained our classifier using **BlazingText** and stored it in a variable called `bt_model`. To deploy the model, we just need to call the `deploy` method stating the number and kinds of machines to use:

```
bt_model.deploy(initial_instance_count = 1, instance_type = 'ml.m4.xlarge')
```

 SageMaker can balance the requests made to the endpoint across the number of instances and automatically scale up or down the depending on the service load. Details can be found at `https://docs.aws.amazon.com/sagemaker/latest/dg/endpoint-auto-scaling.html`.

Once we invoke the `deploy` method, an endpoint should appear in the AWS SageMaker console at `https://console.aws.amazon.com/sagemaker`. The following screenshot shows the endpoint for our BlazingText example:

By clicking on the endpoint in the console, we can find further details:

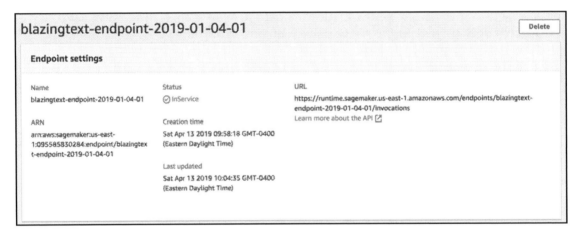

In particular, we can see that the endpoint has a specific URL in which the service is hosted. If we attempt to call this URL directly via HTTP tools, such as `curl`, we would get the following result:

```
curl -X POST \
>
https://runtime.sagemaker.us-east-1.amazonaws.com/endpoints/blazingtext-end
point-2019-01-04-01/invocations \
> -H 'cache-control: no-cache' \
> -H 'content-type: application/json' \
> -H 'postman-token: 7hsjkse-f24f-221e-efc9-af4c654d677a' \
> -d '{"instances": ["This new deal will be the most modern, up-to-date,
and balanced trade agreement in the history of our country, with the most
advanced protections for workers ever developed"]}'
```

{"message":"Missing Authentication Token"}

This is because every request made to SageMaker endpoints must be properly signed to ensure authentication. Only users with role permissions to call the Amazon SageMaker InvokeEndpoint API will be allowed to make calls to SageMaker endpoints. In order for the HTTP service behind SageMaker to be able to identify and authenticate the caller, the `http` request needs to be properly signed. More information about signing requests can be found at `https://docs.aws.amazon.com/general/latest/gr/signing_aws_api_requests.html`. An alternative to signing the requests—if we want to expose our model endpoint publicly—would be to create a lambda function in AWS and expose it behind an API Gateway. More information about how to do that can be found here: `https://docs.aws.amazon.com/sagemaker/latest/dg/getting-started-client-app.html`.

Fortunately, if we are calling the endpoint from within an AWS instance, we can avoid manually signing the requests by using the `sagemaker` library. Let's recap how such calls can be made.

As usual, we first import the necessary Python libraries:

```
import sagemaker
from sagemaker import get_execution_role

sess = sagemaker.Session()
role = get_execution_role()
```

Next, if we know the name of the endpoint, we can create a `RealTimePredictor` instance in order to make real-time predictions:

```
from sagemaker.predictor import json_serializer, RealTimePredictor

predictor = RealTimePredictor(endpoint='blazingtext-
endpoint-2019-01-04-01', serializer=json_serializer)
```

In this case, we are using `json_serializer`, which is a convenient and human-readable format for our example. To invoke the endpoint, we just need to call the `predict()` method:

```
predictor.predict({"instances": ["This new deal will be the most modern,
up-to-date, and balanced trade agreement in the history of our country,
with the most advanced protections for workers ever developed"]})
```

Here is the output:

```
b'[{"prob": [0.5000401735305786], "label": ["__label__1"]}]'
```

You can go back to `Chapter 2`, *Classifying Twitter Feeds with Naive Bayes*, for an interpretation of this output, but the important point here is that the `RealTimePredictor` instance did all the proper authentication, request signing, and endpoint invocation on our behalf.

In addition to the URL and basic information about the endpoint, the AWS console also shows the endpoint configuration:

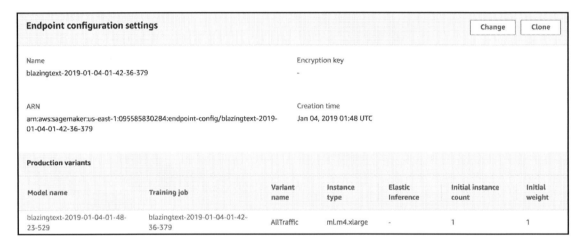

Through the configuration, we can follow the model and training job that originated from this endpoint. Let's follow the link to inspect the originating model. We then get the following screen:

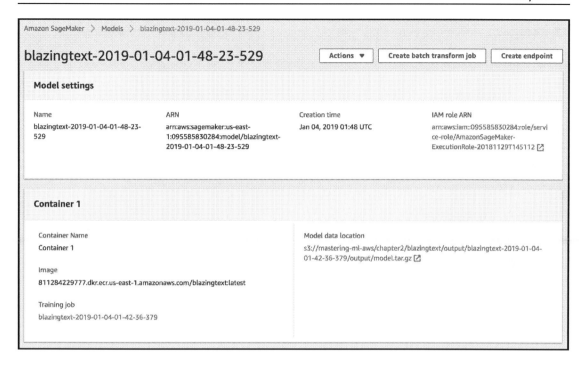

In the model description, we can find details such as the S3 location of the model. This model serialization is specific to each kind of model. In `Chapter 4`, *Predicting User Behavior with Tree-Based Methods,* we saw that the format of such a model was conveniently in an `xgboost` pickle-serialized-compatible format.

You may also have noticed that there is an image associated to this model. SageMaker creates an image of the machine that hosts this model in the Amazon **Elastic Container Registry (ECR)**. Typically these are Docker images under the hood.

> The following link is a great resource on the inner workings of deployment and how containerization works within SageMaker: `https://sagemaker-workshop.com/custom/containers.html`.

Apache Spark model deployment

Apache Spark does not come with an out-of-the-box method for exposing models as endpoints, like SageMaker does. However, there are easy ways to load Spark models on standard web services using the serialization and deserialization capabilities of Spark's ML package. In this section, we will show how to deploy the model we created in Chapter 3, *Predicting House Value with Regression Algorithms*, to serve predictions through a simple endpoint. To do this, we will save a trained model to disk so that we can ship that model to the machine that is serving the model through an endpoint.

We'll start by training our model. In Chapter 3, *Predicting House Value with Regression Algorithms*, we loaded the housing data into a dataframe:

```
housing_df = sql.read.csv(SRC_PATH + 'train.csv',
                          header=True, inferSchema=True)
```

To simplify this example, we're going to use a reduced set of features to build a model that will be exposed as an endpoint. Of all the features, we are going to select just three training features (crim, zn, and indus):

```
reduced_housing_df = housing_df.select(['crim', 'zn', 'indus', 'medv'])
```

You might recall that medv was the actual house value (which is the value we're trying to predict). Now that we have our dataframe, we can create a pipeline just like we did before:

```
from pyspark.ml import Pipeline
from pyspark.ml.regression import LinearRegression
from pyspark.ml.feature import VectorAssembler

training_features = ['crim', 'zn', 'indus']
vector_assembler = VectorAssembler(inputCols=training_features,
                outputCol="features")
linear = LinearRegression(featuresCol="features", labelCol="medv")
pipeline = Pipeline(stages=[vector_assembler, linear])
model = pipeline.fit(reduced_housing_df)
```

With the model instance, we can save it to disk by calling the save() method:

```
model.save("file:///tmp/linear-model")
```

This serialized model representation can then be shipped to the location in which we want to serve predictions (for example, a web server). In such a context, we can load back the model by invoking the `PipelineModel.load()` static method, as follows:

```
from pyspark.ml import PipelineModel
loaded_model = PipelineModel.load('/tmp/linear-model')
```

Let's use this model to obtain predictions for the first few rows of our reduced dataset:

```
loaded_model.transform(reduced_housing_df.limit(3)).show()
```

The output of the preceding command is as follows:

```
+-------+----+-----+----+-------------------+------------------+
| crim  | zn |indus|medv| features          | prediction       |
+-------+----+-----+----+-------------------+------------------+
|0.00632|18.0| 2.31|24.0|[0.00632,18.0,2.31]|27.714445239256854|
|0.02731| 0.0| 7.07|21.6|[0.02731,0.0,7.07] |24.859566163416336|
|0.03237| 0.0| 2.18|33.4|[0.03237,0.0,2.18] | 26.74953947801712|
+-------+----+-----+----+-------------------+------------------+
```

Look at how the `pipeline` model started from the raw CSV and applied all the transformation steps in the pipeline to finish with a prediction. Of course, it's not as interesting to obtain predictions from our training dataset. Realistically, on an endpoint serving predictions, we want to receive arbitrary values of our three features and obtain a prediction. At the time of this writing, Apache Spark can only obtain predictions given a dataframe. So, each time we want to obtain predictions for a few values, we need to construct a dataframe, even if we just need to find the prediction for a single row.

Suppose we want to find the prediction for this combination of features: `crim=0.00632`, `zn=18.0`, `indus=2.31`. The first step is to define the schema of our features as Spark will expect the dataframe to be in the exact format that was used for training.

We define the schema as follows:

```
from pyspark.sql.types import *

schema = StructType([StructField('crim', DoubleType(), True),
                     StructField('zn', DoubleType(), True),
                     StructField('indus', DoubleType(), True)])
```

In the preceding schema definition, we place the names and types of each field. With the schema in place, we can construct a one-row dataframe with the feature values we're interested in:

```
from pyspark.sql import Row

predict_df =
sql.createDataFrame([Row
(crim=0.00632, zn=18.0,
indus=2.31)],
schema=schema)
```

This is how the dataframe looks:

```
+-------+----+-----+
| crim  | zn |indus|
+-------+----+-----+
|0.00632|18.0| 2.31|
+-------+----+-----+
```

With this short dataframe and the loaded model, we can obtain predictions for our arbitrary features:

```
loaded_model.transform(predict_df).show()
```

Here is the output of the preceding command:

```
+-------+----+-----+------------------+------------------+
| crim  | zn |indus| features         |        prediction|
+-------+----+-----+------------------+------------------+
|0.00632|18.0| 2.31|[0.00632,18.0,2.31]|27.714445239256854|
+-------+----+-----+------------------+------------------+
```

So, with the preceding ideas in mind, how can we construct an endpoint capable of serving this model? The simplest way is to use packages, such as Flask, that allow us to easily expose an endpoint on any machine of our choice. Details about flask can be found at http://flask.pocoo.org. To run a flask web service, we just need to write a Python file that knows how to respond to different endpoint requests. In our case, we will just create one endpoint to respond with a prediction given the values of our three features. We will implement a simple GET endpoint in which the three features will be passed as URL params.

The call to the service when running on our local host will be as follows:

```
curl 'http://127.0.0.1:5000/predict?crim=0.00632&zn=18.0&indus=2.31'
```

Here is the output of the service:

27.71

To start the flask service on the machine, perform these three steps:

1. Create a python file that specifies how to respond to the endpoint. We will name this file `deploy_flask.py`.
2. Set the `FLASK_APP` environment variable to point to the python file we just created.
3. Run the `flask run` command.

In `deploy_flask.py`, we put together the preceding ideas regarding how to load the model and construct the dataframe for prediction:

```python
from flask import Flask
from flask import request
from pyspark.ml import PipelineModel
from pyspark.sql import Row
from pyspark.sql.types import *
from pyspark.sql import SQLContext
from pyspark.context import SparkContext

sc = SparkContext('local', 'test')
sql = SQLContext(sc)
app = Flask(__name__)
loaded_model = PipelineModel.load('/tmp/linear-model')

schema = StructType([StructField('crim', DoubleType(), True),
                     StructField('zn', DoubleType(), True),
                     StructField('indus', DoubleType(), True)])

@app.route('/predict', methods=['GET'])
def predict():
    crim = float(request.args.get('crim'))
    zn = float(request.args.get('zn'))
    indus = float(request.args.get('indus'))
    predict_df = sql.createDataFrame([Row(crim=crim, zn=zn,
indus=indus)], schema=schema)
    prediction = loaded_model.transform(predict_df).collect()[0].prediction
    return str(prediction)
```

The only new parts in the `deploy_flask.py` file are the initialization of the flask app and the definition of the `predict` method, in which we extract the three features granted as URL params. Next, we set the mentioned environmental variable and run the service:

```
export FLASK_APP=deploy_flask.py
flask run
```

In the logs, you can see how the service and Spark are initialized, as well as calls made to the service:

```
* Serving Flask app "deploy_flask.py"
* Environment: production
  WARNING: Do not use the development server in a production environment.
  Use a production WSGI server instead.
* Debug mode: off
Using Spark's default log4j profile: org/apache/spark/log4j-
defaults.properties
Setting default log level to "WARN".
* Running on http://127.0.0.1:5000/ (Press CTRL+C to quit)
127.0.0.1 - - [13/Apr/2019 19:13:03] "GET
/predict?crim=0.00632&zn=18.0&indus=2.31 HTTP/1.1" 200 -
```

As the flask logs mention, if you are thinking about serious production load, consider running flask behind a WSGI server. More information about this can be found in the flask documentation.

SageMaker is also able to host any arbitrary model. To do so, we need to create a Docker image that responds to two endpoints: `/ping` and `/invocations`. It's that simple. In our case, the `/invocations` endpoint would use the loaded Spark model to respond with the predictions. Once the Docker image is created, we need to upload it to AWS ECR. As soon as it's loaded on ECR, we can create a SageMaker model just by providing the ECR image identifier.

In the AWS Console (or through the API), choose to create a model:

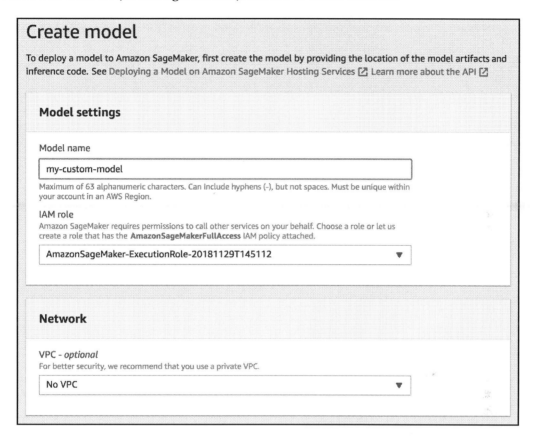

Create model

To deploy a model to Amazon SageMaker, first create the model by providing the location of the model artifacts and inference code. See Deploying a Model on Amazon SageMaker Hosting Services ☑ Learn more about the API ☑

Model settings

Model name

    my-custom-model

Maximum of 63 alphanumeric characters. Can include hyphens (-), but not spaces. Must be unique within your account in an AWS Region.

IAM role

Amazon SageMaker requires permissions to call other services on your behalf. Choose a role or let us create a role that has the **AmazonSageMakerFullAccess** IAM policy attached.

    AmazonSageMaker-ExecutionRole-20181129T145112   ▼

Network

VPC - *optional*

For better security, we recommend that you use a private VPC.

    No VPC   ▼

Once you provide the basic model details, input the ECR location of your custom inference endpoint:

Container definition 1

▼ **Container input options**

    ◉ **Provide model artifacts and inference image location**
       Use this for models trained using built-in algorithms, BYO algorithms, or models trained
       outside Amazon SageMaker.

    ○ **Use a model package resource**
       Use this for model packages that contain inference images and artifacts from AWS Marketplace
       subscribed algorithms.

    ○ **Use a model package subscription from AWS Marketplace**
       Use this for model packages published by vendors from AWS Marketplace.

▼ **Provide model artifacts and inference image**

Location of inference code image
Type the registry path where the inference code image is stored in Amazon ECR.

> *aws_account_id.dkr.ecr.region.amazonaws.com/repository[:tag] or [@digest]*

Location of model artifacts - *optional*
Type the URL where model artifacts are stored in S3.

> *s3://bucket/path-to-your-data/*

The path must point to a single gzip compressed tar archive (.tar.gz suffix).

Container host name - *optional*
Type the DNS host name for the container.

>

Maximum of 63 alphanumeric characters. Can include hyphens (-), but not spaces. Must be unique
within your account in an AWS Region.

Like any SageMaker model, you can deploy it to an endpoint with the usual means. We won't go through the process of the Docker image creation in this chapter, but notebooks are available at our GitHub repository (`https://github.com/mg-um/mastering-ml-on-aws`) under `Chapter 16`, *Deploying Models Built in AWS*, that explain how to do so.

Even if your production environment is outside of AWS, SageMaker and Spark in EMR can be of great use, as models can be trained in AWS offline and shipped to a different environment. Also, the artifacts created by AWS as models can usually be obtained and used offline (this was the case for the `xgboost` model). If you need to port the Spark ML models to an environment in which you can't instantiate a local Spark session or need a very low-latency predictor, consider using the following tool: `https://github.com/TrueCar/mleap`.

Summary

In this chapter, we looked at how models are deployed through SageMaker and covered how the endpoints are defined and invoked. Through the use of Spark's model serialization and deserialization, we illustrated how models can be shipped to other environments, such as a custom web service implementation in flask. Finally, we outlined how your Spark model (or any other arbitrary model) can be served through SageMaker by registering a custom Docker image in AWS ECR.

Exercises

1. Why do SageMaker endpoints respond with a missing authentication token message when you attempt to access the service directly?
2. Name two alternatives to solve the preceding problem.
3. Provide two means to deploy a model built on Apache Spark onto an endpoint.
4. Using our flask example as a basis, construct a Docker image that servers the `/invocations` and `/ping` endpoint and then deploys a model through SageMaker.

Appendix: Getting Started with AWS

Since we will focus on machine learning on AWS it's very important that the you get started with AWS by creating an account if not done already. Please visit `https://portal.aws.amazon.com/billing/signup#/start` . You will need to provide some credit card details, but you will only get charged after you effectively use the different services. Consider that many of the services have a free tier which you can start using at no cost. Once you sign up, the next step is to create a user on the platform which you will use for programmatic access.

Navigate to `https://console.aws.amazon.com/iam/home` and create user:

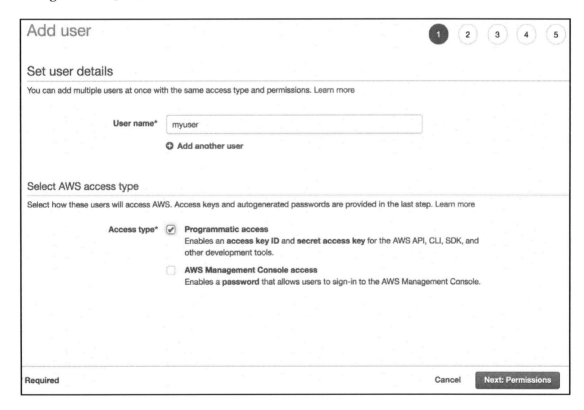

Once you create the user, grant some permissions (in our example we will grant full access):

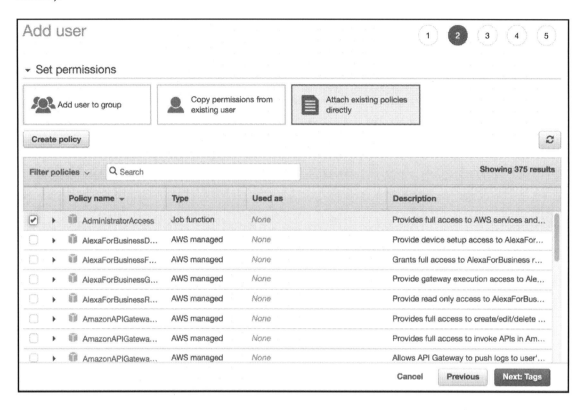

You can optionally set tags to better track costs in case you have multiple users, but we won't focus on that on this book. Once you create the user, you can navigate to that user and create keys:

Once you generate those keys, you can store them in ~/.aws/credentials on your machine, as explained in `https://docs.aws.amazon.com/cli/latest/userguide/cli-config-files.html`. By storing the credentials on that file, the code you run on your machine will know how to authenticate with AWS.

Other Books You May Enjoy

If you enjoyed this book, you may be interested in these other books by Packt:

Effective Amazon Machine Learning
Alexis Perrier

ISBN: 9781785883231

- Learn how to use the Amazon Machine Learning service from scratch for predictive analytics
- Gain hands-on experience of key Data Science concepts
- Solve classic regression and classification problems
- Run projects programmatically via the command line and the python SDK
- Leverage the Amazon Web Service ecosystem to access extended data sources
- Implement streaming and advanced projects

Machine Learning with AWS

Jeffrey Jackovich, Ruze Richards

ISBN: 9781789806199

- Get up and running with machine learning on the AWS platform
- Analyze unstructured text using AI and Amazon Comprehend
- Create a chatbot and interact with it using speech and text input
- Retrieve external data via your chatbot
- Develop a natural language interface
- Apply AI to images and videos with Amazon Rekognition

Leave a review - let other readers know what you think

Please share your thoughts on this book with others by leaving a review on the site that you bought it from. If you purchased the book from Amazon, please leave us an honest review on this book's Amazon page. This is vital so that other potential readers can see and use your unbiased opinion to make purchasing decisions, we can understand what our customers think about our products, and our authors can see your feedback on the title that they have worked with Packt to create. It will only take a few minutes of your time, but is valuable to other potential customers, our authors, and Packt. Thank you!

Index

Made in the USA
Middletown, DE
14 December 2019